POST-INDUSTRIAL

An Economic and Social Su
in the 1980s

Edited by
Fred Robinson

ISBN 0902653 62 8

Published by Newcastle upon Tyne City Libraries and Arts

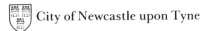 City of Newcastle upon Tyne

FOREWORD

Some 1,850 years ago the emperor Hadrian decided that the north British boundary of the Roman Empire should be marked by a defensive zone including a wall, running between the Tyne and the Solway. At its eastern end he decreed that a bridge be built over the Tyne 'where tide and river meet', almost on the site of the present-day Swing Bridge between Newcastle and Gateshead. While the wall was still under construction it was decided to extend it eastwards to what is now Wallsend, and to build a fort at Newcastle on the site where later (in 1080) the 'New Castle' was built.

This whole area, on both banks of the Tyne down to the sea, several miles upstream and several miles wide, is now a single conurbation of about 840,000 people. Geordies—strictly speaking those born 'within spitting distance' of the Tyne, but let us stretch a point—are highly conscious of their area's distinctive history and identity. That history includes the Roman occupation—although then the main centre was Corbridge, now a delightful village 15 miles upstream from Newcastle. Subsequently, the area became a central part of Northumbria, now only the name of a police force, a water authority and a tourist board, but for a time the dominant Anglo-Saxon kingdom: it had a brilliant Christian culture expressed in widespread missionary work and in works of art and learning, including the Lindisfarne Gospels and, from Jarrow, the Venerable Bede's *Ecclesiastical History*. Tyneside's history also includes Viking settlement which left a local dialect whose accent and vocabulary enable some Geordies, if they wish, to deploy speech as incomprehensible as Lallans to speakers of BBC English.

After centuries of disturbance from feuds and border warring, Tyneside's coal and river began to bring increasing prosperity. Coal and Newcastle became proverbially linked. It was the coal and the river which enabled people in what is now Tyneside to pioneer certain key parts of the industrial revolution. Crowley's iron works at Winlaton and Swalwell was, in the early 1700s, amongst the largest 'manufactories' anywhere. George Stephenson of Wylam built some of the first locomotives, including the *Rocket*, at his works behind what is now Newcastle Central Station. Later, Charles Parsons invented the steam turbine, buying his patents back from his first employers, Clarke Chapman of Gateshead, to found his own firm in Heaton; both firms are now united in Northern Engineering Industries PLC with its group headquarters in Gosforth. Parsons' greyhound-like vessel *Turbinia*, which forced the Admiralty to change their minds about his invention by showing a clean pair of heels to the Royal Navy at

Spithead, is amongst many memorable artefacts on public view locally. At around the same time, it was to the Newcastle Literary and Philosophical Society that a practicable electric lamp was first demonstrated, by Joseph Swan of Low Fell. In the twentieth century, Tyneside shipbuilders held the Atlantic Blue Riband for twenty years with *The Mauretania*, built at Wallsend.

In our own time, the 'Byker Wall' is probably Britain's most highly praised and best known inner city housing development. The area's tradition of running has been continued at world level by Brendan Foster and Steve Cram, and Gateshead Stadium is one of the two premier athletics venues in the UK. Eldon Square in the 1970s was the largest covered shopping centre in Europe, and Gateshead's MetroCentre became Europe's largest out-of-town shopping centre in the 1980s. Jarrow, the core of 'Catherine Cookson Country', provides the setting and inspiration for one of the internationally best-selling novelists of today. Geordie incisiveness and wit are conveyed in a light Geordie accent to the radio-listening nation each morning by Brian Redhead. And then there is the dog that didn't bark: despite exceptionally high levels of unemployment in the 1980s, Tyneside has had no riots—why?

Sixty years ago, in 1928, Ernest Benn published *Industrial Tyneside* by Dr Henry A. Mess, a book of some 180 pages with numerous tables, charts and maps. It was subtitled 'A Social Survey—made for the Bureau of Social Research for Tyneside'. A note explained that 'In 1924, the industrial depression and the social evils apparent in the towns on both banks of the Tyne led a group of men and women to consider what service they might render'. It was as a basis for such service that 'a truthful and comprehensive survey of the facts' was seen as needful, and hence that the Bureau was set up and Henry Mess appointed its director.

The book turned out to be in the finest tradition of early British social investigation established by such men as Booth and Rowntree. What is more, it appears to have been extremely influential. It led directly to the establishment of Tyneside Council of Social Service in 1929 which was set up to foster co-operation and co-ordination between the area's social service agencies. Henry Mess was the Council's first director, a position be held until 1935 when he became Reader in Sociology at London University. Mess, who died aged 60 in 1944, had successfully created a firm foundation for voluntary activity in Tyneside; the Council survived eventually to become the Newcastle Council for Voluntary Service.

It is appropriate that the diamond jubilee of *Industrial Tyneside* should be marked by the appearance of a successor volume. Circumstances have, of course, changed out of all recognition. Staple industries have all but disappeared, local government has been reorganised, a National Health Service has been established, housing conditions have been transformed. Nevertheless, the scourge of mass unemployment is with us again and the gap in living standards, educational provision and social amenities between Tyneside and the south of England remains wide and is currently increasing.

Sixty years ago, though the word 'Tyneside' was in use, it could be thought of as covering a collection of towns on both banks of the Tyne. Today, the conurbation is considerably more unified. The spread of car ownership, an improved road system, and the Metro rapid transit system, have made each part much more accessible to the others. Instead of four County Boroughs and nine other first-tier authorities within two administrative counties, its local government is now carried on by only four Metropolitan Boroughs. Indeed, from 1974 to 1986 there was a single Metropolitan County authority, Tyne and Wear, of which Tyneside formed four-fifths, and which enlarged people's geographical perspectives to an area which was the most appropriate one for many purposes. This book might well have covered Wearside too had it not been for the abolition of the County Council—though, clearly, confining attention to Tyneside does facilitate comparison with Mess's work.

'Post-industrial' has been used to imply an economy in which manufacturing has been so automated that productivity in that sector is hardly a problem any more, and the proportion of the labour force employed in it is negligible. We do not wish to imply that this phase has yet arrived, or is even around the corner, for Tyneside or for the UK. But whilst in the 1920s about 45% of Tyneside's workforce were directly employed in manufacturing and mining, manufacturing today accounts for only about 20% of jobs and mining a mere 2%. In a broad sense, therefore, the term 'post-industrial' does appropriately convey a contrast with the society and economy Mess described.

A notable difference between the 1920s and 1980s lies in the availability of relevant information. Whilst *Industrial Tyneside* made liberal use of published statistics, Mess and his colleagues also undertook considerable investigation on the ground on matters where the facts are now well known to statutory or voluntary bodies. There is still need, however, to bring the facts together so as to provide social concern with a synoptic view.

The earlier book could be written by one person, though its preparation occupied a small team for three years during which they produced a number of working papers on which the book was based. The social sciences today are much more highly developed—and specialised. This suggested a carefully planned and strongly edited symposium rather than a work by a single author. Each of the contributors is an authority in his or her subject, but also possesses an intimate knowledge of Tyneside. Grants for the preparation of the book have come from the Joseph Rowntree Charitable Trust and the Millfield House Foundation, and for its publication from the Sir James Knott Trust. The University of Newcastle upon Tyne, through its Vice Chancellor, gave an early welcome to the proposal, and through Professor John Goddard of the Centre for Urban and Regional Development Studies, made possible the indispensable and skilled work as editor of Dr Fred Robinson.

Personally, I hope very much that *Post-Industrial Tyneside* will be seen as throwing light on the situation of a major British conurbation in the late industrial era; will equip those concerned for the welfare of Tynesiders with a broader understanding of the facts, the problems and the opportunities; and will lead to new initiatives such as, perhaps, the 'Council for the Future' suggested in the concluding chapter.

Grigor McClelland
Newcastle upon Tyne
1988

ACKNOWLEDGEMENTS

I am grateful to the many people who have made this book possible. The original idea for the book came from Professor Grigor McClelland and I would like to thank him for his continuing support and encouragement. It has been a collective effort and I gratefully acknowledge the hard work of all the contributors; their effort, care and friendly co-operation helped considerably in the task of editing this book. On behalf of all the contributors, I would also wish to extend thanks to the various individuals and institutions who provided information and advice. I owe a particular debt of gratitude to the staff of the *Newcastle Journal* press cuttings library; the Tyne and Wear County-wide Research & Intelligence Unit and to colleagues and friends at the Centre for Urban & Regional Development Studies.

I acknowledge the generous support of the Millfield House Foundation, the Rowntree Charitable Trust and the Sir James Knott Trust. I also wish to thank the staff of Newcastle upon Tyne City Libraries and Arts for their commitment and co-operation. I am also very grateful to Denise Weites, Betty Robson and Sue Robson for their unstinting efforts in typing successive drafts. Last, but by no means least, thanks to my wife, Sue, for her support and her helpful comments.

Fred Robinson
Newcastle upon Tyne
1988

CONTRIBUTORS

Professor Grigor McClelland is Visiting Professor at Durham University Business School and is a Trustee of the Joseph Rowntree Charitable Trust. He has served on various public bodies and was Chairman of Washington Development Corporation from 1977 to 1988.

Dr Fred Robinson is a Senior Research Associate at the Centre for Urban and Regional Development Studies, University of Newcastle upon Tyne. His research interests include policy evaluation and the social impacts of economic change. He is editor of the Centre's journal, *The Northern Economic Review*.

Dr Bill Dennison is a Senior Lecturer at the School of Education, University of Newcastle upon Tyne. His main teaching and research interests are in the management of education and he directs a wide range of in-service courses and activities for teaching staff.

Professor Tony Edwards is Head of the School of Education, University of Newcastle upon Tyne. He has recently completed research on the Assisted Places Scheme and is currently involved in an investigation of City Technology Colleges and related government initiatives.

Stuart Cameron is a Lecturer in the Department of Town and Country Planning, University of Newcastle upon Tyne. His main areas of work include housing and urban renewal and he is course co-leader for the Diploma in Housing Policy and Management.

Paul Crompton is a Lecturer in the Department of Economics and Government, Newcastle Polytechnic. His research interests include housing and public policy and he is the course co-leader (with Stuart Cameron) for the Diploma in Housing Policy and Management.

Ann Holohan is a Lecturer in the Department of Social Policy at the University of Newcastle upon Tyne. Her particular interest is in health care and she formerly worked in the University's Health Care Research Unit.

Dr Gordon Pledger became District Medical Officer for Newcastle in 1987, having previously served as Sunderland's District Medical Officer. He received his medical training in Newcastle and worked in the city's hospitals.

Dr David Wilson was District Medical Officer for Newcastle until his retirement in 1987. He has also been an Honorary Lecturer in the Department of Family and Community Medicine at the University of Newcastle upon Tyne.

Peter Hetherington is Northern Political Correspondent of *The Guardian* and is based in Tyneside. Before joining *The Guardian* in 1973, he was Municipal Correspondent for the *Newcastle Journal*.

Professor John Goddard is Director of the Centre for Urban and Regional Development Studies, University of Newcastle upon Tyne. His research interests include technological change and regional and urban economic policy.

CONTENTS

1

INTRODUCTION

Fred Robinson

Tyneside has a distinctive and widely recognised identity even though it comprises towns, villages, industrial and commercial areas each having different characteristics and separate identities. Although the River Tyne is a barrier to movement and interaction it is the key unifying feature of the conurbation, not least because the opportunities for industry and commerce which it once provided gave rise to a common process of economic development. The towns along its banks largely share an economic history dominated by coal-mining, shipbuilding and heavy engineering and have had similar experiences of subsequent economic decline. Closely associated with this shared history are elements of a particular Tyneside 'culture', perhaps difficult to pin down but still evident and maintained by Tyneside's relative isolation.

Any definition of Tyneside must be a matter of judgement and compromise. It can be argued that Tyneside and Wearside are inseparable; that Tyneside's influence is so extensive as to incorporate considerable parts of Northumberland and County Durham; or, conversely, that Tyneside only really embraces places actually adjacent to the River Tyne. Here we have chosen to regard Tyneside as essentially constituting the four Metropolitan Districts of Newcastle, Gateshead, North Tyneside and South Tyneside (Figure 1.1). This is both convenient and straightforward, and has the great merit of encompassing all of Henry Mess's 'Industrial Tyneside'. It is rather more extensive than the area Mess covered,[1] but this correctly acknowledges the expansion of the built-up area of the conurbation since the 1920s.

Tyneside is a relatively small conurbation: in fact, the County of Tyne and Wear is the smallest of the six Metropolitan Counties in terms of both population and area. The four Tyneside Districts comprise an area of about 155 square miles (400 square kilometres) and had an estimated total population of 841,000 in 1985. Like other conurbations, Tyneside has been experiencing population decline. Since the 1960s, the area's population has been falling as a result of net migration to adjacent parts of Northumberland and County Durham and movement to other regions; further decline is forecast—Tyneside's population is expected to fall to 781,000 by 2001.

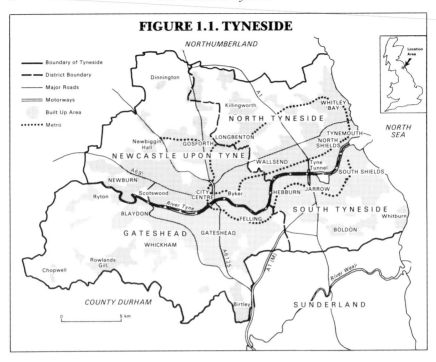

FIGURE 1.1. TYNESIDE

Newcastle upon Tyne is the undisputed centre of Tyneside and has shopping facilities and administrative functions which serve not only the conurbation but also the North East as a whole. But Gateshead, North Shields, South Shields and several smaller towns also have significant commercial centres and distinct identities. The older, inner areas of the conurbation include the Victorian shipbuilding communities like Wallsend and Jarrow to the east and the areas once dominated by heavy engineering in Newcastle's West End. There are long-established middle-class suburbs like Jesmond, Gosforth and, along the coast, Whitley Bay and Tynemouth. There are attractive commuter villages up the Tyne Valley; Council estates which are popular and well-established, others 'difficult-to-let'; and newly-built private housing estates filling gaps left in the built-up area or tacked on to the periphery. Tyneside has the variety and structure of a typical British conurbation and shares many of the same economic and social problems.

The major cause for concern now—as in Mess's time—is the state of Tyneside's economy and, as a consequence, the area's high level of unemployment. At January 1988, there were 61,306 registered unemployed claimants in Tyneside, representing an official unemployment rate of 15.4%, compared with 9.6% for Great Britain as a whole (and even these figures significantly understate the actual level of unsatisfied demand for employment). This situation stems from a number of factors, complex causes and deep-rooted problems. The decline of the traditional industries has led to thousands of job losses, particularly since the onset of deepening recession in the late 1970s and this has been coupled with the inability of the local economy to generate sufficient new jobs to compensate for losses. There are, of course, wide variations in the performance of different economic sectors, industries and firms; in addition, the impact on the different groups in the labour market has also varied considerably. There are examples of firms which have experienced successful growth and there are groups in the labour market little affected by recession. The dominant trend is, however, one of economic decline.

Tyneside's economic difficulties are by no means unique. High unemployment and the collapse of traditional industries are characteristic features of many parts of Britain, especially the peripheral regions of the north. Nor are they new problems—economic decline was clearly visible to Mess sixty years ago, although the direct impact on individuals and communities was in many ways more severe and more apparent then than now. These problems have not been ignored; Tyneside has had half a century of regional policy assistance and over the years has been a testing ground for numerous economic development policy measures. The experience of public policy intervention in the local economy over a long period has demonstrated its usefulness, but also it limitations, ameliorating conditions but not solving fundamental problems. Tyneside cannot recover its former industrial supremacy and there seems little prospect of a return to the kind of full employment experienced in the 1950s. Evidently, this difficult economic context presents important challenges and invites positive, innovative responses, particularly in the area of public policy.

As we show in subsequent chapters, the shortage of employment opportunities in Tyneside has wide-ranging effects. The poor prospects facing many school-leavers, for example, calls into question the function and relevance of traditional educational provision. On the one hand, some argue the need for schooling which helps youngsters cope with unemployment while others look for an education more geared to the needs of employers, to enhance the 'employability' of school-leavers and ultimately to help strengthen the economy. The weakness of the economy obviously hinders the pursuit of a more 'vocational' approach and raises considerable problems for training: it is by no means clear what skills will be needed and it is often uncertain whether training will lead on to employment.

High unemployment and also low pay in weak sectors of the Tyneside economy lead to low household incomes which, in turn, have a direct impact on patterns of consumption. One example is car ownership, which is exceptionally low in Tyneside: at the 1981 Census, only 43% of households in Tyneside had a car, compared with 61% in Great Britain.

Thus in transport—as in education, housing and health services—people in Tyneside rely heavily on public sector provision. In the case of transport provision this has been recognised in the development of public policy, most notably through the construction of the Metro, a new rapid transit system, as well as supportive low fares policies. But in many other areas of public sector provision—housing is a good example—expenditure has been reduced, leading to increasing pressure on public services.

To focus on Tyneside's problems is not to deny the successes and achievements. Using Mess's book as a benchmark serves to remind us of the enormous changes which have taken place over the last sixty years. Most would agree that, in the main, these changes have constituted progress: the people of Tyneside are now much better housed, better fed and better educated than they were then. But current conditions in Tyneside have to be set in the broader context of contemporary norms and expectations and this highlights the fact that Tyneside is relatively disadvantaged and deprived.

A Sketch of Tyneside: The Four Districts

Within Tyneside there are areas of affluence and of serious deprivation, contrasts which parallel the differences between Tyneside and other parts of the country. A brief and generalised sketch of the character of each of the four Districts serves to introduce some aspects of this diversity and indicate the separate identities of Tyneside's communities.

The four Metropolitan Districts were created by local government reorganisation in 1974, incorporating areas previously administered by 21 local authorities. These four, together with Sunderland District, make up the County of Tyne and Wear. The Government's decision to abolish the Metropolitan County Councils in 1986 has, however, left Tyne and Wear as little more than a name on a map and dissolved the sometimes awkward combination of Tyneside and Wearside. Although some functions are still organised on a County-wide basis, local government power now rests with the District Councils.

Of the four Tyneside Districts, **Newcastle** has the largest population (282,000 in 1985). It includes the commercial heart of the conurbation and is the unofficial 'capital' of North-East England. Roads and public transport services converge on the city; it has the region's major inter-city railway station and its principal airport and the city centre is the focus of the Metro rapid transit system. Its shopping facilities attract people from the whole of the North East; it has a University, Polytechnic and the regional offices of private companies and of central government departments. Manufacturing industry is now of secondary importance to the city, with four-fifths of jobs in the service sector—of which half are jobs in public sector services.

Northumberland Street – the busiest shopping street in Newcastle city centre. Major national multiple stores are well-represented here and in the adjacent Eldon Square shopping centre. (*Newcastle City Engineer's Dept.*).

The city centre is small and compact, extending little beyond the line of the old city walls built to protect the medieval city from Scottish marauders. It contains the gracious streets designed and executed by Dobson and Grainger in the first half of the nineteenth century, as well as the vast Eldon Square shopping centre opened in the mid-1970s and an assortment of post-war office developments. Immediately to the south of the city centre the land slopes quite steeply to the Tyne. Here the river, first bridged by the Romans to give access to the Roman Wall, is now spanned by six road and rail bridges (and it is still the lowest bridging point on the Tyne). Undoubtedly the best known is the Tyne Bridge, a suspension bridge built in the 1920s which is now widely used as a symbol of Tyneside itself.

The riverside areas within Newcastle District's boundaries are in some places decaying and derelict, in others undergoing revival and restoration. Close to the city centre, the Newcastle Quayside is now, after years of neglect, witnessing some restoration and new investment, marking the recognition of the historic importance of the few remnants of the medieval city and a new awareness of the potential of this visually exciting area. To the west, extending upriver for four miles, is the Newcastle section of the Enterprise Zone, a mixture of new development—notably Vickers' new 'Dreadnought' factory for the production of tanks—and also dereliction.

The largest area of dereliction is the site of the old Vickers Armstrong plant at Elswick. Here, Tyne and Wear's Urban Development Corporation, in conjunction with a private developer, plans to build a 'high-tech' business park. Above Scotswood Road the riverside communities of the city's West End—Elswick, Benwell and Scotswood—built to accommodate the armaments workers at Armstrong's plants, have undergone substantial redevelopment. New Council estates, on green field sites, have also been built further out to the north and west.

The Town Moor, an extensive area of land on the northern edge of the city centre, has survived the strong development pressures generated by an expanding conurbation. Instead, new housing development took place at Gosforth and then beyond, with post-war expansion channelled northwards into Northumberland, particularly at Cramlington, a local authority-sponsored new town. This northern periphery of the city has witnessed considerable employment growth, notably office jobs at the massive DHSS Longbenton site and at the Regent Centre complex and manufacturing industry on industrial estates at Gosforth and Cramlington.

The eastern edge of the city centre is uncompromisingly demarcated by the urban motorway built in the early 1970s. Beyond this the residential areas of east Newcastle include 'gentrified' terraces and student bedsits in Jesmond; the extraordinary redevelopment at Byker bounded by the flats forming the 'Byker Wall'; and Walker, an appendage of the ailing shipyards.

Across the river and, inevitably, often overshadowed by its traditionally more powerful and prestigious neighbour, is **Gateshead**. Of the four Tyneside Districts, Gateshead covers the largest area but, with 208,000 people, has a smaller population than Newcastle. The town centre of Gateshead is much less impressive than Newcastle or even than the centres of North and South Shields; in fact its shopping provision is limited and it suffered disfiguring redevelopment in the late 1960s and early 1970s. From the town centre, areas of housing—high rise flats, some surviving streets of terraced housing, inter-war villas and post-war estates—extend outwards, with the old Great North Road forming the north-south spine. Gateshead has its share of housing disasters, notably the St. Cuthbert's Village redevelopment close to the town centre which, after only twenty years, has recently been partially demolished. The first multi-storey block of flats on Tyneside was built in Gateshead in 1955 and several other blocks followed. In general Tyneside is, however, fortunate in not having been particularly enthusiastic about high rise flats in the 1960s; it contains fewer high rise flats than most other British conurbations.

Gateshead merges almost imperceptibly into Felling to the east where there is still a significant amount of industrial activity along the river and also the new international sports stadium, reflecting the strong interest in, and encouragement of, athletics in the Gateshead area. Felling has experienced huge slum clearance, accompanied by large-scale rehousing schemes such as the Leam Lane Estate. Next to Felling is Pelaw, a company town built to house workers at the factories of the Co-operative Wholesale Society; almost all these factories and works have now closed.

Immediately to the west of Gateshead is Team Valley Industrial Estate, the single most important industrial area in Tyneside and famous as the first government-financed industrial estate created in the 1930s under the provisions of early regional policy. The estate currently provides jobs for around 15,000 people. The southern part of the Team Valley has Enterprise Zone status, conferring the benefit of a rates 'holiday' until 1991.

The Team Valley Industrial Estate, Gateshead, 1988. The first government-financed industrial estate, created in the 1930s, and now providing jobs for around 15,000 people. The Garden Festival site can be seen towards the top of the photograph and, beyond it, the River Tyne. (*Air Fotos*).

The riverside area from Dunston to where the River Derwent joins the Tyne at Derwenthaugh is remarkable for having become a major focus for policy attention and for both public and private investment in Tyneside. As well as having a huge new 'out-of-town' shopping complex, the MetroCentre, built within the Enterprise Zone, this area is being extensively reclaimed and developed for the National Garden Festival to be held here in 1990. The Derwent Valley itself is also undergoing restoration, with the closure of the Derwenthaugh Coke Works in particular opening up possibilities for environmental improvements and recreational use.

The western part of the Gateshead District is characterised by an attractive rolling landscape in which are scattered former colliery towns and villages and farms. No collieries are now left here, though there has been some opencast mining and also quarrying. In the past coal was taken to the Derwenthaugh and Dunston staiths and loaded onto ships; the Dunston staiths survive as a historical relic next to the Garden Festival site. Some of these settlements have not fully recovered from pit closure, while others have been revived through the construction of new housing estates and some have now become semi-rural 'commuter villages'.

Downriver from Newcastle and Gateshead and extending to the coast are the Districts of North and South Tyneside. The Tyne Tunnel and a ferry service link the two Districts but the river here does form an important physical and psychological barrier which limits the interaction between the two.

North Tyneside, with a population of 193,000 in 1985, contains quite a number of diverse and distinct settlements. Along the river is Wallsend, a town dominated by shipbuilding; the Swan Hunter yards at Wallsend are the main survivors of an industry which was formerly a vital element of the Tyneside economy. North Shields still clings to its long-established fishing industry and its port serves as the main terminal for passenger services to Bergen and Oslo. North Shields is also the District's administrative centre. At the coast, Tynemouth and Whitley Bay are principally dormitory towns, their development originally strongly encouraged by the suburban railway, now replaced by the faster and more efficient Metro system. Tynemouth, with its imposing town houses and picturesque ruined Priory and Castle, still retains an air of Victorian gentility. Whitley Bay, together with Cullercoats and Tynemouth, is also a popular destination for day trips to the coast.

There used to be collieries throughout North Tyneside but all have now gone and landscaping and new development has erased most of the traces of them. The former mining town of Killingworth has witnessed the most dramatic changes, having been completely redeveloped by the local authorities as a new town to cater for Tyneside's 'overspill'; the low-rise housing is reasonably successful but the Killingworth 'Towers' have achieved a degree of notoriety and are now being demolished.

Throughout North Tyneside there has been a considerable amount of new housing development over the last twenty years, with estates added on to such places as Shiremoor and Monkseaton. Wholly new residential areas have been built alongside the new Coast Road north of Wallsend over the workings of the old Rising Sun colliery, the last colliery on the north bank of the Tyne, which closed in 1969.

Mouth of the River Tyne, 1988, with Tynemouth and North Shields to the right and South Shields to the left of the photograph. (*Air Fotos*).

South Tyneside, across the river, is the smallest of the four Districts in terms of population (158,000 in 1985). Like North Tyneside it was formerly a coal-mining area, but only one colliery now survives—Westoe—the last colliery in Tyneside. Along the south bank of the Tyne, little now remains of the once thriving ship repair industry.

South Shields is the District's principal commercial and administrative centre. The riverside extends from Tyne Dock, now the river's main port, followed by disused shipyards and wharves, while the eastern side is a pleasant, if unremarkable, sandy coast which attracts day-trippers in the summer. Shops in South Shields town centre seem to have retained business despite the introduction of the Metro which terminates here and offers a thirty minute link to central Newcastle. Fortunately, the residential districts of South Shields no longer fit Mess's description: 'pitiably squalid, containing both old and dilapidated slums and also interminable rows of decent mean dwellings'. This past is, however, kept alive in the best-selling novels of Catherine Cookson who grew up in this area—South Tyneside is now promoted as 'Catherine Cookson Country'.

West of South Shields are the towns of Jarrow and Hebburn. Both were almost wholly Victorian creations built to house shipyard workers, although Hebburn had a more diverse industrial structure including the Reyrolle electrical switchgear works, an industry which helped Hebburn survive the Depression. Jarrow is of ancient foundation, site of an early monastery where the Venerable Bede lived in the eighth century. It is probably more famous, however, for the Jarrow March, when the unemployed walked to London in 1936 to draw attention to their plight. Jarrow was hit particularly hard by unemployment during the Depression following the closure of Palmer's shipyard, the area's only significant employer which, at its peak, had provided work for 10,000 men.

Beyond Tyneside's four Districts are places which obviously have important links with the conurbation. Sunderland District, the fifth District of Tyne and Wear County, is adjacent to Gateshead and South Tyneside and is quite closely linked to them. Nonetheless, 'Wearside' does have a separate identity and Sunderland itself possesses a fairly self-contained local economy. Washington, in the western part of Sunderland District, is a government-designated new town which has provided housing and employment for both Tynesiders and Wearsiders, but is perhaps more strongly related to Sunderland than to its other neighbours. In County Durham, Chester-le-Street looks to Tyneside for both employment and shopping and is placed on the main north-south axis of the Great North Road, while the towns and villages of north-west Durham—places like Consett and Stanley—are much more loosely linked to Tyneside and have a substantial degree of self-containment, even isolation.

North of the Tyne, Northumberland contains several small towns serving as satellites of the conurbation. Upriver are the settlements of the Tyne Valley, with a significant amount of commuting into Tyneside from places as far away as Hexham. To the north-west of Newcastle and just inside Northumberland is Ponteland and, adjacent to it, Darras Hall—both areas of expensive housing serving as dormitory suburbs. And, finally, north of Newcastle is Cramlington new town which is still, after local government reorganisation, in Northumberland, but is without doubt functionally related to Tyneside.

This, then, gives a brief impression of Tyneside—an area of contrasts, yet a unified and interdependent conurbation.

NOTES

1. Mess defined his 'Industrial Tyneside' as constituting the County Boroughs of Newcastle upon Tyne, Gateshead, Tynemouth and South Shields, the Municipal Boroughs of Wallsend and Jarrow, and the Urban Districts of Newburn, Gosforth, Whitley & Monkseaton, Blaydon, Whickham, Felling and Hebburn. The total population of this area in 1921 was 818,422.

2

INDUSTRIAL STRUCTURE

Fred Robinson

The Rise and Fall of the Tyneside Economy

'Baith sides o' the Tyne, aa remember,
  Was covered wi' bonny green fields,
But now there is nowt but big furnaces
  Down fre Newcastle to Shields.
And what wi' their sulphur and brimstone,
  Their vapour, their smoke, and their steam,
The grass is a' gyen, and the farmers
  Can nowther get butter nor cream.'
  – Local Song[1].

Sixty years ago it was quite easy to provide a simple description of Tyneside's industrial structure. There were the three staple industries of coal, shipbuilding and heavy engineering which together directly employed about one-third of the workforce and constituted the wealth-generating core of the economy, supporting jobs in many other trades. In Mess's book, a whole chapter was devoted to coal-mining and another to shipbuilding, ship repairing and marine engineering. Women represented only about 20% of the workforce and their occupations could be easily listed: domestic servants, barmaids, laundry women, clerks, typists, shop assistants, dressmakers and a few nurses and teachers. Today, the economic structure is much more complex and cannot be so simply described. The three traditional industries are now of minor importance; manufacturing industry is considerably more diverse; public sector services have become major sources of employment and women now constitute about 45% of the employed workforce.

The Tyneside economy in the 1920s was the product of 'carboniferous capitalism', founded on the coal trade and then developing coal-using industries (McCord, 1979). Coal was mined along the banks of the Tyne well before the industrial revolution and shipped to the London market; the area can thus lay claim to being the oldest coal mining area in the country—and, consequently, was one of the first to be exhausted. By the late 1820s, two million tons of coal a year left the Tyne and this trade stimulated Newcastle's commercial development. As demand grew, the active coalfield expanded. New, deeper and more productive pits were sunk with the aid of improved mining technology. The wagonways were replaced by railways, allowing low-cost access to collieries more distant from the Tyne. By the late nineteenth century there were hundreds of collieries across Northumberland and County Durham and shipments of coal from the Tyne reached 15 million tons in 1900. Just before the First World War around 20 million tons of coal left the port of Tyne annually, three-quarters exported to overseas markets.

In the first half of the nineteenth century Tyneside saw the development of some manufacturing industry stimulated by the local availability of coal. Alkali, glass and pottery production became prominent industries. But the second half of the century witnessed a much more vigorous process of industrialisation which was accompanied by the decline of these earlier industries and their replacement by shipbuilding and engineering. In terms of economic power and growth—if not social conditions—this was Tyneside's 'golden age'. The riverside was lined with shipyards and engineering works and the Victorian 'new towns' were then built to accommodate a population which more than doubled in size over this half century[2].

This period was marked by innovation and by the crucial importance of a small number of key personalities, dominant 'capitalists' with great wealth and influence. Shipbuilding, originally established as an adjunct to the coal trade, prospered and diversified with the development of iron ships on the Tyne in the 1850s, and, later, the invention and local manufacture of turbines for ship propulsion. In association with this, ship repairing and marine engineering also expanded. Engineering was likewise originally established to serve the coal-mining industry, producing pumps to allow deeper mining, engines to raise coal and locomotives to transport it to the ports. Subsequently, armaments engineering, with links to naval shipbuilding, developed; the revolutionary Armstrong Gun was invented here and by the end of the nineteenth century Armstrong's works at Elswick and Scotswood in Newcastle's West End employed over 25,000. Men like William Armstrong, Charles Palmer and Charles Parsons were central figures—dynamic businessmen, inventors with reputations for paternalism and philanthropy (Benwell CDP, 1978; Dougan, 1970; McKenzie, 1983). Their wealth was surpassed only by that of the longer-established coal-owning families—notably the Duke of Northumberland, Lord Londonderry and Lord Durham. Out of their Tyneside industries sprang industrial empires with interests in railways, shipping, banking and other manufacturing—interests which supported their Tyneside activities but which also gave opportunities to divert capital elsewhere (Carney *et al.*, 1977).

As Mess pointed out, the basis of Tyneside's prosperity was narrowed during the period from about 1880 to the 1914-18 War, stimulated by the

Rail-mounted 12 inch gun at Armstrong's Elswick works in 1916. This 152 ton gun could throw an 850 pound shell some 33,000 yards. Mess commented that 'Tyneside grew and thrived on the race in armaments – battleships and big guns meant wealth to the captains of industry, work to the rank and file, and dividends to thousands of local investors'. (*Vickers Defence Systems*).

build up of demand for armaments and warships in Britain and overseas, in turn leading to the concentration of investment and of skilled labour in these profitable industries. Tyneside did not share in the development of the new twentieth century industries like cars and aircraft—and local innovations, such as electric lighting, were commercially developed elsewhere (Barke, 1986). Tyneside's over-dependence on a narrow range of industries was subsequently to prove a liability:

'The pre-War position of Tyneside was precarious. Precarious, because it was so largely based upon a few great industries; precarious, also, because it depended to such an extent upon the demands of foreign countries, which might supply themselves; and precarious because so much of the industry was due to the race in armaments which could not continue indefinitely. When the War came, it stimulated still further the shipbuilding and ship repairing industries and the armament industry. Tyneside became a huge arsenal and dock-yard. In the couple of years of trade boom after the Armistice there was a further delirious expansion of shipbuilding, whilst at one time incredibly high prices were obtained for coal shipments. Then came the steepest slump on record, with heavy losses and appalling unemployment'(Mess, 1928, pp.41-3).

The crisis continued until the late 1930s when rearmament again restored demand, revived production and reduced unemployment. The Depression years were grim in Tyneside and, even now, are still recalled and referred to[3]. In the south of England new light consumer industries were being established, heralding a fundamental shift in the country's economic geography from north to south, while Tyneside awaited the recovery of the industrial base which had formerly produced prosperity. By the mid 1920s, the unemployment rate in the shipbuilding industry was over 40% and in coal-mining the situation was possibly worse, aggravated by bitter disputes sparked off by attempts to restore profitability. Armstrong's was forced into an amalgamation with its old rival, Vickers, in 1927 to avoid bankruptcy. Colliery villages and shipbuilding communities like Jarrow (where unemployment reached 74% in the depths of the Depression) were hit hard (Wilkinson, 1939). These areas, in particular, lost substantial proportions of their populations through migration to other parts of Britain and to Australia, New Zealand and Canada.

The government did introduce some limited measures in response to the problems of the 'depressed areas' such as Tyneside, but these really had little impact and were stymied by political opposition to major government 'interference'—intervention—in the economy. Efforts were first made in the late 1920s to encourage migration to other regions, but this fell from favour as a solution, partly because of the lack of job opportunities elsewhere as the Depression deepened. Under the 1934 Special Areas Act, Commissioners were appointed to set up labour-intensive infrastructure projects to provide short-term jobs in Tyneside and other areas, but it was not until 1936 that government measures were introduced to try to bring in new, replacement industries by the construction of factories on industrial ('Trading') estates. The first such estate was established at Team Valley in Gateshead, which provided about 3,000 jobs by the outbreak of War in 1939 (see Loebl, 1988).

The Second World War, like the 1914–18 War, again brought prosperity to Tyneside and again was followed by a period of economic revival—this time longer-lasting, extending beyond immediate post-war reconstruction and continuing through the 1950s. Regional policy was pursued with vigour in the early post-war years by the Labour government; Tyneside was part of the North East Development Area receiving assistance through the construction of further industrial estates while industrial development was to some extent held back in the South and the Midlands. This did help to achieve diversification as new, lighter industries were attracted to the area—attracted mainly by the availability of premises and labour, especially female labour (Allen *et al*, 1957). By 1952 there were 6 industrial estates in Tyneside managed by North East Trading Estates for the Board of Trade, with 145 tenants providing employment for 17,000 people (NETE, 1953).

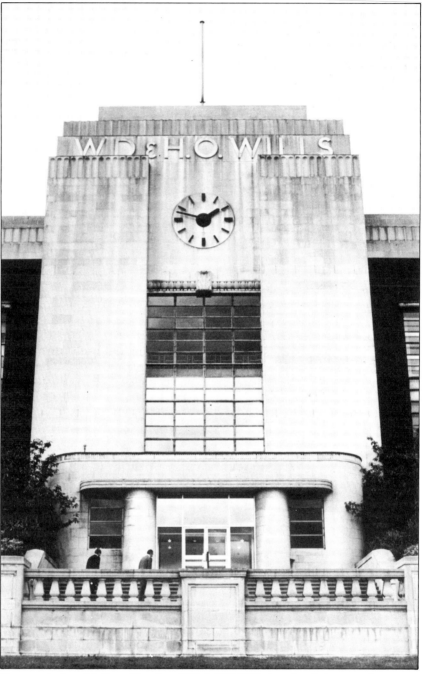

Post-war industrial diversification. WD & HO Wills 'art deco' cigarette factory on the Coast Road, Newcastle – opened in 1950, closed in 1985. (*TUSIU*).

The 'long boom' of the 1950s was accompanied by very low levels of unemployment in Tyneside, with the unemployment rate only occasionally exceeding 3%. This was the last period of strong demand and prosperity for the area's traditional industries. Coal was still, by far, the most important fossil fuel, displaced only by cheap oil imports in the late 1950s. The coal-mining industry, nationalised in 1947, witnessed investment and modernisation. Similarly, the Tyne shipyards also experienced relatively good—but cyclical—demand throughout most of the 1950s. Both industries then began to run down rapidly at the same time as the UK economy as a whole was hit by recessionary conditions in 1957–9. Demand for coal was particularly affected by imports of cheap oil, setting in motion a reappraisal of prospects and a massive closure programme lasting more than a decade. In shipbuilding, effective competition from new, modern and low-cost yards in Japan led to redundancies and closures at British yards, including yards on Tyneside.

In many ways, the period from the late 1940s to the late 1950s was one of false prosperity. Post-war reconstruction at home and abroad, the disruption of industrial production on the Continent and in Japan, and demand for production as a result of the Korean War were all highly beneficial to Tyneside's traditional industries. This, however, only served to conceal the problems of low productivity and postpone the onset of absolute decline while bolstering up a narrowly based industrial structure which was highly vulnerable in times of recession and badly affected by shifts in demand. Some industrial diversification had taken place but it was limited: even by 1961, a quarter of employees in Tyneside worked in engineering, shipbuilding or coal-mining, double the proportion in these three industries in the country as a whole.

Regional policy, in abeyance since 1951, was again implemented in response to rising unemployment. South-east Tyneside, affected by ship-building redundancies, and having an unemployment rate above 6% in 1960, was one of the first areas designated under the 1960 Local Employment Act. By 1963, the whole of Tyneside was designated for regional policy assistance, reflecting increasing unemployment throughout the conurbation. The main concern was to reduce unemployment primarily by inducing companies from the South East and other more prosperous regions to establish branch plants in Tyneside and other Assisted Areas. Factories for rent were provided on industrial estates and financial assistance was also made available to firms.

Lord Hailsham was appointed Minister with special responsibility for the North East and, in 1963, prepared a 'programme for regional development and growth' (Cmnd 2206, 1963). This was concerned with promoting industrial diversification through increased investment in infrastructure which would serve to underpin existing regional policy incentives. There was a strong emphasis on spending on roads—the element of the Hailsham Plan which is probably best remembered—but there were also proposals for more investment in the provision of advance factories, housing, education and training, and derelict land clearance. A key proposal was the development of a new town at Washington (designated in 1964) to provide housing and employment for people from Wearside and Tyneside.

The period from 1963 until the first 'oil shock' which hit the world economy in 1973 was the heyday of regional policy. Under Wilson's 1964–70 Government, expenditure on regional policy measures increased substantially and there was sufficient growth in the national economy to generate branch plant development. Quite a number of new factories were set up in Tyneside and in the North East, coinciding with widespread pit closures throughout Durham and Northumberland. Press headlines about 'new jobs in the pipeline', heralding the movement into the area of new industry, were as frequent then as redundancy announcements were to become in the late 1970s. Efforts were made to 'modernise' both the economic and social structure of the region. Newcastle was in the throes of massive city centre redevelopment, pushed forward by a new breed of powerful politician, notably T. Dan Smith who sought to transform the city into the 'Brasilia of the Old World' (Smith, 1970; Turner, 1969; Davies, 1972).

Nevertheless, the manufacturing sector of the Tyneside economy in 1971 was still heavily dependent on the old industries. Even by then, out of some 147,000 jobs (employees in employment) in manufacturing industry, nearly 31,000 (21%) were in mechanical engineering, 23,500 (16%) in electrical engineering and 22,000 (15%) in shipbuilding and marine engineering. A further 12,500 jobs were in mining and quarrying. New, lighter industries had been established, but Swan Hunters, Clarke Chapman, Parsons, Reyrolle's, Vickers and the National Coal Board remained dominant employers.

The 1960s were, however, characterised in Tyneside—as elsewhere—by a major shift from manufacturing to the service sector. By 1971, the service sector accounted for over 210,500 jobs in Tyneside, representing 53% of all employment. Many of these jobs were in the public sector, with about 80,000 jobs in public sector education and health services and in public administration.

Tyneside in Recession

From 1971 to 1978, total employment within Tyneside was maintained at around 398,000, with further service sector growth compensating—at least numerically—for losses in manufacturing (Table 2.1). By 1978, 59% of jobs in Tyneside were in services, compared with 53% in 1971. Virtually all of this expansion in services was in the public sector—in local authority services, in higher education and in the health service. Within manufacturing, slow decline continued in mechanical and electrical engineering and in shipbuilding. Regional policy had helped to diversify and regenerate the economy, but on a limited scale. By 1978, only 11% of jobs in manufacturing industry in Tyneside were at establishments opened since 1965 (Tyne & Wear County Council, 1982). Thus, the vast majority of those employed in manufacturing industry still worked in long-established plants, primarily in the traditional industries.

TABLE 2.1. EMPLOYMENT IN TYNESIDE, 1971–1984

Sector	Total Employment[1]							
	1971		1978		1981		1984	
	No.	(%)	No.	(%)	No.	(%)	No.	(%)
Primary	13,750	(3)	9,463	(2)	6,714	(3)	5,831	(2)
Manufacturing	147,047	(37)	125,990	(32)	101,106	(29)	77,824	(23)
Construction	26,538	(7)	27,016	(7)	21,824	(6)	20,808	(6)
Services	210,697	(53)	235,123	(59)	224,774	(63)	227,676	(69)
Total	398,032	(100)	397,592	(100)	354,418	(100)	332,139	(100)

Sources: Department of Employment Census of Employment and Tyne & Wear County-wide Research and Intelligence Unit.

Note: 1. Figures refer to employees in employment at workplaces within the Tyneside area (four Districts) and exclude the self-employed (At the 1981 Population Census, Tyneside had 15,640 self-employed residents). The same data is used in Figure 2.1 which gives a breakdown of the various sectors and indicates how they are defined. Percentages rounded.

Deepening recession after 1978 had a severe impact on Tyneside's economy. In the three years 1978 to 1981, *total* employment fell by about 43,000, an overall decline of 11% (twice the national rate), and in *manufacturing* the number of jobs declined by as much as 20%. Employment fell in nearly all parts of the economy, with the biggest numerical losses in mechanical engineering, construction, public administration, distributive trades and shipbuilding (see Figure 2.1). Even the service sector, previously characterised by continual expansion, experienced employment decline, with a total loss of about 10,000 jobs between 1978 and 1981. However, the impact of the recession was much more severe in manufacturing (Townsend, 1983). Consequently the service sector came to account for an even larger share of Tyneside's jobs: by 1981, 63% of Tyneside jobs were in services and only 29% in manufacturing industry. The lack of dynamism in the economy is shown by the fact that only 2,645 jobs in manufacturing in Tyneside in 1981 were provided by plants which had opened during the previous five years—less than 3% of all manufacturing jobs in 1981 (Tyne & Wear County Council, 1986a). This demonstrates both the lack of branch plant moves into the area in conditions of widespread recession and also the small number of jobs generated by new and indigenous small businesses in manufacturing industry.

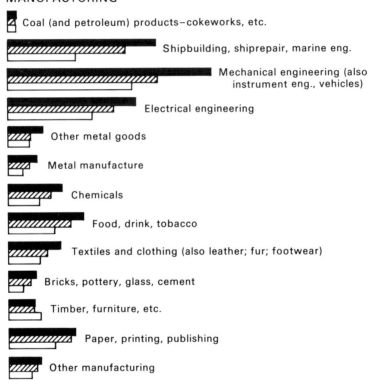

FIGURE 2.1. EMPLOYMENT STRUCTURE OF TYNESIDE, 1978–84

PRIMARY INDUSTRY

Agriculture, (forestry), fishing

Mining (and quarrying)

MANUFACTURING

Coal (and petroleum) products–cokeworks, etc.

Shipbuilding, shiprepair, marine eng.

Mechanical engineering (also instrument eng., vehicles)

Electrical engineering

Other metal goods

Metal manufacture

Chemicals

Food, drink, tobacco

Textiles and clothing (also leather; fur; footwear)

Bricks, pottery, glass, cement

Timber, furniture, etc.

Paper, printing, publishing

Other manufacturing

CONSTRUCTION

Construction

0   10,000   20,000   30,000

Number of Employees

FIGURE 2.1. EMPLOYMENT STRUCTURE OF TYNESIDE, 1978–84 *(cont.)*

SERVICE SECTOR

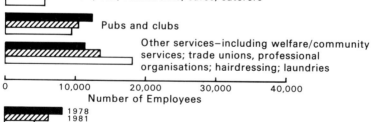

Education

Medical and dental services

National government service (also defence)

Local government service

Gas, electricity, water

Transport–road, rail, (water, air)

Postal services and telecommunications

Retail distribution

Other distribution–wholesale, distbn. ind. materials

Motor repairs, distributors, garages

Insurance, banking, finance, business services

Accountancy, legal services, other professional and scientific services

Leisure services–cinemas, theatres, television; sport; betting; etc.

Hotels, etc., restaurants, cafés, caterers

Pubs and clubs

Other services–including welfare/community services; trade unions, professional organisations; hairdressing; laundries

| 0 | 10,000 | 20,000 | 30,000 | 40,000 |

Number of Employees

1978
1981
1984

Source: Department of Employment: Census of Employment.

Note: Data for 1984 converted to old (1968) Standard Industrial Classification to allow comparison back to 1978.

The Tyneside Economy in the mid-1980s

During the first half of the 1980s, the total number of jobs in Tyneside continued to fall, though the pace of decline slowed down. Between 1978 and 1981, the worst part of the recession, *total* employment in Tyneside had fallen from around 398,000 to 354,000, a decline of 11%. In. the subsequent three year period, decline was more modest: total employment fell to 332,000 by 1984, a 6% decline since 1981 (compared with an employment decline of just over 1% for Great Britain as a whole between 1981 and 1984)

Between 1981 and 1984 there was some recovery and renewed growth in service sector employment, notably in insurance, banking, finance and business services; in accountancy, legal services and other professional and scientific services; and in a variety of miscellaneous services. This growth helped to offset some of the job loss in other activities and slow down the rate of *total* employment decline. However, manufacturing employment continued to shrink rapidly—indeed, at an even faster rate than during the depths of the recession. Between 1981 and 1984, Tyneside's manufacturing employment declined by no less than 23%, compared with a loss of 20% in the preceding three years from 1978 to 1981. The continued decline of the area's manufacturing base in the 1980s is shown not only by the decrease in employment but also by the fall in the value of output. Output decline and job loss have taken place in parallel: 'it is *not* the case that there has been a 'productivity boom' in Tyne and Wear manufacturing which could , in theory, have been the reason for job losses' (Tyne and Wear County-wide Research and Intelligence Unit, 1988, p.5)

TABLE 2.2. KEY ECONOMIC INDICATORS FOR MANUFACTURING INDUSTRY, TYNE AND WEAR[1], 1979–85.

Indicator[2]	1979	1981	1983	1985
Output[3] £m	1,361	1,147	1,095	916
Productivity per employee[4] £	8,902	8,948	10,062	9,484
Operating profit margins[5]	28%	26%	31%	25%
Net investment £m	118	109	77	95

Sources: Tyne and Wear County-wide Research and Intelligence Unit, 1988; Census of Production data.

Notes: 1. Figures available only for Tyne and Wear County, which includes Sunderland as well as the four Tyneside Districts.

2. All financial data adjusted to constant 1980 prices to remove effects of inflation and highlight change in real terms.

3. Output as measured by gross value added.

4. Gross value added per employee.

5. Gross value added minus estimated labour costs.

Manufacturing output in Tyne and Wear amounted to £916 million in 1985, a real fall of 33% since 1979. Even by 1985, the national economic recovery had not revived manufacturing industry in the area. Output was still falling—and as rapidly in the 1983–5 period as in the severe recession years of 1979–81 (Table 2.2). The lull between 1981 and 1983, when output decline moderated and productivity and profitability grew, proved to be short-lived. Productivity in manufacturing, though 7% higher in 1985 than in 1979, actually *fell* in Tyne and Wear at a time when it was *rising* nationally. Moreover, the productivity gap between the local and national performance has widened: in 1979 productivity in Tyne and Wear's manufacturing industry was 5% below the UK average—but by 1985 it was 15% below the UK average. Profitability has also been falling and the only grain of comfort in the figures is the recovery in net investment—but this is still below 1979–81 levels.

'Deindustrialisation' has thus continued during the first half of the 1980s and while Tyneside's manufacturing sector is certainly 'leaner' than in the 1970s it is probably not very much 'fitter'. A 'post-industrial' Tyneside is perhaps in sight. By 1984—the most recent year for which figures are available—the service sector accounted for 69% of jobs in Tyneside, compared with 53% back in 1971. Only 23% of Tyneside's jobs were in manufacturing industry by 1984 (compared with 25% for Great Britain). Tyneside's dependence on manufacturing industry has thus reduced very markedly and rapidly; by 1988 the proportion of Tyneside's jobs in manufacturing industry may well have fallen to around 20%.

In the past few years most of the large companies in Tyneside have continued to shed labour. Job losses in the shipyards have accelerated very rapidly in the 1980s, while in engineering, NEI (Northern Engineering Industries PLC) has been progressively reducing its workforce at the Parsons and Reyrolle plants. In addition, some of the newer branch plants in light industry, like Osram and Levi Strauss, have closed and many others have significantly contracted[4]. Losses from these plants, which were attracted to Tyneside with support from regional policy measures, are perhaps especially disturbing since they constitute a significant reversal in the process of diversifying the economy and reducing dependence on traditional industries which seem set on a course of long-term decline.

There have been few compensating job gains in recent years. The decline of manufacturing in the UK, together with a global transfer of production to low-cost developing countries, has greatly reduced the supply of branch plant projects which Tyneside and the North East might seek to attract. But some new branches have set up in the area, notably Komatsu (a major Japanese company producing earth-moving equipment which has taken over the former Caterpillar plant at Birtley); Findus (a frozen food operation relocated from Humberside to Benton, north

Newcastle) and Dunlop's pipe-making plant at the former naval shipyard in Walker. There have been some new developments to serve the North Sea oil and gas producers, including production of modules and also supply bases. The surrounding area has also seen some inward investment, the largest and most celebrated example being the Nissan car plant at Sunderland which employed 1,300 by 1988 and is planned to grow to 3,500 employees in 1992.

The quite limited supply of major inward investment projects, together with strong encouragement from the government to promote self-employment, has meant that increasingly attention has shifted to the stimulation of local small business development. The local authorities and a wide range of other agencies in Tyneside now provide assistance to people wishing to set up in business; the assistance available includes premises, advice and financial aid. It is clear that this has led to an increase in self-employment and new jobs have been generated: over the 1978–88 period the number of self-employed people in Tyneside has increased by about 6,000. But this is small-scale in comparison with an estimated fall of 60,000 in the number of employees over the decade.

The Current Pattern of Economic Activity

It is difficult to provide an up-to-date picture of the Tyneside economy since the latest employment census figures are for 1984 and there have been some significant changes since then. Nevertheless, we have attempted here to describe the main economic activities, piecing together local information to indicate recent change and the current (1987/88) position of Tyneside's industries.

At the outset, it is worth pointing out that the factors which have led to reductions in employment in Tyneside during the 1980s are multifarious, complex and interrelated. Some of these factors are highly specific, affecting particular types of economic activity; others, notably recession, have had a generalised impact on many industries. Moreover, the problems of the Tyneside economy are very often the local manifestations of difficulties confronting the UK economy as a whole, difficulties which stem from the declining international competitiveness of the UK economy. With these points in mind, we review some of the strengths and weaknesses of the main economic activities in Tyneside.

Mining and shipbuilding

First, Tyneside's longest-established industries—coal-mining and ship-building—have experienced acute competitive pressures. In the case of *coal-mining*, little remained of the industry in Tyneside by the beginning of the 1980s owing to the exhaustion of reserves and the closure of high-cost pits. Subsequently, falling domestic demand, caused partly by recession, and competition from overseas producers, generated pressure to cut more capacity, as did the government's policy of seeking reductions in subsidies to the industry. Productivity improvements have added further pressure. Removal of high-cost pits meant further closures in the North East, including three closures in Tyneside, at Boldon (closed 1982), Marley Hill (1983) and Brenkley Colliery (1985). Today, there is only one pit left in Tyneside, Westoe at South Shields, a 'long life' colliery exploiting undersea reserves. Opencasting, on the other hand, has fared better because production costs are much lower than for deep mining, but the labour input is much smaller and it has a considerable environmental impact. Falling demand for coke, particularly in the declining steel industry, has also led to job losses through the closure of the Norwood cokeworks at Gateshead in 1981 and the Derwenthaugh cokeworks, near Blaydon, in 1986. The 50 year old Monkton plant at Hebburn, employing about 220 people, is now the only cokeworks left in Tyneside.

The *shipbuilding and ship repair industry* is now also, like mining, a pale reflection of its former greatness. Worldwide, the last ten years have been disastrous for the industry, marked by a world decline in the demand for ships coupled with a surplus of ships and considerable over-capacity in shipbuilding (Stone, 1984). In the UK, the industry has not had the same level of government support as in Japan and Korea and UK shipowners, not subsidised to buy from home yards, have often placed orders abroad. The UK merchant fleet is, in any case, shrinking rapidly. Yards on the Tyne have suffered massive cutbacks, with employment falling from about 16,000 in 1984 to about 4,000 in 1987. There are now real fears that the end of shipbuilding and much of the repair industry may be in sight.

The decline of the industry is shown in Table 2.3. Swan Hunter, the only shipbuilding operation now left on the Tyne, has more than halved its workforce over the past five years. British Shipbuilders (BS), the nationalised company created in 1977, sold the yard to a management team, backed by institutional finance from the City, for just £5 million in January 1986. Increasingly concentrating its efforts on building warships, Swan Hunter has had continuing problems winning orders and has seen a series of disappointments as expected work from the Ministry of Defence has been delayed or failed to materialise. In 1985, it had hoped to get orders for two Type 22 frigates but received only one (HMS Chatham); subsequently a promised order for a Type 23 was delayed and, in April 1986, Swan Hunter lost a further order, for an Auxiliary Oil Replenishment ship, to Harland and Wolff. This was followed by the announcement of 825 redundancies, with the possibility of more to come. Currently, the company is building HMS Marlborough (another Type 23 frigate), and a cable ship, and is also undertaking naval fitting-out work and design studies. At the end of 1987 the yard at last gained an order for a

TABLE 2.3. SHIPBUILDING AND OFFSHORE CONSTRUCTION ON THE TYNE, 1981–7

Company[1]	1981	1987	Comments
Shipbuilding and repair			
Swan Hunter	c.10,000	3,300	Walker yard closed; Hebburn yard retained on a 'care and maintenance' basis. Wallsend and Neptune yards remain in operation (but all shipbuilding now to be concentrated at Wallsend). Swan Hunters privatised in 1986. (Employed 11,460 at Nationalisation in 1977).
Tyne Ship Repairers	2,500	c.340	All yards on south bank of Tyne now closed (Middle Docks, Mercantile and Brigham and Young); Wallsend dry dock operation remains. Privatised in 1984 by management buyout—formerly B.S. Tyne Shiprepair Group. (Employed 3,400 at Nationalisation in 1977).
Clelands (BS)	500	—	Wallsend; closed in 1984 and sold to Wm. Press Production Systems [see below].
Clark Kincaid (BS)	1,400	—	Engine building plant at Wallsend. Closed in 1986. Formerly Clark Hawthorn (bringing together Hawthorn Leslie and Geo Clark NEM in 1979) then merged with Kincaid of Greenock in 1984.
Wallsend Slipway Engineering	250	—	Formerly part of BS Tyne Shiprepair Group. Sold to Marske Machine Co. in January 1985, then sold to Howard Doris in August 1985—since closed.
Tyne Dock Engineering	c.100	c.100	South Shields. Went into receivership in 1980, reopened under new owners 1981. Took over the Readheads yard after failure of workers' buyout in 1985.
Smiths Shiprepair	1,300	c.200	Bull Ring Docks, North Shields. Private, local company.
Offshore construction			
Charlton Leslie Offshore	c.500	c.800	Davy Bank yard, Wallsend, opened 1974. Construction of modules. Now leasing McNulty Marine yard at South Shields for conversion of floating crane into production platform.
Wm. Press Production Systems	c.1,000	c.1,300	Operations at Howdon, West Yard, Hadrian Park, former Clelands yard and Howard Doris. Production of modules for offshore oil and gas industry.
Howard Doris	—	—	Established 1985. Parent company in receivership and yard closed in late 1986. Employed 650 prior to closure. Sold to Wm Press in Dec. 1987.

Sources: British Shipbuilders, press and other local sources.
Notes: 1. Small repair yards and contractors not included.

second Auxiliary Oil Replenishment ship which will provide some security and stave off redundancies, but in 1988 was unsuccessful in its bid for an order for another Type 23 frigate—an order which has been seen as vital if further job losses are to be avoided. The yard is also exploring the possibilities of export orders, design work and civil engineering activities. For the first time since privatisation, the company was able to announce a small trading profit in 1987.

The repair yards have also been struggling to find work. Tyne Ship Repairers, privatised in 1984, has moved into profit but many jobs have gone and orders are now reported to be scarce. The company's yards on the south bank of the Tyne have now all closed and activities are concentrated at Wallsend. Tyne Dock Engineering and Smiths Shiprepair, both privately-owned, remain in operation, concentrating on specialised work. With the closure of the Clark Kincaid engine building plant at Wallsend in 1986, British Shipbuilders—which has its headquarters in Newcastle—has now relinquished all its operations on the Tyne.

The development of an offshore construction industry on the river has compensated a little for the massive decline in shipbuilding and repair. William Press Production Systems, now with four construction yards on the Tyne, and Charlton Leslie Offshore at Wallsend, specialise in the production of modules for the offshore oil and gas industry. Both have been successful at gaining orders since their establishment in the 1970s. Press recently bought the former Clelands yard from British Shipbuilders to provide facilities for larger structures and also bought the Howard Doris yard at Wallsend; Howard Doris, set up in 1985 and making steel 'jackets' for rigs, went into liquidation in mid-1986 with the loss of 650 jobs. Press is currently building a production deck for Conoco, modules for BP and platforms for British Gas and has recently won a £30 million deck/module contract for Shell. Charlton Leslie is seeking to enter the market for floating rigs for marginal fields and has gained its first such order, converting a floating crane into a production platform. The future for the industry is uncertain, bound up with the price of oil and hence the level of exploration and production activity. The Tyneside yards have to compete against other companies elsewhere experiencing a shortage of work in the wake of falling oil prices, but at present they do appear to be in a strong position in this difficult market, one which is characterised by considerable overcapacity.

Engineering industries

Engineering covers a wide range of activities, from large-scale capital-intensive heavy engineering through to light engineering of consumer goods and the electronics and information technology production industries. In the two chief areas of engineering production—mechanical

Swan Hunter's shipyard, 1988. The only shipbuilding operation now left on the Tyne. Employment has more than halved over the past five years. (*Stan Gamester*).

Construction of production deck for Conoco's 'V' gas fields project at William Press Production Systems, Howdon yard, 1988. The exploitation of North Sea oil and gas has brought new jobs to Tyneside in offshore construction. (*Newcastle Chronicle & Journal*).

engineering and electrical engineering—employment in Tyneside totalled 29,000 in 1984. Although engineering employment has fallen substantially (see Figure 2.1) it is still of major significance in Tyneside, accounting for 37% of manufacturing jobs and 9% of all jobs in 1984. There are over 200 engineering plants in Tyneside and most are fairly small-scale operations, but there are some 40 to 50 separate plants in the engineering industry each employing more than 100 workers. There was only a handful of giant plants with more than 1000 employees in 1981 (Caterpillar, Vickers, AEI Cables, Plessey, NEI Parsons and NEI Reyrolle) and these have since experienced contraction or, in the cases of Caterpillar and Plessey, complete closure.

The principal heavy engineering company in Tyneside is Northern Engineering Industries PLC (NEI) which is both the largest private sector employer in Tyneside and the largest locally-headquartered company. NEI was formed in 1977 and its Tyneside operations encompass power engineering and heavy marine engineering together with electronics production, project management and research and development; it employs about 7,000 in Tyneside and about 13,000 in the group's other UK plants and overseas subsidiaries.

NEI has suffered considerably from the effects of recession and operates in difficult markets which are both highly competitive and subject to severe fluctuations in demand. It has responded in various ways in an effort to maintain profitability (pre-tax profit in 1986/7 was £23.2 million on sales of £937.5 million). There has been a long series of redundancies and whole plants have been shut down: over the past ten years NEI's Tyneside workforce has been cut by half (TUSIU, 1986). But substantial investment in new technology has also been undertaken to maintain competitiveness and some attempts have been made to diversify within the main areas of the business.

NEI's main focus of activity in Tyneside is power engineering, an industry which has been characterised by a desperately depressed domestic market and fiercely competitive export markets (Lawless, 1988). At home, orders for coal-fired power stations have been deferred and plans for nuclear power stations postponed, held back by the long public inquiry on the Sizewell 'B' station and rendered more contentious by the Chernobyl disaster. NEI Parsons' works at Heaton, which makes turbine generators for power stations, has been quite successful in winning export orders, most recently in India, Singapore and China. It has invested heavily in new technology (£40 million investment during 1980–85, £30 million planned for 1985–90) and maintained a large workforce—Parsons is by far the largest manufacturing plant in Tyneside. But gaining orders is a continuing problem and shortage of work led to the announcement of 600 redundancies in 1986 followed by a further 800 redundancies in 1987, thus cutting the workforce to 3,000. Parsons recently failed to win a major

Turbine assembly at NEI Parsons' works, Heaton. Still the largest manufacturing plant in Tyneside. Parsons designs, develops and manufactures turbine-generators for power stations. (*NEI Parsons Ltd*).

order in China but secured an order for a turbine for Hong Kong in 1988. NEI hopes to secure an order in the next batch of two new coal-fired power stations in Britain.

Other NEI power engineering operations have suffered even more than Parsons. NEI Reyrolle at Hebburn, which manufactures electrical switchgear for power stations and power distribution systems, has experienced major decline since its heyday during the construction of the National Grid. Reyrolle's employed 7,000 in the 1960s; employment fell to 2,000 by the early 1980s and is now around 1,500. After a period of considerable reorganisation and change, Reyrolle's now seems to have stabilised and become stronger, securing a large order in 1987 for substations in Saudi Arabia which will guarantee work into the 1990s. At Gateshead, the lack of orders in the UK nuclear power industry has led to the closure of NEI's Nuclear Systems plant. Employing 2,000 people in the early 1980s, this was one of the most modern boiler making plants in the world, equipped with CNC (Computer Numerically Controlled) machines and robotic welding equipment and extended in 1982 at a cost of £8 million. Since 1984, as work on existing nuclear power stations in the UK ran out—and there was no real prospect of finding orders in coal or oil fired stations—redundancy programmes have been implemented and the plant progressively mothballed until final closure of its production facilities in 1986.

By contrast, NEI Clarke Chapman, engaged in marine engineering, has weathered recession in the last few years and coped with competition. Clarke Chapman's Victoria Works at Gateshead has traditionally built deck cranes for ships, a market undermined by the decline of UK shipbuilding and world overcapacity. Jobs had been lost over a long period, reducing the workforce to 500 by 1982. But diversification into the construction of 'shiplifts' for dockyards (through a joint venture with an Australian company) and the production of jib cranes for the offshore oil and gas industry has opened up new markets, spread the risks and maintained employment. New investment has been undertaken and there is a continuing active search for new markets to achieve further diversification.

NEI's position in highly competitive and shrinking markets, coupled with the need to win big multi-million pound orders, is similar to the situation confronting a number of Tyneside engineering plants. Likewise, product diversification, investment in process technology and securing export sales have often been key factors determining success or failure—although 'success' has frequently meant survival with substantial reductions in employment.

The engineering industry as a whole in Tyneside is oriented towards capital goods and traditional specialisms rather than, for example, 'high technology' consumer goods. In electrical engineering, power plant engineering is the dominant element and there is also some emphasis on cable manufacture (at the AEI Birtley plant and also BICC's Pyrotenax factory at Hebburn making fireproof mineral-insulated cables). Marine engineering, a long-standing Tyneside specialism, embraces NEI Clarke Chapman, module construction yards and also several smaller companies supplying the remnants of the shipbuilding industry and, increasingly, the offshore oil and gas industry. Tyneside also still has a number of firms engaged in mining engineering, notably Huwood, EIMCO (UK), Victor Products (taken over by NEI in 1988), and British Engines. Their fortunes have been tied to a declining domestic coal industry which has resulted in restructuring and heavy job losses.

The production of armaments has become much less significant to Tyneside but is still of some importance. Vickers' new tank plant in the Enterprise Zone at Scotswood has been successful in gaining orders from the Ministry of Defence (MoD) and the Nigerian Army; the works employ about 700, a far cry from the 20,000 employed at Armstrong's Elswick and Scotswood plants at the end of the Second World War. The other main armaments plant is the Royal Ordnance Factory at Birtley (established in 1916) which cut employment from 2,000 to less than 1,000 over the last few years because the MoD placed orders abroad; it has successfully diversified from the manufacture of shells to motors for anti-tank rockets, and, following privatisation in 1987, it is now part of British Aerospace. The MoD is also the major customer for Marconi Radar at Bill Quay, which makes guidance systems for naval missiles and employs 450 workers, and Crompton Vidor's works at South Shields which has a workforce of 230 and produces batteries for NATO's anti-tank missile systems. In mid-1988, however, Marconi announced its intention to close down the company's Bill Quay plant.

Companies producing capital goods for other manufacturing industries and for the construction industry have been hard-hit by recession. The machine tool industry, which was modestly represented in Tyneside, has all but disappeared with the liquidations of Pearson's Machine Tool Company in 1985 and closure of T I Churchill at Blaydon in 1986. Churchill's, one of the area's most advanced plants which made CNC lathes and employed 900 in 1980, fell victim to the corporate rationalisation strategy of parent company Tube Investments which involved retrenchment back to its Coventry base. Some of the other sub-sectors of the engineering industry making machinery for manufacturing production have fared better. Stewart Warner at North Shields, making pneumatic tools, has not only committed new investment but also recently expanded its workforce to 300 by 1987, while Crabtree, employing about 300 at Team Valley, has continued to hold on to its major share of the world market for machines which print onto sheet metal for the canning industry. Formerly part of Vickers, Crabtree was the subject of a management buyout in 1986. Baker Perkins at Hebburn, which manufactures bread-making machinery, has had success in export markets but has witnessed major rationalisation and redundancies since its merger with APV in 1987. Rose Forgrove, which made packaging machinery and was part of the Baker Perkins group, closed its modern Team Valley factory in 1985 having lost markets to Japanese and European competitors.

There were formerly two large companies in Tyneside manufacturing machinery for the construction industry, Caterpillar Tractors and Liner Concrete Machinery. Opened in 1956, Caterpillar's Birtley plant, which made bulldozers and truck bodies, had a workforce of 2,000 in 1980. After a spate of redundancies, blamed on the worldwide recession and a lack of orders, this giant plant closed completely in 1984 making the remaining 960 employees redundant. Subsequently, however, the Japanese construction plant company Komatsu took over the plant in 1986 and employed 275 by early 1988, with annual turnover rising to £50 million. The other company in this sector, Liner, which employed over 500 in the late 1970s producing innovative handling machinery, has experienced a US takeover and repeated restructuring operations which led in the end to closure in 1987.

Electrical engineering is probably as narrowly-based and beset by problems as is mechanical engineering. Employment has fallen substantially since the late 1970s with major job reductions at NEI Reyrolle, the closure of Plessey's outdated telecommunications plant at South Shields, the closure of Osram's Team Valley lamp factory in 1984 and also big redundancies at Ever Ready in Newburn. There are very few firms producing information technology equipment or which could be said to be at the forefront of electronics technology (see Williams and Charles, 1986). Apart from Marconi, which is predominantly geared to the defence market, the only major employer in this category is Burgess Micro Switch of Team Valley which has about 800 employees making electronic switches for a wide range of machines and telecommunications equipment; design and manufacturing processes are computer aided and controlled and 40% of output is exported. At the end of 1987, Mitsumi Electric announced that it would be setting up a components factory at Jarrow which will initially create 80 jobs. But Tyneside still has a long way to go in building up a significant electronics industry. In this industry, as in engineering generally, there has been some growth in new indigenous businesses—but it has been limited and these new firms are often principally contractors to other local companies, thus having to operate in a difficult market environment.

Closely related to engineering is the manufacture of *other metal goods*, a sector employing around 3,000 people in 1984 at about 70 establishments. Many are small companies producing a variety of miscellaneous metal items ranging from metal furniture to springs and components for other products. On the whole, this industrial group seems to have held up reasonably well over the last few years—though many jobs have been lost—and has had the addition of some new small firms. Among the larger establishments are British Ropes (Bridon) which makes heavy duty wire ropes at Willington Quay; Lamp Metals (owned by Thorn EMI and GEC) at Team Valley which has a workforce of 400 making lighting components; and Torday and Carlisle, a growing North Shields-based company involved in electroplating, marine components and the manufacture of safety equipment for the petrochemicals industry. Ronson, with a factory at West Chirton manufacturing cigarette lighters, has been in receivership twice during the last five years but has survived and recovered by introducing new products, vigorous exporting efforts and the centralisation of production. Interestingly, Ronson's new owners have also converted old factory space at the West Chirton site and at Felling into small units for new start-up firms and achieved considerable success by offering low rents and short lease arrangements.

Metal manufacture

Metal manufacture, currently employing less than 2,000, is not an industry of major importance in Tyneside. It includes several small private sector ferrous foundries and mills largely in specialist markets and also a few works dealing with aluminium and lead. Two major closures have taken place in the last few years. Vickers' non-ferrous metals division closed in 1981 and British Steel's Jarrow steel mill finally closed down in 1986 with 240 redundancies. The Cookson Group (formerly Lead Industries) has maintained a significant presence in Tyneside, still operating its long-established lead works at Elswick with a workforce of around 200 together with Cookson Ceramics and Antimony (Anzon) at Willington Quay. At Anzon an important new product, Syalon, has been developed in association with Newcastle University researchers; Syalon is an ultra-heat-resistant and very strong ceramic having a wide range of potential applications.

Chemicals

The chemicals industry in Tyneside, which employed over 4,000 in 1984, has the advantages of being both modern and diverse. In its diversity lies its strength since it is not dependent on one particular market. There have been reductions in employment in virtually all the Tyneside chemical companies primarily as a result of capital investment in new technology but, unlike most Tyneside industries, there have been no large-scale closures. The two largest companies are Sterling Winthrop/Sterling Organics and Procter & Gamble, both subsidiaries of major US multinationals. Sterling Winthrop at Fawdon, Newcastle, employs about 900 in the production of painkillers and other drugs while the Sterling Organics plant at Dudley in North Tyneside has a workforce of around 500 making fine chemicals for drug preparations. Procter & Gamble, which took over the Hedley soap factory at City Road, Newcastle in 1930, has its UK head office in Gosforth, Research and Development facilities at Longbenton, and manufactures toothpaste and hair shampoo at a purpose-built plant on the Tyne Tunnel estate. Other significant chemical plants in Tyneside include Durham Chemicals at Birtley and Rohm & Haas at Jarrow making a variety of industrial chemicals; Berger Elastomers manufacturing sealants for a range of applications; and International Paints (owned by Courtaulds) at Felling which produces heavy duty paints, including innovative marine finishes, and has on-site Research and Development facilities and exports three-quarters of its output. Decorative laminate producer Formica established its Tyneside plant thirty years ago and, despite some redundancies in 1981 and 1985, still employs around 550 at the Coast Road factory in North Tyneside. The chemicals industry on Tyneside does appear to have strengths—not just in terms of diversity but also the emphasis on high value-added production; it is, however, an industry characterised by high levels of investment in process technology which is often job-displacing.

Food, drink and tobacco

With 6,700 employees, the food, drink and tobacco industry was Tyneside's fourth largest manufacturing industry in 1984, after mechanical and electrical engineering and shipbuilding. Since then, there have been some closures and reductions in employment, but also some new openings and expansions in the food industry; and this sector has become a larger source of employment than shipbuilding in Tyneside.

The Tyne has little port-related food production. With the closure of the RHM Baltic Mills, only one flour mill now survives, Spillers' Tyne Mill (see TUSIU 1985a). A well-known landmark on Newcastle's Quayside, the Tyne Mill has received considerable investment since 1980 and is now a computerised and highly-automated operation. In the baking industry, there has been something of a shift to local companies; for example, Crawford's Bakery (part of United Biscuits) closed down in 1984 while Greggs' of Gosforth, a local company, has expanded both its production and its retail outlets. There has been one very large newcomer to the food industry in Tyneside: Findus Foods which makes frozen foods, specialising in French bread pizzas, beefburgers and low calorie dishes. Findus, owned by Nestles, moved from Humberside to its £30 million purpose-built factory at Benton, in the northern suburbs of Newcastle, in 1983. It now employs 1000, of which 600 are part-time women workers.

Other companies in the food industry include Kavli, a Norwegian company which came to Team Valley in 1939 and makes 'Primula' crispbread and cheese, and Northumbrian Fine Foods (formerly Shaws' Biscuits) which manufactures healthy 'crunch bars' at a technologically-advanced plant also at Team Valley. Rowntree Mackintosh's Fawdon plant, opened in 1958, has shed some jobs but still employs over 900, while Welch's toffee factory in North Shields has been introducing new up-market sugar-free products. Another up-market company is Twinings, with a tea packing plant at the Tyne Tunnel estate, employing around 200.

Frozen food production at Findus. The Findus factory at Benton, opened in 1983, now employs 1,000, including 600 part-time women workers. (*Findus UK Ltd*).

Job losses have come not so much from food manufacturing—which is one of Tyneside's more successful industries—as from the drinks industry and tobacco. The tobacco industry has been completely removed by the closure of WD and HO Wills' Newcastle factory at the end of 1985. Wills, established in 1950, had employed nearly a thousand people in 1981; subsequently Imperial Tobacco concentrated sales functions at its other factories and the introduction of new machinery involved some job losses. Falling sales finally led to retrenchment back to the company's other factories and the decision to close the Newcastle branch plant. In the brewing industry, Tyneside has two major concerns, the Northern Clubs Federation brewery and Scottish & Newcastle. Both have invested heavily in new technology. The Federation brewery has relocated from Newcastle to a new plant at Dunston while Scottish & Newcastle has continued to upgrade its Tyne brewery in Gallowgate, at the same time substantially reducing its workforce.

Textiles and clothing

The textiles and clothing industries together employed over 4,700 in 1984 and some subsequent recovery, reorganisation and growth in the clothing industry has maintained this scale of employment. The vast majority of jobs in the clothing industry (89% in 1984) are held by women and this is one of the prime sources of female employment in manufacturing industry. Both the textiles and clothing industries have seen some big closures, notably the Bridon Fibres ropery at Willington Quay, closed in 1982 with 300 redundancies, and the Levi Strauss jeans factory, which closed with the loss of 280 jobs in 1984. But, on the other hand, there have been some striking successes, in particular J & J Fashions and J Barbour & Sons. J & J, founded in Tyneside in 1974, has grown to become a substantial business employing 2,000 at twelve factories (eight of which are in the North East) with an annual turnover of £40 million by 1988. J & J supplies Marks and Spencer and has continually invested in new technology for cutting and production control. Barbours', a family firm founded in South Shields over a century ago, makes waterproof clothing which has become more and more fashionable—as a result of which it has expanded and more than doubled its Tyneside workforce, from 150 in 1981 to 350 by 1987. There are a number of other large clothing factories in the area, including Dukes & Markus and Ramar Dresses, both of which supply Marks and Spencer; Jockey (formerly Lyle and Scott), owned by Courtaulds, which manufactures men's underwear; and the Co-operative Wholesale Society's shirt factory, virtually the sole survivor of the old CWS 'empire' at Pelaw. In addition, the clothing industry is characterised by many small operations ranging from 'sweat shops', to home-working companies, to new small businesses. Recently, efforts have been made to establish workers' co-operatives as well; Precise Fashions, a co-op set up by former Levi Strauss workers, failed to survive, but Louise Argyle at Hebburn has succeeded, becoming a supplier to Barbours'.

Other manufacturing industries

The manufacture of *bricks, pottery, glass and cement* is, of course, linked directly to the construction industry through brickworks and concrete suppliers. But in Tyneside this group of industries is dominated by a few large employers with specialist products—most of which have substantially cut their workforces during the 1980s. At Lemington, Glass Tubes and Components, which makes industrial glass tubing and bulbs—some still hand-blown—has halved its workforce since 1981. The Anglo Great Lakes Corporation, Newburn, produces graphite for nuclear power stations and, like the power engineering industry, has been affected by delays in the nuclear power station programme. At Jarrow, British Steel's refractory brickworks has closed, reflecting the decline of the steel industry. Probably the most encouraging example in this industrial group is Thermal Syndicate, a long-established company based at Wallsend which manufactures fused silica and magnesia products for the semiconductor 'chip' industry and for fibre optics. Recent major reorganisation and modernisation appears to have saved the company from decline; it now employs 600 people, compared with 500 in 1981. Overall, the bricks, pottery, glass and cement industries provided a total of over 2,100 jobs in Tyneside in 1984; today the figure is likely to be under 2,000.

The *timber and furniture industry* is the only manufacturing industry in Tyneside which experienced significant employment growth in the 1981–4 period. It includes saw mills and joinery works associated with the construction industry but the bulk of employment in the industry is provided by a few large furniture factories. By far the largest operation is Universal Bedding and Upholstery, with 800 employees at three Tyneside factories making beds and three-piece suites. Remploy, at Benton and Jarrow, and 'Be Modern', manufacturing fire surrounds and kitchen furniture, are also major employers. Furniture is also one of the industries which provides opportunities for self-employment for people with carpentry and other skills and hence some new businesses, usually serving highly specific markets, have been set up in managed workshops and other small units.

The *paper, printing and publishing industry* is a fairly important sector of manufacturing, employing around one in twelve of Tyneside's manufacturing workers. In 1984, over 6,500 people worked in this industry; since then, there has been some job shedding but also growth of new businesses. The printing trade, in particular, affords opportunities for new firm formation since printing skills learned elsewhere can be used by the self-employed; capital requirements may be relatively modest and there is a multiplicity of specific market niches which can be exploited. Some of the smaller printers serve only the local market but a surprising number do sell nationally, printing labels, packaging or stationery for companies based in other parts of the country.

The largest firms in printing and publishing are Thomas de la Rue, which prints security stationery and banknotes (for over 80 countries) at Team Valley, and Thomson Regional Newspapers which publishes the *Journal* and *Evening Chronicle* in Newcastle. Ben Johnson (formerly HMSO) at Team Valley employs 260, printing telephone directories; Reed International has a modern plant at Killingworth producing cartons and employing over 300; while John Waddington's factory has 125 workers at Team Valley printing labels and wrappers. In general, the industry is characterised by diversity, by a turnover of smaller firms and, increasingly, by an emphasis on investment in computerised machinery which maintains or provides a competitive edge, or perhaps enables a firm to exploit new markets.

Finally, we come to that group of manufacturing establishments listed in the Standard Industrial Classification under '*other manufacturing*' and employing about 3,200 in 1984. Formerly, the largest company in this sector was Dunlop, with plants at Walker and Team Valley manufacturing industrial and hydraulic hoses. Together, these two plants had about 1,200 workers in 1981; the Walker operation closed in 1985 and the remaining Team Valley factory now has only about 200 employees. Dunlop Armaline has, however, opened a new plant at the Newcastle Offshore Technology Park, on the site of the former Walker shipyard. This plant, which started production in 1988, produces high pressure flexible pipe for the offshore oil and gas industry and provides 165 jobs. Also included in 'other manufacturing' is the long-established Team Valley factory of Armstrong World Industries which makes floor and ceiling tiles and employs about 300 people. There are a few medium-sized companies as well; an example is Lion Brush Works, Killingworth, founded by a German Jewish emigré in 1944 and employing over 100, making cosmetic brushes and other beauty care products.

The construction industry

In 1984 there were over 20,000 people employed at over a thousand establishments in the construction industry in Tyneside and probably several thousand others in self-employment. It is a sector characterised by very many small businesses and also some large employers in civil engineering and housebuilding. Several nationally-known housebuilding companies originated in Tyneside, such as Barratt and Bellway—both of which still have their head offices in the area. The local authorities are also large employers in the industry through their public works departments or direct labour organisations. Employment in construction in Tyneside fell sharply during the recession, but may well have experienced some expansion since 1984 in response to the general economic upturn, the construction of some major developments (like the MetroCentre), and the encouragement of self-employment.

The service sector

The service sector as a whole now accounts for about seven out of ten jobs in Tyneside. It is a very diverse sector, encompassing many different economic activities, ranging from education and health services through to pubs and clubs. In Mess's time, mining and manufacturing self-evidently formed the backbone of the local (and also national) economy; today, the service sector is dominant, at least in terms of employment.

In the country as a whole, service sector employment has grown steadily since the war, with a particularly marked increase in the 1970s. Tyneside shared in this growth, with the number of service sector jobs rising from 210,500 in 1971 to over 235,000 in 1978. Subsequently, in the depths of the recession, employment in the service sector in Tyneside declined, falling from 235,000 to 225,000 in the period 1978–81. This 4% decline was, however, much less severe than the 20% decline in manufacturing jobs over the same period. Since 1981, the service sector has experienced some recovery and renewed employment growth—though it is difficult to estimate *how much* growth. Between 1981 and 1984, the service sector as a whole recorded an increase of nearly 3,000 jobs in Tyneside, a rise of just over 1% (though this will be an underestimate because some service employment goes unrecorded). Since 1984, it seems likely that service growth has accelerated, though perhaps generating no more than a 2% to 3% increase in service sector jobs between 1984 and 1987.

Public sector services. Over 100,000 of the 227,500 service jobs in Tyneside in 1984 were in public sector services. This includes jobs in national and local government administration, education, health services, the police and fire service, the utilities, public transport and postal and telecommunications services. These public sector services clearly represent a vital component of the local economy both because of the services they provide and also because they represent a major source of employment. Altogether, these public services account for about 30% of *all* jobs in Tyneside. In Newcastle, the District which has the conurbation's main concentration of offices and hospitals, as well as the Polytechnic and University, about 40% of *all* jobs are in public sector services. Privatisation of British Telecom (in 1985) and British Gas (in 1986) will, of course, have reduced the public sector element within services, but only to a small extent.

Of the 100,000 jobs in public sector services in Tyneside in 1984, more than half were in the *local authorities*. The four Tyneside District Councils, together with the now-abolished County Council, had 51,616 employees in 1985, half of them working in education. Total employment in *education* appears to have remained fairly stable in recent years though there has been some shift from full-time to part-time jobs in ancillary services. In 1985, the four Tyneside local education authorities—the District Councils—employed 25,028 people at schools, colleges and at Newcastle Polytechnic. Of this total, only about half were actually engaged as teachers or lecturers, the rest being employed as ancillary staff (kitchen staff, cleaners, caretakers) or administrative staff within town halls or at the educational institutions themselves. In addition to local authority education services, some 3,570 people are employed at the University of Newcastle and around 1,000 in Tyneside's private sector schools.

Employment in *medical and dental services* stands at around 23,000, including 18,400 working for the National Health Service in Tyneside's hospitals and clinics (in 1986). Of these, half (9,200) are nurses and midwives; another 2,100 are employed in clerical or administrative jobs, and 3,900 in ancillary services. This employment is heavily concentrated in Newcastle (11,000 out of the total of 18,400 work in the Newcastle area) because the major hospitals are located in the city—notably the Royal Victoria Infirmary, Newcastle General and the Freeman Hospital. The vast majority of those working in the medical and dental services work for the NHS, but there is also a small private health sector which includes private practice, nursing homes and the private Nuffield Hospital in Jesmond, Newcastle.

After education and medicine, the third largest source of public sector employment is *national government service*. This includes various local offices such as Jobcentres and unemployment benefit offices (both run by the Department of Employment), the benefit offices of the Department of Health and Social Security (DHSS), and the tax offices of the Inland Revenue. In addition, there are the regional offices of several government departments. But the most important single source of government jobs in Tyneside is the massive DHSS office complex at Longbenton, north Newcastle, which employs about 8,000 people. This is the 'nerve centre' of the country's social security system, with records of everyone who has contributed to the National Insurance Scheme. Here, claimants' eligibility for benefits is checked and this centre is also responsible for administering pensions. In the past, the Longbenton complex employed hundreds of ledger clerks dealing with paper records; today, the routine work is computerised. New technology has enabled the introduction of a more complex benefits system and brought more work to Longbenton, offsetting labour savings brought about through computerisation. Employment has thus remained fairly stable in recent years—a situation which contrasts with the trend of growth experienced in the past. Future employment levels are uncertain but it is evident that there are still opportunities for further computerisation and the possibility of a significant reduction in the number of staff.

'Nerve centre' of the country's social security system – the DHSS complex at Longbenton. Computers have replaced ledger clerks for the routine work. (*DHSS*).

Several other components of the service sector are wholly, or predominantly, within the public sector though affected increasingly by privatisation. Within the utilities, British Gas has been privatised and the electricity and water authorities are to follow. Bus services have been 'deregulated', leading to the increasing involvement of private sector operators, but the railways still remain firmly in the public sector. British Telecom is now a private sector company, while the Post Office remains publicly-owned. The utilities, telecommunications and postal services have all been significantly affected by the introduction of new technology in relation both to the administration of services (e.g. accounts) and delivery (e.g. automated postal sorting, electronic telephone exchanges, electronic fault diagnosis on supply lines). Within the transport industry, British Rail has been strongly affected by a concern to reduce costs and meet cash limits which has resulted in extensive 'de-manning' exercises; the number of jobs on the railways fell by 20% in Tyneside between 1981 and 1984. However, there have been no line closures in Tyneside in the past few years.

Private sector services. The largest single industry in private sector services is *retailing*, which employed just over 30,000 people in Tyneside in 1984, most of them women and many working part-time. Retailing has undergone enormous changes in Tyneside and is, without doubt, a dynamic and successful part of the local economy in spite of economic recession and high unemployment. Several factors seem to account for this apparent paradox. Partly, it stems from the growth in income enjoyed by those in work coupled with the fact that Tynesiders tend to spend money in the shops rather than on housing or cars. The boom in consumer credit has also clearly stimulated the retail sector. In addition, Newcastle city centre and, more recently, the MetroCentre in Gateshead, have succeeded in drawing in shoppers from a large region-wide catchment area.

The development of central Newcastle, involving the completion of the Eldon Square shopping complex in the mid-1970s, served to significantly strengthen the role of Newcastle as a regional shopping centre offering a wide and attractively presented range of consumer durables. The city centre's dominant role was further underlined by the completion of the Metro rapid transit system in the early 1980s which helped to bring in shoppers from the rest of Tyneside and overcome the city centre's car parking problems.[5] Eldon Square has been highly successful and has continued to expand through the incorporation of adjacent areas. Rents are high, reflecting high levels of turnover. Some of the chain stores in central Newcastle are among the most successful in their group: turnover at Newcastle's Marks and Spencer store in Northumberland Street, for example, is only surpassed by their store in London's Oxford Street.

The success of shops in Eldon Square and adjacent streets has had detrimental impacts on some other parts of the city centre—Clayton

Street, for example—which have become marginal and 'down-market'; moreover, Eldon Square and the Metro system have served to strengthen city centre shopping at the expense of some of Tyneside's other shopping areas.

While redevelopment of city and town centre shopping was a feature of Tyneside in the 1970s, the emphasis in the 1980s has been increasingly on the development of new out-of-town shopping facilities. This includes a number of single-store hypermarket developments on the conurbation periphery, but by far the largest of the developments is the £200 million MetroCentre—not on the edge of the conurbation but certainly well away from existing in-town shopping facilities. Despite its name, it is not on the Metro network but it does now have a newly-built railway station and is also well served by buses. It is particularly attractive to car-borne shoppers since it provides some 10,000 free parking spaces.

Built on 115 acres of derelict land next to the Tyne at Dunston—within the Enterprise Zone and thus benefiting from tax allowances on development and rate-free until 1991—the MetroCentre is really an extraordinary development, massive and totally new. Construction started on the site—formerly used as an ash tip for Dunston Power Station—in 1984 and by the end of 1987 over 2 million square feet of retail space had been completed, attracting over a quarter of a million shoppers a week.

The MetroCentre at Dunston, Gateshead, 1988. The largest shopping centre in Europe, with 2 million square feet of retail space, ten-screen cinema, indoor funfair and 10,000 free car parking spaces. (*Air Fotos*).

The main part of the scheme consists of several major stores, linked by covered shopping malls; ultimately there will be 300 shops, large and small, in the development. It is well patronised and apparently popular, a vindication of the faith the developer had in building what is claimed to be the largest shopping centre in Europe (the fourth largest in the world) on a desolate site in a run-down and neglected part of Tyneside. Leisure and recreational facilities are an integral part of the concept, and include a ten-screen cinema and 'Metroland', a large indoor funfair. The MetroCentre has become a major source of employment, providing around 4,000 jobs by 1988, including many part-time jobs.

There is little doubt—though evidence is hard to come by—that the MetroCentre has taken trade from other shopping areas in Tyneside, especially from the less attractive 'secondary' centres like Gateshead town centre but also from Newcastle city centre (Davies, 1988). However, the MetroCentre's catchment is very extensive, bringing in people from as far afield as Lancashire, Yorkshire, Cumbria and Scotland, such that Tyneside does gain from 'exporting' these shopping services in much the same way as an area can reap the advantage of income from tourism. Tyneside's traditional shopping centres are not only experiencing pressure from the MetroCentre but are also threatened by other out-of-town developments such as the new retail park ('Retail World') in the Team Valley section of the Enterprise Zone, providing DIY and other 'bulky goods' stores, and hypermarket developments on the conurbation periphery.

There has been a growing concentration of retailing in large and more efficient outlets, coupled with the decline of the 'corner shop' and secondary shopping centres. Even so, it is worth pointing out that there are still very many small outlets—Tyneside has about 3,000 shops, of which only about 40 employ more than 100 staff and most of these large outlets are in the city centre and the MetroCentre. But growing concentration, increasing efficiency and productivity, led to a steady reduction in employment, at least up to 1984. Since then, new jobs at the MetroCentre will have increased retailing employment—though perhaps only temporarily since the MetroCentre will displace jobs in other shopping centres in Tyneside; this impact is only slowly working through the system.

'*Other distribution*', which includes wholesaling and dealing in industrial materials like building materials and machinery, employed over 12,000 people in 1984 with little decline since 1981. Like retailing, this appears to be a reasonably buoyant activity, and has opportunities for increased productivity and mechanisation. As with many other industries—especially in manufacturing but also in the service sector—an increase in trade and turnover can be accommodated without employment growth as a result of gains in productivity. This is seen, too, in the case of garages—*motor repairers, distributors and filling stations*— which employed 5,600 people in Tyneside in 1984. Employment here fell from 1978 to 1981, followed by a smaller decline to 1984, even though car ownership has grown. The introduction of self-service at filling stations is one obvious example demonstrating how growth in trade may not necessarily lead to growth in jobs.

In Tyneside, as in the country as a whole, there has been recent growth in *insurance, banking, finance and business services* and also in *accountancy and legal services*. These services are concentrated in Newcastle which has a distinct, if rather small, business quarter and they serve both individual 'consumers' and also companies. But while there has been growth it is still the case that Tyneside, and the North East in general, does not have a very substantial representation of these services (see Green, 1985). It has been argued that this is one source of the area's problems. In particular, there is no bank based and headquartered in Newcastle especially concerned to serve the interests of the region; the area has no indigenous and regionally-partisan financial sector—as the Scots have—giving access to finance for local companies. Be that as it may, there is no doubt that Tyneside and the region are 'under-serviced' and that the tendency for accountancy firms or banks to serve the North East from regional headquarters in Leeds, for example, does mean that Tyneside has not shared fully in the growth in this sector.

Since the late 1970s there has been some employment growth in *leisure services*, a category encompassing cinemas, theatres, television, sport and betting. Nearly 7,000 worked in these services in 1984, a similar number as in 1981. Since then, there may well have been further growth stemming from increasing provision of sports facilities in particular. Nevertheless, despite the current emphasis on the prospects for growth in the 'leisure industries' it is difficult to envisage this becoming a major source of employment. The same can be said of *hotels, restaurants, cafés and catering*, providing about 5,700 jobs in Tyneside in 1984—fewer than in 1981. Tyneside's 'night life' is developing and lifestyles are changing, with more people going to restaurants; but the prospects for growth must be quite limited—dependent on rising incomes or, alternatively, the development of tourism. The declining number of jobs in *pubs and clubs* no doubt reflects changing life styles but the demise of this recreational activity is certainly not in sight: spending on alcohol in Tyneside is still well above the national average and, with 9,500 working in pubs and clubs (as well as two major breweries) this is the largest component of the leisure 'industry'.

Finally, we come to '*other services*' which, as Figure 2.1 shows, is the fastest growing source of jobs in Tyneside. This is really a diverse miscellany of activities including welfare and community services; trade unions and professional services; and services like hairdressing and laundries. Here, the greatest growth has been in community and welfare services, including voluntary sector organisations, growth which has been primarily stimulated by the expansion of MSC-funded activities. Dry cleaning, laundries and personal services like hairdressing have also witnessed growth. Again, it would probably be over-optimistic to expect *major* additional expansion of employment in these activities over the short to medium term.

This, then, completes our somewhat lengthy—though still necessarily limited—review of the various industries of Tyneside. It is a complex picture, diverse and difficult to encapsulate. In the next section we try to establish some of the salient characteristics of this complex picture and then turn to policies and prospects.

Key Features of the Tyneside Economy— a Summary

The Tyneside economy has evidently been under severe pressure in the past few years. Tyneside has been particularly hard-hit by recession and jobs have been lost, on a large scale, in virtually all parts of the economy. Economic recovery has been weak and patchy—in fact, many industries are still trying to recover from recession.

The *manufacturing sector* has witnessed major decline: in the worst years of the recession, 1978–81, employment in Tyneside's manufacturing industries fell by 20%. The long-term decline of Tyneside's traditional industries continued and accelerated: between 1981 and 1984, manufacturing employment declined by a further 23%. Mining has all but disappeared while shipbuilding has seen massive job losses (employment fell from 21,000 in 1978 to about 4,000 in 1987), and heavy engineering has been struggling to win orders and be competitive. But even in the 1980s, Tyneside was still heavily dependent on traditional industries which were undergoing long-term (perhaps terminal) decline and which bore the brunt of recession.

There are, of course, some 'success stories' as well. Chemicals, the food industry, timber and furniture and the clothing industry have fared reasonably well and there are successful and progressive companies in these industries. In addition, a few new large scale manufacturing developments have come to Tyneside—Findus, Komatsu and Dunlop Armaline. The existence of some buoyant components of the manufacturing sector suggests that Tyneside will continue to have a significant role as a manufacturing centre, but neither the 'success stories' nor inward investment seem likely to reverse the decline in manufacturing jobs.

Tyneside's manufacturing industry is predominantly externally-owned and externally-controlled. Most of the larger manufacturing establishments in the area are branch plants of national and multinational companies with headquarters elsewhere—principally in London. The experience of recent years does suggest that this is a source of weakness (Smith, 1986). Branch plants are often poorly integrated into the local economy in terms of their inputs and outputs and may be perceived as expendable 'outposts' (Austrin and Beynon, 1979). The closure of T.I. Churchill and Wills, for example, seem to indicate retrenchment back to base and underline the marginalised role of the branch plant. On the other hand, in the absence of a sufficiently large and dynamic indigenous sector, attracting branch plants (however short their survival) is generally regarded as vital to the maintenance of Tyneside's manufacturing industry. The alternative—the stimulation of self-employment and encouragement of local small businesses—has received a great deal of attention in the past few years and is, no doubt, worthwhile. In particular, it acknowledges the problem of dependence on the branch plant sector. The main trouble is, however, that small businesses generate few jobs, many fail and very few show significant growth.

Falling employment in manufacturing is a feature of the UK economy as a whole and, indeed, of all advanced economies, with the progressive shift towards the service economy. Tyneside has shared this experience—though suffered more than many other areas, losing a larger proportion of manufacturing jobs and witnessing less growth in the service sector. The service sector, which actually lost employment during the 1978–81 period in Tyneside, has not compensated for jobs lost in manufacturing. But the service sector has become the major source of employment in Tyneside, accounting for 69% of jobs by 1984.

Around 44% of Tyneside's service jobs are in *public sector services*—in education, health, local and central government services, the utilities, transport and communications. These activities have been undergoing change as a result of government pressure to reduce public expenditure and carry through policies of privatisation and deregulation. Even so, these changes have not been as traumatic as those experienced in manufacturing. Unlike shipbuilding or heavy engineering, there can be no doubt that these essential services will survive and will provide employment. What is far from clear is how much employment they will provide, given the growing impact of technological change on office work (see Foord and Gillespie, 1986) and the continuing effort to contain or reduce public expenditure. It is also not clear which of these services will remain within the public sector and which will be privatised.

Private sector services include retailing which, as we have shown, has been dynamic and witnessed considerable change. Again, Tyneside has followed national trends and developments, including increasing concentration as a result of the growing domination of national chain stores and the decline of the small trader and even regional chains. As elsewhere, out-of-town shopping has grown—despite the planners' efforts to restrain it—and become more and more important. The MetroCentre is certainly the most striking example of the trend, extraordinary for its scale and location.

Few economic activities in Tyneside showed growth in employment in the early 1980s. Some personal services, leisure, catering, finance and various business services did, however, witness growth of outlets and employment. There may well be scope for further growth—for financial services as shareholding widens, for example, or for hotels and restaurants as social habits change and perhaps as tourism develops. Such growth does, however, substantially rely on rising disposable income—by no means guaranteed in Tyneside.

Economic Policies and Prospects

Policies

The decline of the Tyneside economy has been accompanied by a proliferation of public policy measures aimed at arresting decline and regenerating the economy. Both central and local government have been developing and implementing a variety of new policies since the late 1970s. Tyneside has become a policy 'laboratory', subject to a complex array of economic policies with varied (if sometimes unclear) objectives and focussing on different components of the economic structure and different parts of the conurbation (Robinson *et al.*, 1987).

The longest-established economic development policy is the government's *regional policy* which has been in operation for most of the past fifty years. It is salutary to reflect that Tyneside was among the 'Depressed Areas' subject to regional policy in the 1930s and is still receiving regional policy aid in the 1980s because of its high level of unemployment. The whole of Tyneside has 'Development Area' status and companies undertaking investment have thus been able to apply to the Department of Trade and Industry for financial subsidies in the form of Regional Development Grant (abolished in 1988) and Regional Selective Assistance. Expenditure on regional aid has been generally declining in recent years and further reductions are planned. In 1983/84 Tyneside companies received around £18.4 million regional policy assistance and by 1985/6 this had fallen to £13.9 million.

Regional assistance has, until recently, had a strong emphasis on support for large-scale investment projects and capital-intensive manufacturing industry. Historically, regional policy aid was seen primarily as a means for inducing companies to establish branch plants in the area and policy was, in this way, instrumental in creating the 'branch plant economy'. While the encouragement of such inward investment is still a significant part of regional policy it has become less important, at least in terms of expenditure, as the supply of inward investment projects has declined. Over the last decade or more, much of the assistance has in fact gone to help companies already in the area—helping firms like NEI and Scottish & Newcastle Breweries to modernise and develop their production facilities—often without generating additional jobs (indeed, sometimes displacing employment).

Significant revisions to regional policy were made in 1984 and again in 1988. In 1984, Regional Development Grant was restyled so that it was focused on job-creating investment and aided more smaller firms. Subsequently, in 1988, RDG was abolished entirely, though Regional Selective Assistance was retained. At the same time, a new Regional Enterprise Grant for smaller firms in Development Areas was introduced, along with new grants to help meet the costs of consultancy assistance for business development. Regional policy may have become more sensitive to needs but expenditure has been cut and policy action has shifted to other measures and forms of intervention in the economy.

Up until the early 1970s, economic development policy in Tyneside was fairly simple and could be described quite easily. At that time it basically comprised regional assistance measures together with the government-funded factory construction programme undertaken by *English Estates*. In addition, inward investment was encouraged by the *North of England Development Council*, a region-wide promotional organisation financed by central and local government. Some of the local authorities also sought to attract industry to their areas through their own promotional efforts and advertising.

Today, the picture is far more complex. These long-established activities continue—with some changes in emphasis and scope—but to them have been added a range of new initiatives, agencies and measures. In the early 1970s the local authorities in Tyneside, as elsewhere, did relatively little in terms of economic development; since then, they have become more and more involved in this field and some of the Tyneside authorities have become widely recognised for successful policy development and implementation. In the last few years, central government has also sought new approaches to economic development, including the designation of an Enterprise Zone and, more recently, the establishment of an Urban Development Corporation in the area. Regional policy has been eclipsed by a steady stream of new measures and a shift of attention and resources from regional to urban policy. At the same time, the strong focus on small businesses and the creation of an 'enterprise culture' have been key features of central and also local government policy initiatives and have brought about the establishment of enterprise agencies, training courses for potential entrepreneurs and advisory services. As well as all this, central government intervention in the labour market has grown enormously as a result of the expansion and widening role of the Manpower Services Commission.

The 1980s has thus been a period characterised by a great deal of policy activity; it has not been particularly easy to keep track of new policies and institutions and this proliferation has led to ritual calls for more co-ordination. Funding for policy measures has also become much more complicated, especially since the European Community has become an increasingly important source of finance.

Here we have not attempted to describe in great detail all these policy measures and institutions but, rather, give an indication of the main elements of policy. This serves to show the principal concerns of policy and where attention is concentrated, thus revealing the strengths and weaknesses of current public policy intervention in the Tyneside economy.

To begin with, the *local authorities* now make a major contribution to local economic development policy in Tyneside, though some Councils are very much more active than others[6]. A major thrust of policy has been to pursue 'physical' measures—the acquisition and servicing of industrial sites and the construction of small factory units to rent. Much of this activity has been concentrated in the 23 Industrial Improvement Areas which the local authorities have designated right along the banks of the Tyne; the aim here has been to restore the viability of these older industrial areas through a combination of physical measures and so help maintain inner city employment.

Without doubt, the construction of small factory units by the local authorities has been of considerable importance, meeting the needs of smaller firms and compensating for the lack of interest shown by private developers. Moreover, the Tyneside local authorities also developed innovative forms of provision, notably a wide range of 'managed workshops' projects which offer on-site advisory services, shared facilities and cheap space for new businesses in a 'sheltered' environment. As well as these physical measures, a further important area is the provision of financial assistance, representing about a quarter of the economic development expenditure of Tyneside's local authorities. Much of this assistance takes the form of small grants to help new and small businesses, often tenants of local authority units. In addition, there has been an increasing emphasis on policies designed to stimulate particular sectors of the economy such as offshore technology, the media industries and, most recently, tourism (e.g. South Tyneside's 'Catherine Cookson Country' promotion).

Nearly half the local authority expenditure on economic development policy in Tyneside is financed specifically by central government through the Department of Environment's Urban Programme. Newcastle and Gateshead are 'Partnership Authorities', receiving major funding from the Urban Programme (totalling £18.4 million in 1986/7), while North and South Tyneside receive smaller amounts of aid as 'Programme Authorities' (£7.9 million between them in 1986/7). The Urban Programme supports a wide range of economic, environmental and social projects in the inner areas of Tyneside and also includes the Urban Development Grant scheme which subsidises private sector development projects. £42m out of £111m received by Tyneside's local authorities from the Urban Programme in 1979–84 has been earmarked for economic projects and this has clearly been an important stimulus to the development and maintenance of policy activity at a time when mainstream central government support through the Rate Support Grant has been progressively reduced. As well as securing funding from the Urban Programme the local authorities have also been active in seeking funds from other sources, notably from the European Community. The European Social Fund has provided finance for wage subsidy schemes operated by the local authorities, while the Community's Regional Development Fund has supported the provision of industrial premises and other infrastructure projects.

The bulk of local authority economic development expenditure in Tyneside (including expenditure funded from the Urban Programme and the European Community) is largely focused on help for new and small businesses. There is little large-scale or strategic policy, especially since the demise of the County Council. Local authority economic development policies in Tyneside are generally conventional and non-controversial in comparison with the more radical and interventionist policies of authorities like the old GLC and Sheffield City Council.

A new small business – making gates and doors. One of the tenants of the TEDCO workshops at the former Plessey factory, South Shields. (*Newcastle Chronicle & Journal*).

Local authority factory units at Maurice Road, Wallsend. Units like this, rented to small businesses, have been built throughout Tyneside by the public sector to stimulate the development of small businesses.
(*North Tyneside MBC*).

The Tyneside authorities have held back from developing more interventionist approaches (like equity investment in local firms through Enterprise Boards) and instead have sought to maintain, refashion, and improve upon, the more conventional measures formulated in the late 1970s and early 1980s.

Alongside this local authority activity there are a number of agencies which also are mainly concerned with the small firms sector. ENTRUST, (Tyne and Wear Enterprise Trust), gives help to entrepreneurs and advises on business development, in part funded under the DTI's Business Improvement Services Scheme which is, in turn, financed by the European Regional Development Fund. ENTRUST has become a key agency in the small business field and has offices in each of the four Tyneside Districts. Enterprise agencies set up by British Coal and British Shipbuilders have also been active in Tyneside, both seeking to help create jobs in areas where they have implemented redundancies, principally by offering advice and some financial help to people setting up in business in conjunction with other agencies. In South Shields another enterprise agency, the Tyneside Economic Development Company, provides workshop space for small businesses in the former Plessey factory and in Newcastle a Youth Enterprise Centre has been developed by Project North East. Both these initiatives receive significant private sector support. At a former clothing factory in Gateshead, a new managed workspace development for design-oriented businesses called 'Design Works' has been set up with funding from the Burton Group, the construction firm McAlpine, and central and local government. The Northern Region Co-operative Development Agency, formed to encourage the establishment of workers' co-operatives, and the North East Media Development Council which promotes the media industries, were both originally set up with the encouragement and support of the former County Council and now receive funding from the District Councils. Local authorities have also supported several initiatives and agencies aiming to promote technological development, such as the Tyne and Wear Innovation Centre, the Micro-electronics Applications Research Institute (MARI) and the Newcastle Technology Centre. Both MARI and the Technology Centre have strong links with the University and the Polytechnic and now receive major funding from central government sources.

Meanwhile, as local policies and projects have grown and developed, central government has been pursuing several new initiatives to promote economic regeneration. In 1981, the Tyneside *Enterprise Zone* was designated, one of 25 such Zones in the UK where firms enjoy an exemption from rates for ten years (up until 1991) and can claim 100% capital allowances against Income Tax and Corporation Tax on industrial and commercial buildings. There are also fewer planning restrictions in the Zones, with developers given considerable freedom within a broad land use specification. The costs of the Zones are substantial. Exemption from rates (reimbursed to local authorities by the Exchequer) cost £7.3 million in the Tyneside Zone between 1981 and 1984; the tax allowances will have been even greater and the public sector has spent large sums on infrastructure.

The Tyneside Enterprise Zone covers 1,100 acres of riverside land in west Newcastle and Gateshead, together with the southern part of English Estates' Team Valley Industrial Estate. So far, industrial development has been limited; the largest industrial project is Vickers' new tank factory at Scotswood which moved from the adjacent Elswick site and there are also new small factory units at Team Valley. Most movement of activity into the Zone has involved short distance moves of firms from other parts of the area to take advantage of the rates holiday; a recent case in point is the movement of the Bonas Machine Co. from Sunderland—also hard-hit by unemployment—to the Team Valley Zone. And the Zone's incentives, though partly eroded by rises in rentals and land values in the Zone, have served to reduce interest in development at other Tyneside locations. But commercial development has been stimulated by the Zone; the rates and tax advantages were of considerable importance in the development of the MetroCentre retail project at Dunston and the 'Retail World' development at Team Valley. The MetroCentre is the largest and most apparent 'success' to result from the Zone's designation but it is also the case that the policy has helped to restore and bring back into use derelict and difficult riverside sites. This will be helped further by the landscaping and development of adjacent land for the 1990 National Garden Festival in Gateshead. But job generation has been disappointing—apart from jobs associated with the MetroCentre which may be expected to lead, ultimately, to the displacement of some retailing jobs elsewhere in Tyneside.

The actual implementation of the Enterprise Zone policy—which includes the formulation of planning guidelines, management and promotion—has largely been the responsibility of the local authorities.

Artist's impression of the £50 million Newcastle Business Park to be developed at the old Vickers site at Elswick. The project involves collaboration between a private developer and the new Tyne & Wear Urban Development Corporation and is planned to provide industrial and commercial premises and also waterfront pubs and restaurants. (*Newcastle Chronicle & Journal*).

Likewise, implementation of policies within the Department of Environment's Urban Programme has largely rested with the local authorities. More recently, however, this balance between local and central government has shifted in favour of more direct central government involvement in implementation as well as finance. This is apparent in relation to the new *Tyne and Wear Urban Development Corporation* established in 1987, which aims to support the economic regeneration of the conurbation's riverside areas by undertaking projects which will 'lever' private sector investment. The Corporation is a 'quango' run by a board appointed by the Environment Secretary and is thus quite separate from local government (see Byrne, 1987). Its creation marks an attempt by central government to assume more direct control and more fully incorporate private sector interests. The Urban Development Corporation has a budget of about £150 million spread over five or six years, to be spent on land acquisition, site servicing and subsidies for private sector property development. The Corporation is involved in the Offshore Technology Park at Walker; the planned Business Park at Elswick; Barratt's riverside village and marina project at St Peter's Basin, Walker; and hotel and redevelopment schemes on Newcastle Quayside. The aim is to stimulate a strong private sector reponse and rejuvenate some of the most run-down parts of the area.

Alongside the regional and urban policies of central government are the labour market measures pursued by the *Manpower Services Commission* (MSC) which are of major importance. The MSC's expenditure in Tyneside is now considerably greater than either regional aid or spending on the Urban Programme. The main elements are the Youth Training Scheme, for school-leavers, and the Community Programme, a 'make-work' scheme for the long-term unemployed. Both of these (discussed more fully in Chapter 3) make some contribution to economic development, though it can be argued that there is often little co-ordination between these MSC schemes and other economic policy measures. A third, but much smaller, part of MSC policy is the Enterprise Allowance Scheme which offers an allowance to unemployed people starting a business; this is more clearly tied into broader economic development objectives, especially the various measures aimed at stimulating the creation of small businesses. Linked to this, the MSC also now has responsibility for the Small Firms Service which provides information on self-employment and a counselling service for small businesses.

The proliferation of policies and agencies in Tyneside has reached the point where co-ordination is becoming more and more necessary. This is perhaps especially so in the small business field, where the potential entrepreneur can certainly be forgiven for being confused by the variety of agencies and schemes offering help. But co-ordination also seems essential in bringing together broad areas of policy—linking training provision with industrial development, for example.

Some steps have been taken towards policy co-ordination. In 1984, the government set up a '*City Action Team*' in an effort to ensure more effective co-ordination of central government policy measures in the inner areas of Tyneside. In 1986, a new region-wide agency, the *Northern Development Company* (NDC) was established with the support of the business community, trade unions and the local authorities. The NDC is the successor to a long line of regional institutions, stretching back over fifty years, concerned with articulating and ameliorating the region's economic problems (Cousins *et al.*, 1974). It is intended to provide a 'one-stop shop' for industrialists considering locating in the North (it has incorporated the long-established North of England Development Council) and is also concerned to change the 'image' of the region and co-ordinate sections of industry. Its budget, at £2.3 million for 1988/9, is relatively modest. In 1988, another attempt at co-ordination was launched: the CBI's '*Newcastle Initiative*', which involves bringing together representatives of the private and public sectors to promote various urban regeneration schemes in Newcastle. The main schemes are the rejuvenation of Grey Street as a commercial centre, the creation of a 'theatre village' area in Newcastle's West End and fostering cultural and commercial ties with Japan. Yet, for all these efforts, critics justifiably point out that there is still no *major* development organisation in the region like the Scottish Development Agency which could take a lead role in economic policy and there remains a great deal of scope for more co-ordination and possibly even a rationalisation of policy measures and organisations.

What, then, have these policies achieved so far in Tyneside? New sources of economic activity and jobs have been generated by the various policies aimed at encouraging self-employment and small businesses. The many small businesses now occupying enterprise workshops and nursery factory units are evidence of the success of policy and the relative vitality of the small firms sector. This sector is, however, characterised by high failure rates and few small firms grow to become significant employers, nor have employment gains in small firms done much to compensate for the job losses experienced by Tyneside's large firms. But this sector is widely seen as the key to economic regeneration in the future and its encouragement has been as much a feature of the policies of the Labour local authorities as of the Conservative government. Old expectations of lifelong employment in large companies have been shattered by economic change (Pyke, 1982), but the new values of the 'enterprise culture' and self-employment are only beginning to be established.

Regional policy has helped to bring new activities and jobs to Tyneside. Despite criticisms of an approach creating a dependent and externally controlled 'branch plant economy', the attraction of inward investment remains a major part of policy. The attraction of such projects has become more and more difficult, though there have been a few notable successes in recent years. It does seem clear, however, that the attraction of new branch plants, while providing a useful addition to the economy and employment is unable to compensate for job losses in Tyneside's existing industries.

Within the manufacturing sector, lack of competitiveness has long been identified as a basic weakness—both in Tyneside and in UK industry as a whole. Policy has gone some way towards remedying this, through regional aid for investment and technology initiatives. Investment to raise productivity has been essential to the survival of many firms in Tyneside, though it has often meant reductions in employment. Despite major investment, competitiveness has been difficult to achieve in Tyneside's traditional industries like shipbuilding and power engineering where international competition is severe; these industries also remain heavily dependent on favourable government decisions on defence spending and power station orders.

The regeneration of industry and creation of new jobs is a slow process and difficult to evaluate. Tyneside still seems to be recovering from the recession and it is unclear how far new initiatives and small firms will be able to make up for the losses of the older industries.

While the impact of industrial measures is debatable and difficult to establish, it is apparent that policy measures have succeeded in promoting the *physical* regeneration of some of Tyneside's inner areas. Supported by central government, the local authorities have cleared and restored large areas of derelict land, while the Garden Festival will turn dereliction into a tourist attraction and parkland, subsequently to be used for housing. Urban Programme funding has been used to rejuvenate Industrial Improvement Areas, build new factory units and develop infrastructure. Urban Development Grants have helped to stimulate new housing and commercial development in the inner areas, helping to bring new life to Newcastle's Quayside, for example. This process will be further promoted through the activities of the new Urban Development Corporation which, it is hoped, will encourage private investment and create new economic activities. Enterprise Zone designation has also brought about the development of derelict and difficult riverside sites. Some of the problems of the physical fabric of the conurbation are thus being tackled; it remains to be seen whether this will be accompanied by an economic regeneration sufficient to substantially ameliorate Tyneside's unemployment problems.

Prospects

Successive reports analysing the economic problems and prospects of the North East[7] have pointed to the inherent weaknesses of the region's economy and the considerable difficulties which lie ahead. The government's recent submission to the European Regional Development Fund, for example, stated:

'Despite signs of a continuing upturn in the UK economy, there are few indications of recovery in the North East where employment continues to decline contrary to the national trend. The prospects for the regional economy in the short term are likely to be affected by a number of constraining factors, notably:

(i) an unfavourable industrial structure and a continuing loss of employment in the Region's basic industries (particularly coal-mining);

(ii) a limited amount of footloose industry as a result of low economic growth and high unemployment nationally and internationally;

(iii) a poor image of the North East amongst industrialists, developers and investors;

(iv) continuing restraint on public expenditure restricting direct employment in public services and indirect employment arising from public investment.

All these factors will affect the region's ability to respond to an upturn in the national economy, and reduce the likelihood of any significant increase in the overall level of employment in the North East in the short term. Much of the region's progress over the next few years will depend on the ability of local firms and entrepreneurs to generate new sources of employment, and the efforts of local and other public authorities to create the right conditions for growth in the indigenous sector and the attraction of mobile industry. It will be particularly important in this context for the region to exploit its full potential in the promotion of high technology industries and other important growth sectors such as tourism, and to ensure continued improvement in the rate of new firm formation'. (DTI, 1986, para 7A, 1.31).

For the most part, these observations (this 'gloomy prognostication') are directly relevant to the situation of Tyneside. However, Tyneside does, at least, have the advantage of being the region's principal conurbation and service centre. It is the largest shopping and commercial centre between Leeds and Edinburgh and this generates a substantial amount of economic activity and employment.

Over the next few years, Tyneside seems set to continue the transition from a manufacturing economy to a service economy. Employment in the area's traditional manufacturing industries and large companies may be expected to decline further, both through competitive pressures and technological change. The introduction of new technology could well reduce employment in some parts of the service sector such as clerical work and retailing. But some new jobs will be created in the small firms sector and in the growing 'low-tech' and low-paid personal services. This growth is not likely to be sufficient to increase the overall level of employment and significantly narrow the gap between labour supply and demand.

NOTES

1. Local song quoted in Heslop, 1899.
2. A detailed account of Tyneside's economic and social development in the nineteenth century and earlier is given in McCord, 1979; see also Hepple, 1976. For a photographic record, see Atkinson, 1980; and for maps, with commentaries, showing the growth and development of Newcastle, see Barke and Buswell, 1980. The important contribution of Grainger, Dobson and Clayton to the development of Newcastle city centre is discussed by Wilkes and Dodds, 1964. Local histories include Middlebrook, 1968 (on Newcastle); Manders, 1979 (Gateshead); Richardson, 1923 (Wallsend); Letch, 1970 (Birtley) and Simpson, 1988 (North Shields and Tynemouth). Gateshead, past and present, is shown in the *Gateshead Domesday Book* (1986), while the County Council's *Tyne Guide* (1986) is an excellent pictorial guide, commentary and history of development along the river.
3. The Depression still provides the setting for a considerable amount of writing on the region—for example, the novels of Catherine Cookson. For memories of the 1930s in the North East see also Armstrong and Beynon, 1977.
4. A detailed list of redundancies in Tyne and Wear over the period 1979 to 1987 is given in TUSIU, 1987.
5. The impact of the Metro rapid transit system on shopping and urban development is discussed in *The Metro Report* (Metro Monitoring and Development Study, 1985).
6. For a review of economic initiatives pursued by Newcastle see the *Annual Report of the Economic Development Committee* (Newcastle City Council, 1987). South Tyneside's economic development policies are presented in their *Quarterly Economic Digest* (South Tyneside MBC, 1975–).
7. The annual *State of the Region Report*, prepared by the Northern Region Councils Association, provides an up-to-date review of the economic and social situation in the North. See also *Economic Prospects for the North* (Robinson and Goddard, 1982). For a comprehensive analysis of the region's problems and prospects in the 1970s—together with policy recommendations—see the *Strategic Plan for the Northern Region* (NRST, 1977). A wide-ranging review of economic and social conditions in Tyne and Wear is given in the *County Structure Plan: Report of Survey*, prepared by the former County Council in 1979, and the *Structure Plan Annual Reports* (Tyne and Wear County Council, 1981–84).

REFERENCES

Allen, E., Odber, A.J. and Bowden, P.J. (1957) *Development Area Policy in the North East of England*. Newcastle: North East Industrial and Development Association.

Armstrong, K. and Beynon, H. (1977) *Hello, are you Working? Memories of the Thirties in the North East of England*. Whitley Bay: Strong Words Publications.

Atkinson, F. (1980) *North East England. People at Work, 1860–1950*. Ashbourne, Derby: Moorland Pubs.

Austrin, T. and Beynon, H. (1979) *Global Outpost: The Working Class Experience of Big Business in the North East of England, 1964–79*. Discussion Document (mimeo), Department of Sociology, University of Durham.

Barke, M. and Buswell, R.J. (1980) *Historical Atlas of Newcastle upon Tyne*. Newcastle: Newcastle Polytechnic.

Barke, N. (1986) Newcastle/Tyneside 1890–1980 *in* Gordon, G. (ed) *Regional Cities in the UK*. London: Harper & Row.

Bean, D. (1971) *Tyneside: A Biography*. London: Macmillan.

Benwell Community Development Project (CDP) (1978) *Making of a Ruling Class*. Newcastle: Benwell CDP.

Byrne, D. (1987) What is the Point of an Urban Development Corporation for Tyne and Wear? *Northern Economic Review*, 15, 63–75.

Carney, J., Lewis, J. and Hudson, R. (1977) Coal Combines and Interregional Development in the UK *in* Massey, D.B. and Batey, P.W. (eds.) *Alternative Frameworks for Analysis*. London: Pion.

Cousins, J.M., Davis, R.L., Paddon, M.J. and Waton, A. (1974) Aspects of Contradiction in Regional Policy: The Case of North-East England. *Regional Studies*, 8, 133-144.

Davies, J.G. (1972) *The Evangelistic Bureaucrat: A Study of a Planning Exercise in Newcastle upon Tyne*. London: Tavistock.

Davies, R. (1988) Retailing in the Year 2000: The Future for Tyneside. *Northern Economic Review*, 16, 17–23.

Department of Trade and Industry (DTI) (1986) *UK Regional Development Programme 1986–90*. London: DTI.

Dougan, D. (1970) *The Great Gun Maker: The Story of Lord Armstrong*. Newcastle: Frank Graham.

Foord, J. and Gillespie, A. (1986) Office Work and New Technology in Tyne and Wear. *Northern Economic Review*, 12, 69–29.

Gateshead Domesday Young Enterprise Board (1986) *The Gateshead Domesday Book*. Gateshead MBC.

Green, A.E. (1985) Recent Trends in the Service Sector in Tyne & Wear and Berkshire. *CURDS Discussion Paper 71*. Newcastle: Centre for Urban and Regional Development Studies.

Hepple, L.W. (1976) *A History of Northumberland and Newcastle upon Tyne*. Chichester: Phillimore.

Heslop, R.O. (1899) 'A Tyneside Tragedy', in *The Banks of the Tyne*. South Shields: Daily Gazette.

Lawless, J. (1988) Twixt the Devil and the CEGB [A business portrait of NEI]. *Business*, May 1988, 58–68.

Letch, H. (1970) *Birtley*. Newcastle: W.L.Large.

Loebl, H. (1988) *Government Factories and the Origins of British Regional Policy, 1934–1948*. Aldershot: Avebury.

Manders, F.W.D. (1979) *A History of Gateshead*. Gateshead Corporation.

Mess, H.A. (1928) *Industrial Tyneside: A Social Survey*. London: Ernest Benn Ltd.

Metro Monitoring and Development Study (1985) *The Metro Report*. Newcastle: Tyne and Wear Passenger Transport Executive.

McCord, N. (1979) *North East England: An Economic and Social History*. London: Batsford.

McKenzie, P. (1983) *W.G. Armstrong*. Longhirst Press.

Middlebrook, S. (1950) *Newcastle upon Tyne: Its Growth and Achievement*. Newcastle: Newcastle Journal.

Newcastle City Council (1987) *Economic Development Committee Annual Report 1986/1987*. Newcastle: Newcastle City Council.

North East Trading Estates (NETE) (1953) *Industrial Estates: A Story of Achievement*. Gateshead: NETE.

Northern Region Councils Association (1988) *State of the Region Report*. Newcastle: NRCA. [This Report has been published annually since 1979].

Northern Region Strategy Team (NRST) (1977) *Strategic Plan* (5 vols). London: HMSO.

Pyke, F. (1982) A Job for Life? The Closure of Vickers, Scotswood. *Northern Economic Review*, 3, 9–17.

Richardson, W. (1923) *History of the Parish of Wallsend*. Newcastle: Northumberland Press.

Robinson, F. and Goddard, J.B. (1982) *Economic Prospects for the North*. Newcastle: BBC North East.

Robinson, F., Wren, C. and Goddard, J.B. (1987) *Economic Development Policies: An Evaluative Study of the Newcastle Metropolitan Region*. Oxford University Press.

Secretary of State for Industry, Trade and Regional Development (1963) *The North East: A Programme for Regional Development and Growth*. Cmnd, 2206. London: HMSO.

Simpson, R.C. (1988) *North Shields and Tynemouth: A Pictorial History*. Chichester: Phillimore.

Smith, I. (1986) Takeovers, Rationalisation and the Northern Region Economy. *Northern Economic Review*, 12, 30–38.

Smith, T.D. (1970) *Dan Smith: An Autobiography*. Newcastle: Oriel Press.

South Tyneside MBC (1975–   ) *Quarterly Economic Digest* (formerly *Quarterly Industrial Review*). South Shields: South Tyneside MBC.

Stone, I. (1984) The Crisis in Shipbuilding and the North East. *Northern Economic Review*, 9, 2–12.

Townsend, A.R. (1983) *The Impact of Recession*. London: Croom Helm.

Trade Union Studies Information Unit (TUSIU) (1985a) *Bad Taste: the Food, Drink and Tobacco Industry in Tyne and Wear*. Newcastle: TUSIU.

Trade Union Studies Information Unit (TUSIU) (1985b) *Tyne and Wear in Crisis*. Newcastle: TUSIU.

Trade Union Studies Information Unit (TUSIU) (1986) *The Future for NEI in Tyne & Wear*. Newcastle: TUSIU and Tyne & Wear District Councils.

Trade Union Studies Information Unit (TUSIU) (1987) *Plant Closures*. Newcastle: TUSIU.

Turner, G. (1967) *The North Country*. London: Eyre and Spottiswoode.

Tyne and Wear County Council (1979) *County Structure Plan: Report of Survey*. Newcastle: Tyne and Wear County Council.

Tyne and Wear County Council (1981–4) *Structure Plan Annual Report*. Newcastle: Tyne and Wear County Council.

Tyne and Wear County Council (1982) *Manufacturing Employment Change in Tyne and Wear Since 1965*. Newcastle: Tyne and Wear County Council.

Tyne and Wear County Council (1986a) *Manufacturing Employment Change in Tyne and Wear 1965–81*. Newcastle: Tyne and Wear County Council.

Tyne and Wear County Council (1986b) *Tyne Guide*. Newcastle: Tyne & Wear County Council.

Tyne and Wear County-wide Research and Intelligence Unit (1988) *Manufacturing in Tyne and Wear 1979–85: An Analysis of the Census of Production*. Newcastle: Tyne and Wear County-wide R & I Unit.

Wilkes, L. and Dodds, G. (1964) *Tyneside Classical: The Newcastle of Grainger, Dobson and Clayton*. London: Murray.

Wilkinson, E. (1939) *The Town that was Murdered: The Life Story of Jarrow*. London: Gollancz.

Williams, H., and Charles, D. (1986) The Electronics Industry in the North East: Growth or Decline? *Northern Economic Review*, 13, 29–38.

3

THE LABOUR MARKET

Fred Robinson

The last chapter examined the industrial structure of Tyneside, looking at the development of the various economic activities and efforts to promote economic regeneration. We now turn our attention to the relationship between this economic structure and Tyneside's workforce. Patterns of employment are described, focusing especially on the occupational structure and the job opportunities for men and women. We then look at unemployment, the gap between labour supply (people in the workforce) and labour demand (the availability of jobs). Finally, we discuss the growth of government intervention in the labour market through the provision of youth training and temporary work by the Manpower Services Commission.

It is very clear that the labour market has undergone enormous changes since Mess's time. The much greater diversity of the industrial structure today—and particularly the growth of the service sector—has produced a much more complex and varied mix of occupations. New occupations have been created while others have become extinct. Women have become a much larger part of the workforce. And the 'occupational communities' built around mining and shipbuilding have largely disappeared. But it remains the case that the different 'socio-economic groups', defined by occupation, income and 'class', generally live in separate residential areas of Tyneside. And unemployment, job insecurity and low pay are still major features of the Tyneside labour market.

Labour Supply and Labour Demand

According to the last Census of Population in 1981, the total resident workforce of Tyneside was then 400,000. This comprised people living in the Tyneside area who were in employment (nearly 344,000), or seeking work (the unemployed—50,000), or temporarily not working because of sickness (6,000). Since 1981 the figures will have changed; in particular, there has been population loss from the area through migration and an increase in the numbers seeking work owing to rising unemployment. Nevertheless, the 1981 figures are reasonable indicators of overall magnitudes of labour supply and its component elements.

FIGURE 3.1. COMMUTING FLOWS TO AND FROM TYNESIDE, 1981

(a) Workplaces of Tyneside residents in employment

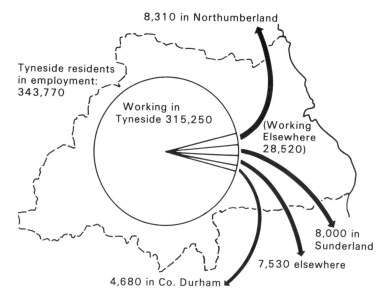

8,310 in Northumberland

Tyneside residents in employment: 343,770

Working in Tyneside 315,250

(Working Elsewhere 28,520)

8,000 in Sunderland

7,530 elsewhere

4,680 in Co. Durham

(b) Residence of people working in Tyneside

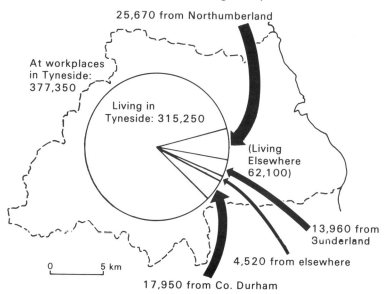

25,670 from Northumberland

At workplaces in Tyneside: 377,350

Living in Tyneside: 315,250

(Living Elsewhere 62,100)

13,960 from Sunderland

4,520 from elsewhere

0   5 km

17,950 from Co. Durham

Source: 1981 Census of Population: Economic Activity Tables (based on 10% sample data)

The relationship between labour supply and demand is not simply a matter of comparing the resident workforce of Tyneside with the number of jobs in the area, since Tyneside is not a self-contained labour market. There are significant numbers of people commuting into, and out of, the area for work. Of the 344,000 people living in Tyneside and in work in 1981, over 315,000 worked in Tyneside itself while nearly 29,000 travelled to jobs outside the conurbation—mainly to workplaces in the adjacent areas of Sunderland, Northumberland and County Durham (see Figure 3.1).

The flow of commuters *into* Tyneside is considerably greater than the flow *out* of the conurbation. In 1981 62,100 people travelled into Tyneside to work whereas 28,520 travelled out. Tyneside is evidently an important source of jobs for people living outside the conurbation, with particularly large commuting flows of men into Newcastle from Northumberland, and into Gateshead from County Durham.

Not surprisingly, the largest commuting flows *within* Tyneside are journeys to work in Newcastle city centre, with large numbers of people commuting in to the centre from North Tyneside and Gateshead. Both in Tyneside and in the country as a whole, men commute longer distances than women because women are more reliant on public transport and many work in part-time and low-paid jobs relatively close to home.

Patterns of Employment

Men and women in the Tyneside labour market[1]

In the 1920s, women accounted for only about 20% of Tyneside's workforce. Tyneside did not have the textile mills which, in Lancashire and Yorkshire, employed large numbers of women and employment opportunities for women in Tyneside were very limited; women married early and very few married women (only about 4%) went out to work. Most married women had more than enough (unpaid) work to do in the home. Moreover, jobs that men did often involved hard physical effort, long hours and shift work, necessitating a large input of domestic labour. Women had to be there to keep the home fires burning, feed and take care of the breadwinner, bring up the children and generally manage household affairs. In *Our Kate*, Catherine Cookson describes well the attitudes of men:

> '....in those days a man went out to work and that, to his mind, was enough; the house and all in it was the woman's task, and it lowered a man's prestige if he as much as lifted a cup .... Both me granda and me uncle Jack would have let their clothes go rotten on their backs before they would have washed them; as for cooking a meal, even if they had known how to, they wouldn't have lowered themselves to the level of the fire, or the gas stove. Man's rightful standing in the house was a thing to be guarded, to be fought for; no weakness or emotions or kindly instincts must touch it' (Cookson, 1969, p.25).

Such attitudes have obviously not disappeared. Traditional male chauvinism is still prevalent in Tyneside, but perhaps not so stridently expressed nor so widely accepted as in the past. The traditional divisions between the respective roles of men and women, both in the economy and the society, have undoubtedly been challenged and at least partially eroded.

Probably the single most important challenge has come from the changing structure of employment. On the one hand there has been a substantial reduction in male employment, linked closely to the decline of the old male-dominated heavy industries. This reduction is a well-established and long term trend (see Table 3.1), manifested in redundancies, earlier retirement and high levels of male unemployment. On the other hand, female employment was growing up until the late 1970s and since the early 1980s has stabilised. The majority of Tyneside women, single or married, now seek paid work outside the home. Today, around 45% of those in paid employment in Tyneside are women. And, with further decline in manufacturing and with any growth concentrated in the service sector, there could well be more women in work than men within the next ten years or so. Certainly, the economy could not now function without the participation of women as paid workers and their earnings form a vital part of household income.

TABLE 3.1. TOTAL EMPLOYMENT IN TYNESIDE BY GENDER, 1961–84					
	1961	1971	1978	1981	1984
Males	(265,410)	249,704	235,955	205,014	183,200
Females	(119,450)	148,328	161,637	149,404	148,939
Total	(384,860)	398,032	397,592	354,418	332,139
Females as % of Total	(31.0)	37.3	40.7	42.1	44.8

Sources: Department of Employment Census of Employment, 1971–84: figures for employees in employment *working* in Tyneside itself. The 1961 figures are from the Census of Population and refer to employed residents *living* in the old local authority areas of Tyneside; hence the 1961 data are not directly comparable with later figures.

Industries and occupations

The labour market remains strongly segmented by gender. The industrial and occupational structures of male and female employment differ considerably. Women are clustered in jobs generally characterised by low pay, low skill levels and low status, often with poorer conditions and fewer prospects for promotion. Moreover, a large proportion of women work in part-time jobs, which usually means lower rates of pay and poorer conditions than in comparable full-time jobs.

Manufacturing industry in Tyneside is largely male-employing. Three-quarters of *manufacturing* jobs are held by men (compared with 55% of *all* jobs) and this is largely a result of the high proportion of jobs which are held by men in the engineering and shipbuilding industries, dominant elements of Tyneside's manufacturing sector (Figure 3.2). In addition, nearly all those working in the primary industries and in construction are men. This concentration can be expressed another way: in 1984, 45% of men working in Tyneside were in manufacturing, primary industries or construction, compared to only 14% of women.

This perhaps serves to put into clearer perspective the common assumption that regional policy has produced a major increase in factory jobs for women in Tyneside; the fact is that the vast majority of women who go out to work in Tyneside are employed in the service industries. Only a few manufacturing industries—in particular clothing, but also textiles, and paper, printing and publishing, have a large proportion of female workers. In the manufacturing sector, in primary industry and construction, traditional patterns of gender segregation have persisted and women have, quite clearly, *not* been 'displacing' men. Women's share of jobs in manufacturing actually remained much the same—at around 25%—between 1971 and 1984.

The occupational structure of male employment in Tyneside underlines the importance of manufacturing industry as a source of jobs for men but also indicates the significance of managerial and professional occupations which are still largely male preserves. The top ten occupations for *men* in Tyneside[2] in 1981 were:

- Metal and electrical goods manufacture and repair
  (operators, fitters, etc.)   23%
- Other processing, making and repair, excl. metal
  and electrical goods   7%
- Construction, mining, etc. workers   7%
- Managerial staff–in production, distribution, etc.   7%
- Professional and related in science, engineering, technology, etc.   6%
- General labourers   5%
- Bus, coach, lorry drivers, etc.   5%
- Clerks   5%
- Professional (e.g. legal, finance) and related supporting
  staff and managers, including central and local government
  managers   4%
- Storekeepers, warehousemen, etc.   3%

These ten occupational categories accounted for nearly three-quarters of men's jobs. Occupations within the mechanical and electrical engineering industries are dominant, followed by manual work in other

FIGURE 3.2. MALE AND FEMALE EMPLOYMENT IN TYNESIDE, 1984

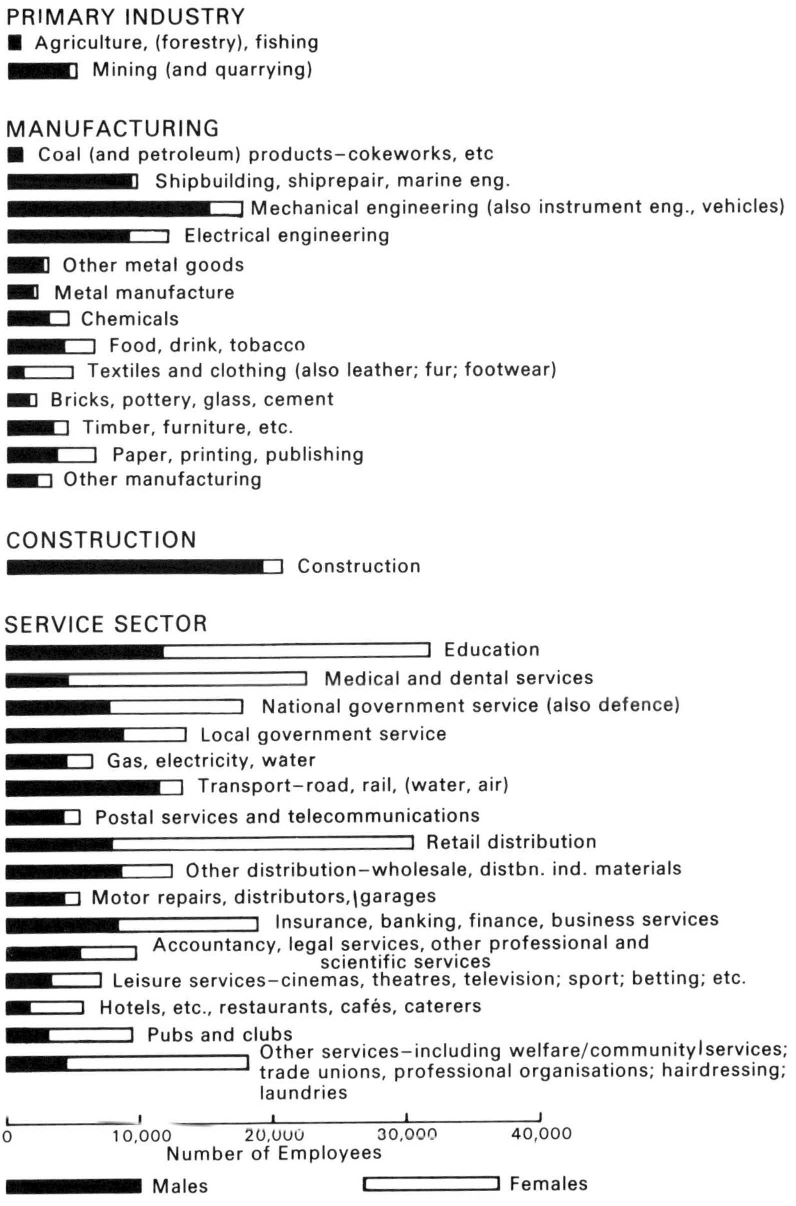

PRIMARY INDUSTRY
■ Agriculture, (forestry), fishing
▆ Mining (and quarrying)

MANUFACTURING
■ Coal (and petroleum) products–cokeworks, etc
▆ Shipbuilding, shiprepair, marine eng.
▆ Mechanical engineering (also instrument eng., vehicles)
▆ Electrical engineering
▆ Other metal goods
▆ Metal manufacture
▆ Chemicals
▆ Food, drink, tobacco
▆ Textiles and clothing (also leather; fur; footwear)
▆ Bricks, pottery, glass, cement
▆ Timber, furniture, etc.
▆ Paper, printing, publishing
▆ Other manufacturing

CONSTRUCTION
▆ Construction

SERVICE SECTOR
▆ Education
▆ Medical and dental services
▆ National government service (also defence)
▆ Local government service
▆ Gas, electricity, water
▆ Transport–road, rail, (water, air)
▆ Postal services and telecommunications
▆ Retail distribution
▆ Other distribution–wholesale, distbn. ind. materials
▆ Motor repairs, distributors, garages
▆ Insurance, banking, finance, business services
▆ Accountancy, legal services, other professional and scientific services
▆ Leisure services–cinemas, theatres, television; sport; betting; etc.
▆ Hotels, etc., restaurants, cafés, caterers
▆ Pubs and clubs
▆ Other services–including welfare/community services; trade unions, professional organisations; hairdressing; laundries

0	10,000	20,000	30,000	40,000

Number of Employees

▆ Males   ▭ Females

Source: Department of Employment: Census of Employment.

Excavator assembly at Komatsu, Birtley. Engineering continues to be an important source of jobs for men in Tyneside. (*Komatsu UK Ltd*).

Ship design offices at Swan Hunter's shipyard. New technology is being introduced in Tyneside's traditional industries – but the workforce remains, traditionally, male. (*Newcastle Chronicle & Journal*).

manufacturing, the construction industry and mining. Managerial and professional occupations (in production, distribution, legal and financial services, central and local government) accounted for nearly a fifth of male jobs. Labouring, transport and warehouse jobs are also important–and are also occupations predominantly undertaken by men.

The occupational structure for *women* is very different, with a strong concentration on the service sector and largely low status, low-paid occupations. Clerical work accounts for 18% of women's jobs, followed by jobs in retailing (11%). The top ten occupational categories accounted for two thirds of jobs:

– Clerks	18%
– Sales staff, shop assistants, shelf fillers, forecourt attendants, etc.	11%
– Caretakers, Cleaners, etc.	8%
– Secretaries, typists, receptionists	7%
– Domestic staff and school helpers	6%
– Nurses	5%
– Teachers (primary and secondary)	4%
– Counter hands, assistants, kitchen porters, etc.	3%
– Waiters and bar staff	3%
– Tailors, dressmakers and other clothing workers	2%

A striking feature of this list is the similarity with Henry Mess's description of women's employment in Tyneside in the 1920s:

'Roughly 76,000 women were returned [in the Census of Population] as occupied in 1921. About 17,000 of these were indoor domestic servants, and another 10,000 were engaged in other forms of personal service, e.g. barmaids, laundrywomen. About 9,000 were clerks or typists, and about 11,000 were shop assistants or saleswomen. Rather more than 6,000 were dressmakers, tailoresses, or in some other way engaged with clothing. There were about 5,000 professional workers, mainly teachers or nurses. This accounts for about three-quarters of the whole number. It will be seen that the number of industrial workers was small: the 10,000 or so who were so engaged were in a number of occupations no one of which employed a great number. Food industries, printing and stationery, light metal-work, and rope work, absorbed a certain number; but the outstanding feature of the area is the absence of any considerable industrial occupation for women'(Mess, 1928, p.47).

Of course there are now very few 'indoor domestic servants'—though the nanny is returning and employment agencies advertise in the Tyneside press for local girls and women to work in the south. Aside from this, women then—as now—were concentrated in routine office work, shops and catering. Nursing and teaching are still the most significant professional occupations available to women in Tyneside. Thus, despite the large increase in the numbers and proportions of women going out to work, the overall occupational structure has changed relatively little. There are still substantial barriers and constraints on women in the labour market, including discriminatory recruitment—a recent study of the recruitment practices of employers in Newcastle found that there was 'widespread, blatant and potentially unlawful discrimination between men and women' (Curran, 1985). There remains a widespread expectation that women's primary role is to run the home and care for children (Vyse, 1983). There are signs of change, but change is coming more slowly and is less apparent in the depressed labour market of Tyneside than in the more dynamic local economies of southern Britain.

Full-time and part-time jobs

Only a very small proportion—about 4%—of *men* working in Tyneside have part-time jobs. By contrast, more than four out of ten *women* going out to work in Tyneside are part-timers. Much of the increase in female employment has taken the form of part-time jobs and this seems likely to continue, especially since employers often see part-time work as offering 'flexibility' and providing an opportunity to reduce costs. In many parts of the service sector, like retailing and particularly catering, part-time work is the norm; in some industries, too, there has been a noticeable shift from full to part-time work.

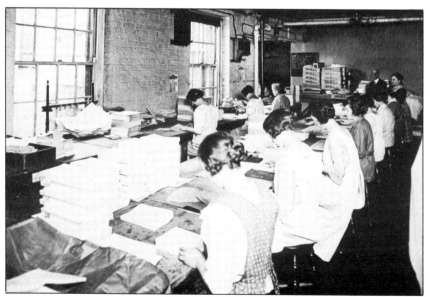

Bookbinding at Andrew Reid's printing works, Newcastle, 1926. Printing was one of the few manufacturing industries providing production jobs for women in the 1920s. (*Newcastle upon Tyne City Libraries and Arts*).

'Women's work' in the 1980s – clerical staff operating VDUs at the DHSS complex, Longbenton. (*DHSS*).

'Women's work' in the 1980s – clothing factory, J & J Fashions, South Shields. (*Newcastle Chronicle & Journal*).

Official figures undoubtedly understate the scale of part-time employment since some part-time jobs will be in the informal sector, the so-called 'black economy', unrecorded and involving cash in hand payment. Nevertheless the official figures do provide an indication of the structure of part-time work. Of the 63,000 *part-time women workers* recorded in the 1984 Census of Employment in Tyneside, 58,000 were in the service sector. And these workers are concentrated in just a few parts of the service sector, with 13,600 in retailing, 9,600 in education, over 7,000 in health services, 5,700 in pubs and clubs and 2,500 in hotels, restaurants, cafés and catering. Many of these jobs are low-paid, including a large number of those in education and health, most of which are found in ancillary services such as cleaning and catering. Over the past decade or so, the proportion of part-time workers has increased, especially in the private sector service industries. In retailing, for example, while *total* employment declined between 1971 and 1984, the number of *part-time* jobs increased; in 1984, 60% of women working in retailing in Tyneside worked on a part-time basis compared with 44% in 1971. In pubs and clubs there are now very few *full-time* female employees; 87% of women employees working in pubs and clubs in 1984 were part-timers, compared with 70% in 1971. Part-time employment certainly does offer women the opportunity to combine paid work with work in the home. On the other hand, it is generally low paid and offers poorer conditions than full-time jobs. Moreover, for many women in Tyneside there is no question of choice since the *only* jobs available to them are part-time.

Earnings in Tyneside

In many industries, rates of pay are negotiated at the national level and this reduces regional variations in earnings. There are, however, industries and occupations where pay rates are locally negotiated and reflect local conditions of supply and demand for labour; this serves to depress wages in areas of high unemployment like Tyneside and push up pay rates in more prosperous parts of the country.

Average gross weekly pay levels for full-time *male manual workers* in Tyne and Wear match the national average (£174 a week gross in 1986), a reflection of the prevalence of nationally-agreed rates and relatively good wages in industries like engineering (see Table 3.2). The engineering sector, together with shipbuilding, provides an important source of relatively well-paid jobs for manual workers and brings average male manual earnings up to the national average. The decline of this sector therefore has an especially serious impact on local earnings.

Both nationally and locally, *male non-manual workers* in full-time jobs are the highest paid category. In Tyne and Wear, half of them were paid more than £200 a week (over £10,400 a year) in 1986. The main categories of high earners are professional workers in fields like education, health, science and technology; lawyers and accountants; and managers both in manufacturing and in the service sector. But there are fairly low-paid male non-manual workers as well, notably in clerical jobs and retailing, many of whom receive less than manual workers in the engineering industry. There is a substantial gap between local and national average levels of pay: male non-manual workers in Tyne and Wear earn 10% less than the national average and nearly 20% less than their counterparts in the South East. They do, however, have the advantage of considerably lower housing costs.

A large proportion of women are low-paid, both nationally and in Tyne and Wear, and on average they earn substantially less than men. This derives primarily from the occupational structure of women's employment, but there is also an element of wage discrimination. Over half of Tyne and Wear's *female manual workers* in full-time jobs earn less than £100 a week and average weekly pay (£100.5 gross in 1986) was below the average for the country as a whole (£107.5). Women working in *non-manual* full-time jobs do rather better, but again earn less than the national average. Only about a third of full-time non-manual female workers in Tyne and Wear received more than £150 a week, most of them professional workers in education and the health service. The lowest paid occupations for full-time female workers are in retailing, catering, cleaning and in personal services like hairdressing.

TABLE 3.2. PAY: FULL-TIME WORKERS IN TYNE & WEAR AND GREAT BRITAIN, 1986

Average Gross Weekly Pay (£)		Tyne & Wear as % of GB	Tyne & Wear: gross weekly pay, per cent earning:	
Tyne & Wear[1]	GB		*Less than* £100 p.w.	*More than* £200 p.w. (males) *or* £150 p.w. (females)[2]
Male manual	174.0	174.4	99.8	7.1%	27.8%
Male non-manual	220.5	244.9	90.0	3.4%	50.4%
(All males)	(193.3)	(207.5)	(93.2)	(5.6%)	(37.2%)
Female manual	100.5	107.5	93.5	56.0%	6.9%
Female non-manual	136.5	145.7	93.7	27.2%	32.1%
(All females)	(129.0)	(137.2)	(94.0)	(33.2%)	(26.9%)

Source: *New Earnings Survey*, 1986.

Notes: 1. Figures available only for Tyne and Wear County, which includes Sunderland as well as the four Tyneside Districts.
2. Percentages earning above £200 a week for men, above £150 a week for women.

The lowest paid group in the labour market are those women working part-time—a large group since around four out of ten women in paid employment are part-timers. As Table 3.3 shows, part-time female workers in Tyne and Wear are particularly disadvantaged. 63.2% of those in manual jobs in the area earned *less than* £2.20 an hour in 1986, compared with 47.5% for Great Britain. Those in non-manual jobs are not quite so badly off; even so 34.0% earned less than £2.20 an hour in Tyne and Wear—above the national level of 23.0% who were so poorly paid. Less than a third of the non-manual and only about 6% of the manual female part-time workers in the area earned *more than* £3.00 an hour (equivalent to more than £120 for a forty-hour week).

TABLE 3.3. PAY: PART TIME[1] FEMALE WORKERS IN TYNE & WEAR AND GREAT BRITAIN, 1986.

	Percent earning *less than* £2.20 an hour		Percent earning *more than* £3.00 an hour	
	Tyne & Wear	GB	Tyne & Wear	GB
Female manual	63.2	47.5	5.7	10.6
Female non-manual	34.0	23.0	30.0	39.2

Source: New Earnings Survey, 1986; unpublished data.

Note: 1. Part time workers are defined as those working less than 30 hours a week.

Among the lowest paid part-timers are shop assistants, cleaners and women working in catering; in these jobs the going rate for part-time work in 1987 was well below £2 an hour. These occupations are noted for low pay in general, but part-timers are often further disadvantaged, being paid even less per hour than full-time workers. Many of these low-paid part-time jobs are in the public sector—ancillary staff in health and education for example, sectors which are especially important components of the Tyneside economy. In the private sector, low-paid part-time jobs are being generated in industries such as retailing, resulting from the shift from full to part-time employment.

The general picture that emerges, then, is that many people in employment in Tyneside earn less than the national average for their occupation, the prime exception being some male manual workers. Many are low-paid, especially women and, above all, part-time women workers. The outlook for the future is not optimistic. Two key trends serve to further depress wages in Tyneside: the decline of engineering and other relatively well-paid male manual jobs, and also the tendency for growth in the service sector to be translated into part-time jobs. By these processes the area's economic problems could well be exacerbated by reduced spending power in the local economy in the future.

Unemployment

Unemployment in the 1980s

Unemployment is undoubtedly the most important economic, social and political problem confronting Tyneside today. It has profound impacts on material welfare, on health, education, crime and, indeed, on the whole social fabric. Memories of the 1930s have been rekindled: thus the re-enactment of the Jarrow March in 1986 was not a nostalgic celebration of a fiftieth anniversary, but rather was intended to demonstrate that unemployment is again a major problem which needs to be tackled. And even for many in work, the economic climate is often one of insecurity, with the ever-present possibility of becoming unemployed.

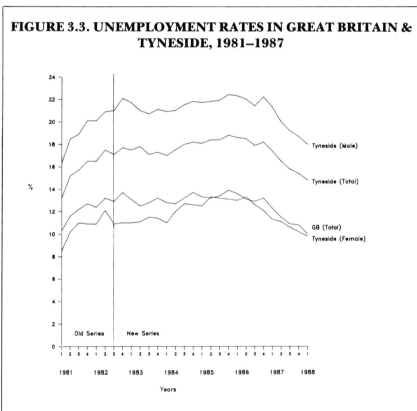

FIGURE 3.3. UNEMPLOYMENT RATES IN GREAT BRITAIN & TYNESIDE, 1981–1987

Source: Department of Employment and Tyne & Wear County-wide Research and Intelligence Unit.

Note: Unemployment rates for Tyneside represent numbers unemployed (unemployed benefit claimants) as a percentage of 'economically active' residents in 1981 (as enumerated in the Census of Population). The rate for Great Britain represents numbers of unemployed (claimants) as a percentage of the total labour force for each mid year, and excludes the self-employed.

During the 1970s the level of unemployment in Tyneside rose steadily, with a sharp increase during the recession from 1978/9 to 1982/3. Subsequently, the official unemployment rate remained fairly stable, at between 16% and 18% until 1986. Some recovery since then produced a gradual decrease, down to 15.4% at the start of 1988, and male unemployment fell below 20% for the first time since 1981. Throughout the 1980s, unemployment in Tyneside has stayed about five percentage points above the national rate (Figure 3.3).

The official unemployment figures give a useful indication of the relative scale of unemployment and its characteristics but do not show the full extent of joblessness. In the last few years repeated revisions to the methods used to count the unemployed and calculate rates have served to depress the figures by excluding various groups such as men over 60 and married women ineligible for benefit. The official figures now only cover unemployed people in receipt of benefit and do not take into account those on short-term training and 'make-work' schemes who would wish to have a 'real' job. The growth of these schemes has certainly been an important contributory factor in countering increases in unemployment and has helped, along with modest economic recovery, to produce a fall in the official figures since late 1986.

But discussion about the figures and the extent to which they understate the actual level of unemployment should not obscure the fact that unemployment is very high in Tyneside, well above the national average. In January 1988, there were 61,306 unemployed claimants in Tyneside, representing an official unemployment rate of 15.4%, and almost one in five men in Tyneside was out of work. The problem is one of massive proportions and it is far from certain whether there can be a return to the conditions of full employment which even Tyneside experienced in the 1950s (Benwell CDP, 1978).

Patterns of unemployment: age, duration and geography

Unemployment affects some groups in the labour market more than others and, consequently, the incidence of unemployment varies from one part of Tyneside to another. Essentially, those with few skills or redundant skills run a high risk of being unemployed and areas with lesser skilled and manual workers suffer high rates of unemployment (North Tyneside CDP, 1978; Cousins *et al.*, 1982). The 'working class' bear the brunt of unemployment while some 'middle class' areas of Tyneside have unemployment rates well below the national average.

New entrants to the labour market, often with few skills or qualifications, are at a severe disadvantage. The under-18 age group has the provision of the Youth Training Scheme which holds down the official unemployment rate (17.8% for the under-18s in January 1988). However, as Table 3.4 shows, unemployment is at a very high level for the 18-24 age group; nearly a quarter of Tynesiders in this age group are out of work. The 'prime' age group (25–54) is less severely affected by unemployment; this group includes people who are well established with employment in the labour market—even so, just under one-fifth of men in this group are unemployed. The situation for older workers, aged 55 and over, is difficult to judge since many men aged over 60 are no longer counted in the figures and some will have voluntarily opted for early retirement. The particular problem for this age group is to be found in competing for jobs against younger applicants when recruitment practices often involve limitations on age.

Long term unemployment is an acute and growing problem, one which has intensified as unemployment has stayed at a high level over several years. At January 1988, 44.8% of unemployed claimants in Tyneside had been out of work for over a year and long-term unemployment is highest for older workers, reflecting their difficulty in securing new employment. There is no doubt that in Tyneside there is now a substantial section of the population experiencing long periods of unemployment and with little prospect (in fact, a declining probability) of finding work.

TABLE 3.4. UNEMPLOYMENT IN TYNESIDE: AGE AND DURATION ANALYSIS, JANUARY 1988

Duration	Age				Total	%
	Under 18	18–24	25–54	55+		
Less than 1 month	367	1957	2825	354	5503	(9.0%)
1 to 6 months	1588	6834	9056	1252	18730	(30.6%)
6 months to 1 year	354	3303	5056	944	9657	(15.8%)
1 to 3 years	312	3463	7719	1971	13465	(22.0%)
Over 3 years	0	1701	9629	2621	13951	(22.8%)
(Total)	(2621)	(17258)	(34285)	(7142)	61306	(100.0%)
Rates[1] by age group						
– all unemployed	17.8%	23.1%	13.9%	—	15.4%	
– males	19.6%	28.0%	17.7%	—	18.7%	
– females	16.1%	16.9%	8.0%	—	10.2%	

Source: Department of Employment and Tyne & Wear County-wide Research and Intelligence Unit.

Note: 1. Unemployment rates (by age group) represent numbers unemployed (unemployed benefit claimants) as a percentage of 'economically-active' residents in 1981 (as enumerated in the Census of Population). Rates for the 55+ group are not calculated owing to the exclusion of many older men from the unemployment figures.

Finally, we turn to the geography of unemployment within Tyneside. As Figure 3.4 shows, the unemployment rate varies considerably across the conurbation, with some wards experiencing rates in excess of 30% while others have less than 15% unemployment. Broadly, the highest levels of unemployment are found in the old 'working class' areas close to the Tyne, though peripheral Council estates like Newbiggin Hall also suffer very high unemployment. The more 'middle class' and white collar suburbs have (relatively) low unemployment; these areas include well-established residential areas like Gosforth, Jesmond and Tynemouth and also recently-built private estates on the northern fringes of Newcastle and North Tyneside and on the western side of Gateshead District.

The striking contrasts in unemployment within Tyneside are probably often not fully appreciated. The worst affected ward, Newcastle's West City, which includes the high-rise flats at Cruddas Park, had an official unemployment rate of 39.4% in April 1987 and a male unemployment rate of 49.8%. Across town, less than four miles away, South Gosforth has only a 7.0% unemployment rate, the lowest of all wards in Tyneside. In twelve Tyneside wards (out of a total of 88 wards), more than 25% of the workforce were unemployed in April 1987 while, at the other end of the spectrum, 12 wards had less than 10% unemployment. And high unemployment is, of course, linked to other forms of deprivation and disadvantage, just as areas of low unemployment and relative affluence enjoy other advantages such as better education and health service provision.

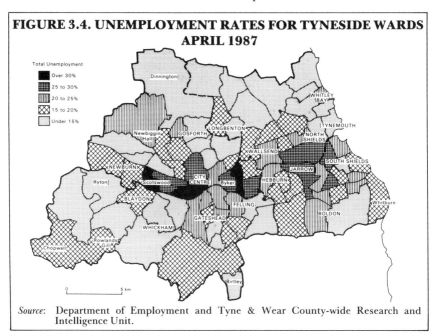

FIGURE 3.4. UNEMPLOYMENT RATES FOR TYNESIDE WARDS APRIL 1987

Source: Department of Employment and Tyne & Wear County-wide Research and Intelligence Unit.

Labour Market Intervention: the Youth Training Scheme and the Community Programme in Tyneside

Since the late 1970s, the national unemployment crisis has fostered a massive increase in the activities of the government's Manpower Services Commission (MSC). In areas of high unemployment like Tyneside, the majority of youngsters now join the MSC's Youth Training Scheme (YTS) when they leave school because jobs are just not available. And, for many long-term unemployed adults, the MSC's Community Programme (CP) has provided the best chance (often the only chance) of work—albeit temporary and low-paid. Expenditure on YTS and CP has become very considerable and many organisations which provide places on these schemes, especially those in the voluntary sector, have come to rely heavily on MSC funding.

The MSC (re-named the Training Agency in 1988) was established in 1974 as a 'quango', separate from government but accountable to the Secretary of State for Employment. Its functions include the provision of adult training at colleges, Skill-centres and, increasingly, supporting training within firms.[3] MSC also now has a significant involvement in secondary school education through its Technical and Vocational Education Initiative (TVEI) for 14 to 18 year olds (see Chapter 4). But the bulk of the MSC's expenditure is directed towards YTS and CP.

YTS and CP have developed from a whole series of schemes which originated in the mid-1970s and which have provided temporary jobs or training for the unemployed, MSC paying sponsors of these schemes both the running costs and allowances or wages for the participants. First came the Job Creation Scheme, launched in 1975, which provided temporary work for the unemployed, particularly the young unemployed. In the following year, the MSC introduced the Work Experience Scheme which supported employers giving youngsters first-hand experience of employment. In 1978, the Job Creation Scheme was replaced by the Special Temporary Employment Programme offering work 'of benefit to the community' to unemployed adults; this, in turn, was replaced by the Community Enterprise Programme in 1981 and then the Community Programme was introduced in 1982. Alongside this provision, new schemes were established for school-leavers; the Youth Opportunities Programme was created in 1978, later replaced by the Youth Training Scheme brought in by the MSC in 1983.

There have been repeated changes to MSC schemes—they have been revised, renamed and restructured, changing in terms of duration and emphasis. Aside from change, a constant underlying feature has been growth, especially since the early 1980s. In 1979–80 an average of 80,000 were on the Youth Opportunities Programme at any one time in the country as a whole, and 10,500 adults were on the Special Temporary

Employment Programme in March 1980. Total national MSC expenditure on the two schemes in 1979/80 was £175.7 million. By March 1987 there were around 435,000 youngsters on YTS and around 245,000 adults on CP, and the MSC's budget for the two schemes in 1986/7 had grown to £2,093 million.

Tyneside has shared in this massive expansion. By 1988, YTS provision in Tyneside had grown to nearly 8,000 filled places—twice as large as the former Youth Opportunities Programme (which had about 4,000 places in Tyneside in 1980). YTS is, however, also of much longer duration—now two years—compared to six months on the old programme, and YTS also has a stronger commitment to training. But the biggest expansion has been seen in the schemes for adults, with about 1,000 on the Special Temporary Employment Programme in 1980 compared with well over 11,000 on the Community Programme in 1988 in Tyne and Wear. Between 1984 and 1988 the number of people on CP in the area nearly doubled (See Table 3.5). Today, the MSC is one of Tyneside's biggest 'employers', albeit an indirect provider of employment which is managed by others and is combined with some training elements. By 1988, the MSC's two major schemes had more than 19,000 participants in Tyneside, a figure similar to the total number (18,000) employed by Newcastle City Council. By 1988 the MSC was spending over £50 million a year on YTS and CP in Tyneside alone (though the net cost is much smaller when savings on benefits are taken into account—and a large part of it is financed by the European Community).

TABLE 3.5. THE MSC's YOUTH TRAINING SCHEME (YTS) AND COMMUNITY PROGRAMME (CP) IN TYNESIDE/ TYNE & WEAR, 1984–8

	Filled places (no. on schemes)	
	Youth Training Scheme (YTS) Tyneside[1]	Community Programme (CP) Tyne & Wear[2]
Sept.1984	N/A[3]	5,978
April 1985	4,400	N/A
Oct.1985	5,180	6,834
April 1986	4,002	9,183
Oct.1986	6,411	10,505
April 1987	5,396	11,487
March 1988	7,900	11,300 (est.)

Sources: Manpower Services Commission, Newcastle, and Tyne and Wear County-wide Research and Intelligence Unit.

Notes: 1. YTS figures refer to numbers of trainees at schemes operated in the four Tyneside Districts. YTS formerly lasted a year; the two-year scheme was introduced in April 1986.
2. CP figures only available for Tyne & Wear County (the Tyneside figure would be about four-fifths of the County total).
3. N/A = Not Available.

The Youth Training Scheme. Most youngsters leaving school in Tyneside now go on to the YTS and relatively few refuse a place. Leaving school at 16 and going straight into a job is now rare; in Gateshead, for example, only 10% of leavers went straight to a job in 1986—and mainly into poorly paid jobs with no training.[4] Traditional apprenticeships have also become rare and most of those apprenticeships which have survived . have become integrated into YTS.

YTS has been expanded to provide two years of training and work experience for 16 and 17 year olds. Schemes are run by public and private sector employers, local authorities, voluntary bodies and training organisations and these 'managing agents' receive grants from the MSC to cover administration, training and the cost of paying allowances to participants. In 1987, youngsters received £28.50 a week in their first year on YTS, £35 a week in their second year.

Without doubt, YTS has had an enormous impact on the youth labour market in Tyneside and in other areas where jobs are scarce. YTS has almost completely displaced the traditional youth labour market and is widely used by employers as their only method of youth recruitment. To them, it has the advantage of a free probationary period and free labour. Not surprisingly, YTS has been subject to criticism: in particular, that it amounts to cheap labour; that 'real' jobs have been displaced by YTS and that it depresses wages; and that YTS provides inadequate or low quality training. The MSC has been concerned about such criticisms and sought to upgrade the training element, and certainly the scheme generally provides better and more training that its predecessor, the Youth Opportunities Programme (during their two years on YTS, youngsters receive at least 20 weeks off-the-job training at a college or workshop). However, most youngsters on YTS judge its success or failure according to whether or not they get a job at the end of it—and many are disappointed. In Tyneside, only about 40% to 50% are in employment six months after leaving YTS, while the rest find themselves unemployed or else seek more training.[5] School leavers are well aware that there are good and bad schemes—the good ones being those where employers subsequently give jobs to a substantial proportion of their YTS 'graduates'. The bad schemes are regarded as 'slave labour', have little real training and lead nowhere.

Nowadays, Tyneside's Careers Offices (run by the local authorities) are generally only able to offer youngsters a place on a YTS scheme since there are so few 'real' jobs available. The situation is not quite so bad at the Jobcentres which cater for adults seeking work. Even so, a considerable number of the opportunities for work displayed at the Jobcentres are for Community Programme vacancies, while many of the 'real' jobs on the vacancy boards are low-paid, part-time or require specific skills and experience which few unemployed people possess.

The Community Programme. In April 1987, a fifth of the vacancies notified at Tyneside's Jobcentres were for places on the MSC's Community Programme and a total of 11,487 people in the county were then on CP schemes. CP provides work for long-term unemployed people, for up to a year, on projects deemed of benefit to the community. Projects include activities like clearing derelict land, decorating the homes of elderly or disabled people, insulating lofts, running play-schemes and community care projects. Most CP schemes are sponsored and administered by local authorities and voluntary sector organisations; as with YTS, sponsors are paid for overheads and administration and they are reimbursed their payroll costs by the MSC.

To be eligible for a place on CP, those aged 18 to 24 usually have to have been out of work for at least 6 of the previous 9 months, while those aged 25 and over must have been unemployed for at least 12 of the preceeding 15 months. They must also have been receiving State benefits—the benefit rule excludes most unemployed married women not receiving benefit in their own right. Thus, only about a quarter of those on CP are women. Wages are very low since the MSC requires that wages must *average* only £67 a week (1987 rate) per participant. And, since scheme sponsors also have to pay the going rate for the job, many CP workers (about three quarters of them) can only be employed on a part-time basis. For those with children this can often mean that a wage on the CP differs little from the income they would receive from benefits, but for single people CP wages are normally considerably more than State benefits. Taken together, these aspects of CP mean that the majority of participants are young, single men.

Temporary work for the unemployed on the MSC's Community Programme. Labour-intensive work on environmental improvement schemes has been a major component of the Community Programme. (*Newcastle City Engineer's Department*).

CP only lasts for a year, it provides little or no training and it is low-paid. It has, however, offered a real lifeline to many long-term unemployed people, boosting their morale, using their time—often on worthwhile work—and restoring self-confidence. Because of this, there is no shortage of applicants for CP. But, like YTS, CP often does not lead on to a 'real' job; national surveys have shown that only about a quarter of those leaving CP went straight into employment and only a third were in work 7 to 8 months after leaving. The position could well be even worse in Tyneside. Quite simply, there are just not enough jobs available. In this depressed labour market a new pattern has emerged of people working on CP for a year, then going back to CP after a period of unemployment (6 months or a year) which makes them again eligible for a place. CP cannot be a solution to unemployment any more than the public works schemes of the 1930s, but it has became a large and well-established feature of the labour market on Tyneside and it does give individuals temporary respite from the despair of unemployment.

Future developments. There seems little doubt that schemes like YTS and CP are permanent features of the labour market. The names of schemes may change; but some large-scale training provision for school-leavers and 'make-work'/training schemes for unemployed adults will continue in Tyneside and other economically depressed areas. The continuing fall in the numbers of 16 to 19 year olds and the growth of service sector jobs will help to improve prospects in the youth labour market but YTS (or a successor scheme) will still be needed in areas like Tyneside to bridge the large gap between labour supply and demand. Moreover, there is now strong and widespread support for a period of training for early school-leavers to ensure that they are more 'employable', better trained and better prepared for work. YTS has effectively served to raise the (school) leaving age in Tyneside and in other areas of high unemployment.

The CP is being replaced in 1988 by a new Employment Training scheme which, as its name implies, is intended to have a much stronger training element than CP (see Department of Employment, 1988). Like the abortive and short-lived 'new Job Training Scheme' which preceded it, the Employment Training scheme is much less generous than CP since it will pay participants only £5 to £10 above their existing level of benefit. Not surprisingly, the new scheme has been severely criticised as being exploitative, representing a way of introducing 'conscript' labour, serving to depress wages and substitute for 'real' jobs. It has been likened to the Workfare system in the US where the unemployed are directed to work for their welfare benefit, and it is highly unpopular with trade unions—but it does provide an inexpensive way of both reducing the unemployment rate and providing some training.

Conclusion

This Chapter has dealt with a number of interlocking themes: changing patterns of employment; levels of pay; unemployment and MSC measures. The economic structure of Tyneside has undergone some profound changes, notably the shift from a male-dominated manufacturing-based economy to a service economy employing large numbers of women, many on a part-time basis. This shift is continuing, in turn fostering changes in the position of women at home as well as in the labour market, changes in the expectations people have of jobs and even in the structure of communities in Tyneside.

The role of government in relation to the labour market has a major bearing on the job prospects and opportunities for people in Tyneside. Aside from the impact of decisions concerning public sector jobs and services, the government also plays a significant part in structuring the way in which the labour market operates. The present government is concerned to promote flexibility and labour market deregulation, a process which may encourage employers to take on workers but which also tends to reduce conditions of employment. Deregulation may have a substantial impact on pay, notably with the introduction of wage differentials in the public sector to reflect local conditions—this would mean lower wages in areas of high unemployment like Tyneside.

Alongside deregulation and an emphasis on market forces, the government has, by contrast, undertaken more and more labour market intervention through the MSC. In the main, this has been a reaction to rising unemployment though there has been a growing emphasis on the provision of training in response to the now well-accepted view that the workforce in the UK is poorly trained or has inappropriate skills.

The central problem of the Tyneside labour market in the 1980s is, however, that the supply of labour is considerably greater than demand. Deregulation, local economic development activity and more training will not, in themselves, solve this problem. The gap between the employed and unemployed is widening, with the burden of unemployment falling disproportionately on the 'working class'. New ways of easing this burden through efforts to affect the distribution of jobs (work sharing, earlier retirement, a shorter working week, and so on) may eventually be explored but, as yet, have not been accorded the serious consideration that they undoubtedly deserve.

NOTES

1. This section draws heavily on an earlier paper, 'Some Reflections on the Role of Women in the Tyneside Economy' by Hardill and Robinson, 1987.
2. Data on 'top ten' men's and women's occupations from 1981 Census of Population, *Economic Activity Tables* for Tyne and Wear.
3. The MSC's training provision for adults includes a variety of short courses to help the unemployed acquire skills; training to help people become self-employed; and training employees within firms, supported by MSC grant aid. At any one time about 5,000 adults in Tyneside are receiving such training supported by MSC (1987), about two-thirds of them receiving training as employees in firms. Total annual expenditure on this adult training provision in Tyneside is estimated at around £4 million in 1986/7. MSC also runs the Enterprise Allowance Scheme which pays £40 a week for a year to help unemployed people set up a business; total expenditure on this scheme in Tyneside was around £2 million in 1986/7. Both these elements are small in comparison with YTS and CP, which together involve expenditure of more than £50 million a year in Tyneside.
4. In 1986 the average weekly wage for 16-18 year olds going into jobs in Gateshead was only £42.72 and nearly half paid less than £40. The Careers Office notes that YTS and the New Workers Subsidy serve to depress wages, as does the recent removal of young people under 21 from the scope and protection of Wages Councils (Gateshead MBC Careers Guidance Service Report to 31 March 1986).
5. MSC undertakes a follow-up survey of those who have participated on YTS. In the MSC's Newcastle (including Northumberland) and South Tyne areas, 61% responded to the survey in 1986. Of these, half were in full-time jobs 6 months after leaving YTS, the majority of them (58%) working for the employer they were placed with on YTS. Nearly a third were unemployed (the rest were on another YTS, on courses, etc).

REFERENCES

Benwell Community Development Project (CDP) (1978) *Permanent Unemployment*. Newcastle: Benwell CDP.

Cousins, J., Curran, M. and Brown, R. (1982) *Working in the Inner City: A Case Study* [of Newcastle]. London: Department of the Environment

Cookson, C. (1969) *Our Kate*. London: MacDonald

Curran, M.M. (1985) *Stereotypes and Selection: Gender and Family in the Recruitment Process*. London: HMSO.

Department of Employment (1987) *New Earnings Survey*, 1986. London: HMSO.

Department of Employment (1988) *Training for Employment*, (Cmnd 316). London: HMSO.

Hardill, I. and Robinson, F. (1987) Some Reflections on the Role of Women in the Tyneside Economy. *Northern Economic Review*, 14, 12–23.

North Tyneside Community Development Project (CDP) (1978) *In and Out of Work: A Study of Unemployment, Low Pay and Income Maintenance Services*. North Shields: North Tyneside CDP.

Vyse, H. (1983) *Women on Work*. Newcastle: TUSIU.

4

EDUCATION

Bill Dennison and Tony Edwards

Along with health care, education is the most important publicly provided service in Tyneside. Since the publication of Henry Mess's book, there have been both substantial increases in the scale of education provision and tremendous changes in the practices of teaching and the arrangements in schools and colleges. The situation existing in the 1920s still reflected the unsystematic and incremental ways in which the state, through local agencies, took over from charities and churches in the organising and financing of education. To compare this situation with that of the 1980s it is necessary to describe the effects of the main events in the intervening period—most notably the 1944 Education Act and the reorganisation of local government, of which education is an integral part. Education on Tyneside is a relatively small element in a national service which is locally administered. Many aspects reflect this national character, but as many are idiosyncratic and unique to Tyneside.

The Administration and Structure of Education

Sixty years ago the pattern of Local Education Authorities (LEAs) in Tyneside was much more complicated than it is now. Then there were ten LEAs, six of them responsible for both elementary and 'higher' education and four (called Part III Authorities) responsible only for the elementary stage. Now there are only four LEAs (Gateshead, Newcastle, North Tyneside and South Tyneside), responsible for educational provision. This rationalisation and simplification of the administrative structure occurred in two stages. First, the Education Act of 1944 eliminated the Part III Authorities (although Wallsend continued as an 'excepted district', with certain limited powers, for another thirty years). And subsequently, in 1974, local government was completely reorganised, creating Tyneside's four new Metropolitan District Councils, each of which has LEA functions. The new authorities incorporated former County Borough LEAs but also took over educational responsibilities in some areas which had previously been administered by Durham and Northumberland County Councils. In the main, the new LEAs used the existing infrastructure of schools, offices and personnel.

The duties and powers of the LEAs are defined in the 1944 Education Act and subsequent amending legislation. Principally, they are to provide compulsory education for those aged 5–16, organise further education, manage special services and run the numerous activities which support the work of the schools. Between them the four Tyneside LEAs employ nearly 8,500 teachers, and spend over £200 million a year in maintaining 460 schools, four further education colleges, and one Polytechnic (Newcastle). By national standards, all four Tyneside LEAs are small: South Tyneside, North Tyneside and Gateshead being respectively the first, fifth and seventh smallest of the 75 mainland English LEAs outside London. They are also much smaller than was originally envisaged; evidence presented to the Royal Commission preceding the 1974 reorganisation about the effectiveness of local government favoured large LEAs with populations of approximately one million, because of the high quality of support activities that would be possible and the likelihood of recruiting good staff to senior positions (RIPA, 1968). An early draft of the Local Government Bill of 1972 envisaged that the much larger Metropolitan Counties would become LEAs, but this proposal met with firm opposition nationally. As a result, in Tyne and Wear it was the five Metropolitan Districts (including Sunderland) which became the LEAs rather than the County of Tyne and Wear itself. Three of the new LEAs had populations of less than 200,000, similar to the kind of small County Borough which had been the focus of much criticism in studies of the size and effectiveness of LEAs.

While the administrative framework may be simpler than it was sixty years ago, the arrangement of schools is considerably less straightforward. Back in the 1920s, the majority of children attended elementary schools from the ages of 5–14, with only a minority changing to secondary schools of some form at eleven, and many of these paying fees. The 1944 Act eliminated fee-paying in the public sector and obliged LEAs to provide secondary education for all children, from the age of eleven. Meeting that obligation was difficult, because it coincided with a massive building programme to repair the damage and neglect of the War years and the large post-war 'bulge' in the birth-rate. By the mid-1950s, however, most elementary schools had become primary (5–11), infant (5–7) or junior (7–11) schools, while secondary education had divided between a selective component (grammar, high or technical schools) and the non-selective secondary moderns. Nationally, the proportion thought suitable to be selected for grammar schools was estimated at 20% of the age-group, but that proportion varied widely between LEAs. Labour-controlled authorities were especially likely to regard grammar schools as a means of enhancing opportunities for able working-class children (Parkinson, 1970), so that Gateshead, for example, raised the percentage of eleven year olds entering grammar school from 8% to 40% by building three new schools (Batley *et al.*, 1970). Here, as elsewhere in Tyneside, comprehensive reorganisation came late for the same reason—the strong attachment of many local politicians to grammar schools as the main 'ladder' of opportunity for the working-class boy and girl. It was not until the Labour administration of 1964 and the DES (Department of Education and Science) Circular 10/65 asking LEAs for their reorganisation plans, that comprehensive schools began to be introduced, although Newcastle had previously opened two comprehensives in areas of new housing.

As the LEAs struggled to complete their secondary school building programmes, they were told in the Circular that the 'all-through' 11–18 school was the 'simplest and best' solution to comprehensive reorganisation. However, a number of different ways of achieving non-selective schooling were also suggested. Several of the Tyneside LEAs found that their selective and secondary modern schools were too small to be reconstructed as 11–18 comprehensives, especially if they were to have reasonably-sized sixth forms. With capital spending restricted, they looked to other ways of using existing buildings as the Circular also suggested. Thus, the former Tynemouth LEA turned its secondary moderns into 11–16 schools and opened a sixth form college. Northumberland essentially used its existing buildings to establish a three-tier system (first schools for pupils aged 5–9; middle schools 9–13; and high schools 13–18). Gateshead introduced junior high schools (for those aged 11–14) in its secondary modern buildings, linked to senior high schools for pupils aged 14–18. Only Durham, Newcastle and South Shields chose the government's preferred 11–18 pattern.

These various arrangements withstood local government reorganisation, resulting in three of the new LEAs inheriting dual or multiple systems which have yet to be disturbed and which would be incomprehensible to anyone without some knowledge of the past. Gateshead has junior and senior highs in the old borough, but 11–18 comprehensives in the areas it took over from Durham; Newcastle has 11–18 schools, alongside the three-tier system in the area which it inherited from Northumberland; whereas North Tyneside has 11–16 schools in Tynemouth and North Shields with a sixth form college, and three tiers elsewhere. Only in South Tyneside is there a relatively tidy predominance of 11–18 comprehensives, with a few residual 11–16 schools. In the Roman Catholic sector progress towards reorganisation was slower, because to retain their voluntary-aided status (and some freedom from LEA control) the Church authorities had to find 15% of the capital costs for new and adapted buildings. After some delay, the Church has been able to introduce 11–18 schools in each of the four LEAs.

Expenditure Patterns

Educational finance is now considerably more complex than in Mess's time, and it would be impossible to discuss how much the Tyneside LEAs spend outside the context of national arrangements for funding LEAs. For all four District Councils, sustaining an education service tends to dominate other resource issues. In South Tyneside, for example, net LEA expenditure represents 66% of the Council's total expenditure, while for the remaining Districts the equivalent figures are just below 60% (CIPFA, 1987).

Apart from some fees and charges, the only source of local revenue available to the Councils is income from the rates and this is insufficient to finance their full range of statutory responsibilities. As education is the most substantial of these responsibilities, its funding represents the paramount issue in central government subsidy provided through the Rate Support Grant. Since the mid-1970s the size of this grant has been of critical importance in the government's determination to restrict local spending. At its peak in 1975–76, Rate Support Grant provided 66% of net local authority expenditure. Gradually this figure has been considerably reduced, the national average in 1986/87 being 46%. Simultaneously, other constraints on local autonomy were introduced, the most important being the 1980 Local Government Planning and Land Act, which brought a new method of distributing grant to authorities, including penalties (grant reductions) for overspending. Subsequently, the Rates Act of 1984 has empowered the government to limit rate rises in local authorities by the process known as 'rate-capping'.

The effects of these developments on all four Districts have been marked. Three (Newcastle, North Tyneside and Gateshead) are among the handful of authorities which have been rate-capped. All four, however, are more dependent on the Rate Support Grant than the national average because of the low rateable value of properties in their areas. Each has had to restrict spending, not only on education but also on all other services. For there is no earmarked grant. The Rate Support Grant is a block grant to the whole authority, and although its calculation relies upon adding together the figures government thinks ought to be spent on each service, the authority is free to determine its own spending pattern. In fact, so tight are the financial constraints and so great is the combination of statutory duties and previous commitments that none of the four Districts perceive much freedom. Indeed, the main thrust in education budget-making since the late 1970s has been towards standstill or reduced budgets, with the principal issue being whether all statutory responsibilities can be fulfilled in these circumstances, especially when the government is simultaneously adding new duties.

All LEAs have needed to evolve retrenchment strategies, and their adverse effects on buildings, the curriculum and teaching equipment have been highlighted by successive annual reports from Her Majesty's Inspectorate (DES, 1986). Against this background of under-provision, detailed statistics suggest, however, that the Tyneside LEAs fare none too badly in *relative* terms. In 1983–84, for example, Newcastle was the second highest spending LEA per pupil on primary education, with South Tyneside fifth and Gateshead seventh. Because teaching is so labour intensive (teachers' salaries account for over 70% of primary school costs) such relatively high expenditures reflect PTRs (pupil to teacher ratios) which are significantly more generous than the national average—around 19 to 1 for the four Tyneside LEAs compared to 21.8 to 1 for other Metropolitan Districts and 22.9 to 1 for all English LEAs. More detailed figures for 1984/5 (Table 4.1) show that at both primary and secondary level the four LEAs spend above the national average per pupil in almost all of the main expenditure categories. Only occasionally does one of them drop below the national average, but even this must be compared to factors such as high spending on non-teaching support staff by Newcastle LEA and, to a lesser extent, by North Tyneside.

TABLE 4.1. EXPENDITURE PER PUPIL AND PUPIL TO TEACHER RATIOS (PTRs), 1984/5

Local Education Authority	Primary Education					Secondary Education				
	Expenditure per pupil (£)				Pupil to Teacher ratio	Expenditure per pupil (£)				Pupil to Teacher ratio
	Total Net	Teaching Staff	Other Staff	Books/ Equipment		Total Net	Teaching Staff	Other Staff	Books/ Equipment	
Gateshead	855	603	93	26	19.2	1,106	788	78	48	15.4
Newcastle	910	585	157	19	19.3	1,288	859	136	39	14.4
North Tyneside	838	567	115	28	19.1	1,212	829	105	51	14.1
South Tyneside	832	565	115	21	20.8	1,184	841	92	55	14.6
Provincial Met. Districts (outside London)	779	533	102	21	21.8	1,112	770	107	39	15.8
All English LEAs	776	531	96	23	22.2	1,134	766	112	43	16.1

Source: *CIPFA Education Statistics Actuals, 1984–85.*

The spending pattern for 1984/85 (the most recent figures available), is still no more than a snapshot. Because the financial manoeuvrability of LEAs has always been limited, and has become dramatically more so recently, the 1984/85 expenditures demonstrate the culmination of annual budget decisions going back to the formation of the new LEAs. Then, and for much of the 1970s, the pressure from unions, headteachers and school governors to adopt generous staffing levels was formidable; it was also in line with LEA policy. Each of them, but particularly Newcastle, was determined to give priority to educational spending, partly to overcome the social disadvantages of many pupils, and partly to make good the earlier deficiencies in provision of the kind reported by Mess. Their success must be judged by the fact that, in the mid-1980s, the four Tyneside LEAs were on average spending around 5% to 10% more on education than other Provincial Metropolitan Districts (these are the LEAs with which comparisons ought to be made, rather than the Shire counties, because they face not dissimilar problems).

Looking ahead, though, the Tyneside LEAs will find it increasingly difficult to sustain above-average spending on education. First, because rate-capping is just a further step in the government's efforts to control local authority expenditure by curbing 'overspenders', and as the Tyneside LEAs are heavily reliant on Rate Support Grant, they will be specially vulnerable to additional curbs. Second, even if an authority as a whole manages to 'overspend', the demands of other services, particularly those associated with social welfare in an area of high unemployment, will compete strongly for local authority resources.

In addition, as for other LEAs, those on Tyneside have been subject to an increasing tendency to centralise finance. More particularly, the government has used resource constraints as a means of implementing their educational policies. With less Rate Support Grant, but more government money available from Education Support Grant; and various projects like TVEI and Low Attainers (described in detail later), LEAs have naturally been inclined to accept money even if it involved them in practices contrary to their own philosophies. Always such extra resources are only provided by government departments if what the LEA proposes receives approval. Usually, the LEAs must bid competitively for resources, with government as sole arbitrator. All four Tyneside LEAs have been involved in such processes.

However, the expenditure picture certainly remains a good deal more optimistic than that drawn by Mess. Sixty years ago, looking at elementary education, he compared spending on teachers salaries and the total expenditure per pupil of each of the Tyneside authorities with national figures. At that time, none of them was better than 10% below the average for comparable authorities, while Hebburn and South Shields were both more than 20% below average. In addition, in absolute terms the present situation demonstrates other positive features. As elsewhere, a wide range of support activities have been developed in Tyneside, such as special schools, careers and psychological services and school meals. Here, comparative measures of LEA expenditure have to be interpreted carefully. The Tyneside LEAs, for example, provide a much higher proportion of free meals than the national average, but that in itself is a measure of relative deprivation, with more children belonging to low income families. For similar reasons, greater spending on special schools and other support services is likely to occur, while in an area of high unemployment above-average expenditure on a careers service is also to be expected.[1]

Schooling Conditions in the 1920s and the 1980s

Any potential complacency about above-average spending ought to be dispelled by two questions. First, do the Tyneside LEAs have to spend more even to offer an average service because the needs of their children are greater? Second, are they spending effectively? All the expenditure figures and PTRs so far mentioned are input measures; they give no indication about whether the LEAs achieve value for money.

Both of these questions are extremely complex, and satisfactory answers await research which is very difficult to carry out. A recent study of LEA expenditures on secondary education considered the effects of pupil needs, 'involuntary measures' (factors over which the LEA had no control) and discretionary measures in comparing actual expenditure per pupil with what LEAs might be expected to spend. According to these calculations Newcastle 'overspent' by a few per cent, while Gateshead and North Tyneside 'under-spent' by similar margins (Jesson *et al.*, 1986). Such calculations though, tell us nothing about the effects of actual expenditure on outcomes, (but in a later section we discuss how the achievements of school leavers have been used as an indicator of effectiveness of spending).

Looking at the way the four Tyneside LEAs deploy their resources is also informative. In the *primary sector* each LEA has its own distinctive staffing policy. Gateshead aims for reception classes of no more than 27 pupils, rising to 29 for other classes, plus a headteacher. In practice many classes are much smaller. Newcastle, by contrast, awards a teacher for every 30 children, a headteacher, plus an additional one or two non-class based teachers if school size is above certain thresholds. Also a social priority index is used to assess those schools deserving between 0.5 and 2 extra teachers. North Tyneside uses this notion of socio-economic needs to band their primary schools into nine groups, in which Band 1 schools in socially deprived areas have an average class-size of 18.2, climbing to 28.4 for Band 9 schools. The headteacher is additional, as is an extra weighting of 20% for reception class children. Additional too is a pool of class teachers used at the discretion of the LEA. South Tyneside has a basic PTR of 21.9 to 1, including the headteacher, with a lower ratio sought in schools with special factors as identified by educational psychologists and school advisers.

The contrast between these staffing levels and the conditions in elementary schools described by Mess is remarkable. Sixty years ago, over a third of classes had more than fifty pupils; indeed, in Newcastle nearly half the classes, and in Hebburn almost two thirds, were in this category. The practicable ideal of the Board of Education over the next few years, as Mess reported, was to reduce the maximum class-size for children under eleven to 50 pupils, and for over-elevens to 40.

Direct comparisons of staffing levels in *secondary schools* are more problematic as all older pupils are now in secondary schools; but even so, the contrast with sixty years ago seems quite remarkable. Gateshead negotiates directly with each of its secondary schools on the basis of PTR and the need to protect an established curriculum. Also each school has a permanent supply teacher to cover for staff absence and course attendance. Newcastle uses a basic ratio of 20 to 1 for Years One and Two, 18 to 1 for Years Three, Four and Five, and 12 to 1 for the sixth form. Additionally there are some special allowances and a measure of curriculum protection. North Tyneside negotiates staffing with each school and intends to introduce a curriculum-led staffing policy. South Tyneside has already achieved this situation, and here the curriculum model which the LEA agrees to staff is also weighted to take account of special needs identified within each school.

An overall PTR of around 15 to 1 for secondary education in each of the LEAs (Table 4.1) does not, of course, mean an average class size of fifteen. First, all secondary school teachers have some non-contact time, while the headteacher and senior staff with management responsibilities often have much lighter teaching timetables. Secondly, individual teachers may be absent because of illness or (increasingly) are away on in-service training. Thirdly, optional courses from Year Three, and particularly in the sixth form, tend to introduce small teaching groups. The combined effect of these factors is often large classes of more than 30 in Years One and Two. But in certain circumstances, such large groups can sometimes be an advantage. Their existence may allow the school more freedom in designing option arrangements as they free teacher time, and they also signify that the school is not affected too drastically by falling rolls.

Falling rolls. The pressure of falling rolls, together with demands to reduce or contain expenditure, represent the two most significant influences on school staffing in the 1980s. Nationally, the birth rate declined by about a third from 1964 to 1977; since then there has been a small increase. The decline has been particularly marked in the main conurbations, including Tyneside. And because of more localised movement by families with school age children out of the older housing areas of Tyneside, many schools have found their rolls falling very much faster and further than the national average. For most secondary schools in Tyneside, these decreases will not finish before the early 1990s. Fewer

Percy Main School, near North Shields, in the 1920s. This class had over 40 pupils – but at the time a third of primary classes had over 50 pupils. (*Local Studies Centre, North Shields*).

Infants' reception class at St Cuthbert's School, North Shields, 1986. The atmosphere is more relaxed, less formal – and classes are also smaller – than in Mess's time. (*Stan Gamester*).

pupils may of course offer an opportunity for better PTRs, and without the pressures of financial retrenchment these might have been achieved. However, the combination of even a constant PTR with falling rolls, which with rate-capping is the best that Tyneside LEAs can achieve, has certain adverse effects. In primary schools it means fewer teachers, the same class sizes, but increased likelihood of mixed-age teaching groups. For secondary schools it involves the disappearance of minority subjects like Music or German, simply because there are fewer teachers in the school.

In both sectors, the combination of fewer pupils and financial constraints has produced school mergers, closures, and the redeployment or early retirement (though not redundancy) of staff—often with deleterious consequences for pupil and teacher morale. In one respect the Tyneside LEAs are advantaged by their smallness in that the LEA can negotiate with each school individually over staff redeployment or the level of curriculum support it can offer. Conversely, their size reduces flexibility of possible response. In secondary education, particularly, they have relatively few schools, many are small and shrinking and curriculum protection at the level the LEA might judge prudent is inhibited by finance. Above the school leaving age the problems of Tyneside LEAs are further exaggerated by low participation rates in Further Education. Not surprisingly, two LEAs, Gateshead and South Tyneside, plan a system of 11–16 schools and tertiary colleges as a solution to their difficulties.

Falling rolls generate space, but at a price. Buildings are a fixed cost, and without closures, premises-related costs per pupil rise, meaning less to spend on other items. However, it is rare for any closure proposal by the Tyneside LEAs not to meet sustained community resistance. The decline in the number of children also means that arguments for new buildings receive little attention. The result, at a time when local authority capital expenditure continues to be severely restricted, is that the four LEAs have opened only a handful of new schools during the last ten years. Even so, the overall position today is enormously better than that described by Mess. His main concerns were about shared classrooms, premises lacking modern requirements, and temporary buildings. There are still many examples of old buildings, but only a few were not improved or added to with specialist rooms during the 1960s and 1970s. These were the decades of substantial school building programmes, first in the primary sector, and the Tyneside LEAs had their share of national developments. The main disadvantage of current policies is not the cessation of the building programme, but its accompaniment by considerable restrictions on minor improvements and even routine maintenance schemes. In many schools, the fabric of the buildings is deteriorating, and there seems little likelihood of any additional finance to improve the situation.

Teachers. Apart from the fact that the Tyneside authorities had too few teachers, the prime concern of Mess about the teaching force was the relatively large number of uncertificd tcachers. Again, that situation has been transformed over the past sixty years in line with national events. In 1961 the minimum length of training for teachers was raised to three years, and in 1977 to four years of study, including the B.Ed. degree. The proportion of staff entering schools after a degree course and a postgraduate teaching certificate has grown steadily, first in secondary then in primary schools. If we accept Mess's assumption that, as a whole, certificated teachers were superior to non-certificated, then there can be few doubts that the present teaching force is of better quality than that of sixty years ago. (Unfortunately, there are no readily available statistics to compare the qualifications of teachers employed by the Tyneside LEAs with the national situation).

A further issue which concerned Mess was the tendency of the Tyneside authorities to employ locally-educated teachers, since he argued that their lack of standards of comparison could induce an unimaginative outlook on education and make them malleable to the demands of the Local Education Office. It is conventional wisdom to argue that the Tyneside LEAs employ a larger proportion of staff without experience elsewhere than do other LEAs. However, there has been no reliable research that might substantiate this view, let alone to confirm whether the conclusions of Mess still pertain.

Nursery and Special Education. Perhaps, though, the greatest contrast in schooling between the 1920s and the 1980s is in the provision made for children under the age of five and those with special educational needs. Mess reported that none of the Tyneside authorities had established nursery schools, and apart from a few private kindergartens, all children started school at five. There are still relatively few nursery schools, although South Tyneside had eleven in 1986 (with 807 children) and Newcastle seven (with 593 children). However, the situation has been transformed mainly because of the number of nursery classes attached to primary schools, and the policies of the LEAs to permit under-fives to start school. LEAs have this power, and both Newcastle and Gateshead, for example, have a single intake arrangement—in the September before the child's fifth birthday. Two factors influenced this increased provision, even during a time of retrenchment. The first was pragmatic—using the spare capacity resulting from falling rolls. The second was the increasing realisation of the importance of schooling to this age of child, particularly those living in areas where the home environment was less likely to be conducive to intellectual and emotional development. In terms of numbers the results are impressive. Out of a total primary school population of about 68,000 children, nearly 12,000 under-fives attend school full-time and more than 7,000 attend on a part-time basis.

Provision for pupils with special educational needs expanded in the years following 1944. Between them, the four LEA's now maintain 24 non-boarding and 4 boarding schools for pupils with learning difficulties, emotional and behaviour problems, and special handicaps (e.g. blind, deaf, etc.). In total over 2,000 pupils attend these schools and, as would be expected, they are very demanding in resources— pupil to teacher ratios, for example, range from 5 to 1 to 7 to 1 across the LEAs. Since the late 1970s, and more particularly since the Education Act 1981, the main emphasis in policy has, however, been to integrate as many of these pupils as possible into 'mainstream' primary and secondary schools.

The School Curriculum

In his account of the curriculum, Mess referred to 'a somewhat unimaginative and utilitarian outlook' in the schools of Tyneside, attributing it to over-recruitment of teachers from within the region and to the 'rather heavy hand' of some Education Offices. The outcome was a predominance of teaching which was conscientious but dull. Sixty years later, the curriculum never seems to stand still long enough to be dull. Indeed, teachers' representatives often complain that the frequency and pace of innovation threaten to exhaust the profession, and to make it impossible to consolidate one initiative before another rushes in.

To an extent which any commentator in the 1920s would have found astonishing, the impetus behind many of the changes has been central government. In the 1920s, fears that a future Labour Government might seek to indoctrinate the young if the government's Board of Education were given powers which could be misused in this way helped to support the autonomy both of local authorities and of teachers. But during the last ten years, traditional assumptions about who should control the curriculum have been strongly challenged. Teachers and headteachers are losing their 'freedom' to determine what is taught, although at the secondary stage the overlapping demands of higher education and of employers have always made it a largely illusory freedom. The 1986 Education Act requires governing bodies to be actively involved in shaping the curriculum, it encourages consultation with representatives of the 'community', and it insists on a regular accounting to parents for the content and quality of what is taught. There are obvious possibilities of conflict at this local level where the 'partners' fail to agree—for example, about such sensitive issues as sex education. But local accountability has to be placed in the wider contexts of local authority curriculum policies which themselves have to take account of national 'guidelines'.

Until 1981, LEAs might produce declarations of intent for particular subjects or even age-groups, but the decision to do so was theirs. They are now *required* to submit to the Department of Education and Science statements of policy for the whole curriculum 5–16, together with their arrangements for making that policy known and for ensuring that the work of their schools is consistent with it. For example, Newcastle and South Tyneside met the first target date of 1983 by producing general and unobjectionable statements of intent which left their schools considerable room for manoeuvre. Both statements were revised in 1987, and in some areas were hardened. North Tyneside's comprehensive set of 1983 guidelines is typical in combining 'broad guidance' with an insistence that the curricula of individual schools could not be prescribed in detail. Similarly, Gateshead's 1987 statement sets out the criteria against which schools should 'review their curriculum provision and frame their own statement'. Such guidelines refer to concepts of breadth, balance and relevance which were certainly part of curriculum debate sixty years ago, and even their references to 'areas of experience' rather than to subjects would not have been altogether unfamiliar. What are new are the lengthy statements in all four LEA curriculum policies about the obligations of schools to (i) prepare children to live in a multicultural society; (ii) offer equal opportunities to boys and girls to take subjects and gain qualifications in any area of the curriculum; (iii) assimilate children with special needs, as far as possible, into 'mainstream' provision; and (iv) take account of new technology, especially information technology.

More generally, the sections of these policy statements on primary education mark a great advance from the utilitarian narrowness which Mess noted especially in the elementary schools. Even in the 1920s, there was a growing movement to extend (or enrich) the elementary curriculum and to encourage more active forms of learning. A view of that curriculum which emphasised a broad range of learning experiences rather than an excessive preoccupation with basic skills dominated the *Hadow Reports* of 1926 and 1931[2], but there were then few schools which could have been chosen to exemplify it. There are now many schools in Tyneside which display that commitment to active collaborative forms of learning which are associated with the 'best' primary practice, and provide visually colourful and attractive environments for young children which are very different from the often gloomy instructional 'barracks' of sixty years ago.

As the various LEA Policy Statements make clear, however, the schools face increasingly difficult decisions about what to include and exclude in a curriculum which is increasingly expected to meet needs far beyond the 'Three R's', while at the same time satisfying demands for children to acquire the necessary basic skills in literacy and numeracy. Two particular innovations deserve mention in this context of basic skills. The teaching of reading has been transformed in many schools by an emphasis on children 'reading for understanding' rather than being drilled too early in word-by-word accuracy, and using books which are much more imaginative and pleasurable to read than the 'Janet and John' books which were previously the standard reading manuals. Similarly, practical work and problem-solving are now much more likely to be emphasised in the teaching of mathematics.

There are particular innovations to note in secondary education which are local manifestations of national developments—for example, the increasing emphasis on Personal and Social Education exemplified in the Newcastle LEA's development project launched in 1986; the introduction of the Certificate of Pre-Vocational Education in school sixth forms as well as in Further Education (together with other forms of business and technical education); and the widespread changes in curriculum content and in teaching methods which are demanded by the new '16+' examinations, the GCSE (General Certificate of Secondary Education). We concentrate in the rest of this section, however, on local effects of a major change in the funding of education in recent years. This is the allocation by the Department of Education and Science (DES), and on a very much larger scale by the Manpower Services Commission (MSC), of funds for which LEAs bid in accordance with centrally-specified criteria. We focus on two major central government initiatives here: the MSC's Technical and Vocational Education Initiative and the DES Lower Attaining Pupils Project.

The MSC's *Technical and Vocational Education Initiative (TVEI)* was announced by the Prime Minister in November 1982, apparently without consultation either with the DES or with local authorities. Indeed, the 'new institutional arrangements' for TVEI were made the responsibility of the MSC and were only described as having to be 'in association with local authorities......where possible'. The idea was to offer newly designed courses to a small cohort of children in a relatively few schools of collaborating LEAs. The courses were to start for pupils aged 14 and extend over four years, either in school or further education colleges, and they were intended to cater for all ability levels and both sexes. No Tyneside LEA was included in the first group of fourteen TVEI pilot projects, but Newcastle, South Tyneside and North Tyneside were successful in their bids for the 'second wave' of funding for the period 1986–89. (Gateshead's TVEI bid was delayed by its participation in the slightly earlier DES-funded Lower Attaining Pupils Project). TVEI is now to be extended to secondary schools throughout the country, with substantially reduced levels of earmarked funding in relation to this greatly enlarged scope. But in the 'second wave' of its development, now involving all four Tyneside Authorities, the emphasis was still on piloting a 'wider and richer curriculum' in a limited number of schools which received considerable extra money for their efforts. Newcastle, for example, received an additional £400,000 a year for projects directly involving five of its comprehensive schools; under the terms of TVEI's national extension, it will receive £650,000 a year to fund developments in which all its thirteen comprehensive schools will be involved. Until now, some schools have been receiving as much additional money for their involvement in TVEI as they were receiving from their LEA for the whole of the rest of their work. In return, they had to be seen to be emphasising the application of skills and knowledge to 'real world problems', and to be constructing for their pupils an earlier and more substantial bridge to the 'world of work'. They had to meet criteria drawn from more general statements of curriculum policy—for example, the avoidance of sex stereotyping in the courses they offered. But there were also specific demands for more provision of information technology, more work experience, more explicit orientation of courses to areas of employment, and an emphasis in pupil assessment on recording positive achievements in a wide range of activities and (where appropriate) negotiating those assessments with the individual pupils themselves.

The *Lower Attaining Pupils Project (LAPP)* was initiated by the DES, just before TVEI in 1982, as an expression of the then Secretary of State's concern for the 'bottom 40%'—those 'for whom the existing public examinations at 16+ are not designed'. It has lacked the glamour and publicity attached to TVEI, and its total budget of £3 million a year has been small compared with that MSC-controlled enterprise. Gateshead was one of the fourteen LEAs selected initially to participate in LAPP, and the first year was given to careful planning by teams of teachers drawn from the three comprehensive schools in which the Project began. Its main objective was to 'improve self-respect and motivation' among academically unsuccessful older pupils by constructing a curriculum specifically adapted to their needs and their 'world'; by teaching methods which were more inventive, challenging and less teacher-centred; and by developing methods of assessment which recorded what pupils *could do* rather than listing their failures.

In that last respect, Gateshead was, in fact, already well advanced, even before its involvement with LAPP, through its prominent part in the Unit Accreditation System devised by Northern Education Authorities. Gateshead was the first Tyneside Authority to be involved in the Northern Partnership for Records of Achievement—a joint enterprise by LEAs and Examination Boards to record the proficiency of pupils in a wide range of academic, practical and personal skills. The first such records were issued to pupils leaving the LAPP project in the summer of 1986; and the experiences gained from this system are likely to prove invaluable when all schools have to produce records of achievements for their pupils in the early 1990s.

While the main base for the LAPP innovations as a whole was initially the three comprehensives chosen to launch the project (Highfield,

Dunston and Ryton), the innovations in curriculum, teaching methods and assessment are intended for dissemination throughout the LEA. Similarly, Newcastle's involvement from 1986 has been initially centred in one school (Blakelaw), which recruits from a social priority area and has a high proportion of 'low attainers' as defined by national objective tests. But the project objectives of improving attendance, morale, certification, and participation rates in post-sixteen education are clearly relevant to all the city's comprehensive schools, as are the intended changes in curriculum towards more concentrated units with short-term, explicit objectives and in teaching methods towards more 'autonomous' forms of learning.

There are important common features in both TVEI and LAPP. More adventurous and challenging forms of teaching, learning and assessment are being sought, and there is a greater emphasis on both residential experience and work experience. Within schools, pressures towards team-teaching have been strong and both Projects have made exceptionally heavy demands on the teachers chosen to co-ordinate them. The need for collaboration between schools has done much to challenge their traditional autonomy.

When TVEI is extended to all secondary schools in the four LEAs during the next few years, there is a likelihood that some benefits can be transferred to all schools. Opportunities for courses, meetings, and other contacts between staff from different schools will grow, helping to provide mechanisms for the exchange of experiences and ideas on records of achievement, pupil profiling, and so on. As part of these processes, and as a result of local and national developments, some parts of the curriculum will become more modularised—broken down into smaller components. In this way the curriculum should appeal more to the less academic pupils, and be the basis for negotiable programmes of learning between the pupil and the teacher.

On the debit side, the greatly increased resources available to some schools within an LEA has caused some resentment among the less favoured, while also carrying a 'price' in that the schools have been scrutinized by 'outsiders' (LEA advisers, HMI, local and national project evaluators) with quite unusual frequency and intensity. There is also the deeper problem that schools may again be expected to find educational solutions for intractable economic problems. The introduction of both of these Projects has coincided with rapidly rising youth unemployment. Hence, serious questions persist about what any changes in the school's curriculum and in methods of teaching and assessment can do to improve the 'employability' of young school leavers in a region facing such severe economic decline; we return to this matter in the final sections of this chapter.

Independent Schools

Except for the new common examinations at 16+ (the GCSE), the
curriculum innovations outlined in the previous section have left the
independent schools largely untouched. While the government has urged
LEAs to promote technology in their schools, and to prepare pupils more
fully and explicitly for the 'real world' and 'working life', the independent
schools have been actively encouraged to remain as bastions of traditional
academic standards and subjects. Nationally, the private sector contains
6% of the total school population, and 7% of pupils in secondary schools.
Those averages conceal considerable differences between different parts of
the country—differences which, at the secondary stage, often reflect the
philanthropic activities of wealthy individuals and merchant companies
centuries ago, the more entrepreneurial ventures which created so many
new 'public' schools in Victorian times, and the decisions of some
endowed grammar schools in the 1920s to receive public funds directly
from central government rather than through a local authority.

In 1926, eight of Tyneside's secondary schools were 'under trusts or
private management'. Seven of these were in Newcastle itself, one of them
(the Royal Grammar School) being a 'public' school whose headmaster
was a member of the Headmasters' Conference. The significantly lower
proportion of 'free places' in Newcastle than in many other parts of the
country, which Mess noted, was a consequence of this relatively high
density of private secondary schools. Sixty years later, Tyneside has no
'public' school in the traditional sense of a fee-paying boarding school, the
nearest such schools being at Durham, Barnard Castle and Sedbergh, and
only three boys' Preparatory schools explicitly geared to preparation for
the common entrance examination to such schools at thirteen. However,
Newcastle does have four former direct-grant grammar schools which are
now independent (the Royal Grammar, the Central High School for Girls,
and the two Dame Allen's Schools) together with two girls' independent
grammar schools (Church High and La Sagesse).

Although two former direct-grant schools in Newcastle are now
maintained comprehensive schools (Sacred Heart and St. Cuthbert's),
those that remain represent one of the highest concentrations of
prestigious independent day schools in the country, although it should be
noted that all of them (and to some extent the two Catholic
comprehensives) recruit some of their pupils from outside the city itself.
Elsewhere in Tyneside, there are six private secondary schools in the area,
the best known of which is the King's School at Tynemouth. Of the eleven
schools catering for younger children which are listed in the 1983–4
Parents' Guide to Independent Schooling, three are traditional Preparatory
schools; four are junior departments of the former direct-grant schools;
and four are part of schools taking pupils from 9–16 or 9–18. As remains

true of most of the private sector, the most prestigious schools are single-sex. But some independent secondary schools are co-educational so as to widen their market appeal, although King's has followed what is now a common practice in 'public' schools of admitting girls as sixth formers.

Independent schools are often described as complementing provision in the maintained sector, adding to the range of schools and to parental choice without additional costs to public funds. Fee-paying parents are then likely to be described as saving public money in so far as they pay 'twice' for their children's schooling—through normal rates and taxes, and then through fees—while not taking up places in maintained schools to which they are entitled. From another perspective, independent schools (or at least the more academically reputable of them) are seen not only as being in competition with the public sector, but also as 'creaming off' many able pupils who would otherwise have been a stimulating presence in primary, middle or comprehensive schools. For example, the 1970 report by Benn and Simon on the progress of comprehensive re-organisation cited Newcastle as a prominent example of an LEA seriously damaged, especially in relation to its planning of sixth form education in its comprehensive schools, by the high concentration of direct-grant and independent grammar schools. Their argument was open to an obvious counter-argument—which applies similarly to criticisms of the present Assisted Places Scheme—namely, that those grammar schools were non-local in character and drew their intakes from a wide geographical area and from several LEAs. Thus the Newcastle grammar schools continue to recruit fee-paying pupils from the other three Tyneside LEA areas.

The direct-grant system was phased out by the Labour Government in 1976, schools on the list having to make a straight choice between 'full' independence or being absorbed into the educational plans of their local LEA. The subsequent Conservative Government did not restore the direct-grant list. Instead, it introduced an Assisted Places Scheme, implemented in 1981, through which financially eligible parents of academically eligible children could have all or part of their fees remitted at selected independent secondary schools. Five Newcastle schools joined the Scheme from its outset, and were initially allocated 157 places a year, together with another 25 at the sixth form stage. The Royal Grammar School's annual allocation of 55 places was the largest in the country, and only London, Manchester, Liverpool and Bristol had larger numbers of places than Newcastle. The take-up of those places has varied between schools, with the Central High School having its quota reduced, but the total number of assisted place pupils in 1985 was 660. Put another way, and with due regard to the point about considerable non-local recruitment, the Scheme caters each year for a number equivalent to the entire intake of a large comprehensive school.

The Royal Grammar School, Newcastle – one of Tyneside's independent schools. (*Newcastle City Engineer's Department*).

The effects of the Scheme have been hotly contested. The benefits promised to, and obtained by, individual pupils have to be balanced against the possible disadvantages to children in maintained schools, and that accounting exercise is extremely difficult. More generally, the relatively high level of independent school provision in Newcastle affects the *apparent* performance of the LEA. Newcastle has 10% of its secondary pupils in independent schools, and 16% of its school leavers in 1985 were from such schools compared with a national figure of 6%. If most of those pupils would otherwise have gone to Newcastle's own comprehensive schools, and if most of them are assumed to be able pupils with a high probability of substantial examination achievements at sixteen and of staying on into the sixth form, then the LEA's performance as measured by success in public examinations at sixteen will be significantly depressed. The effect is substantial; in one recent and well-publicised analysis, taking this 'creaming off' into account raises Newcastle from being an apparently under-achieving LEA into the 'top ten'.

Further and Higher Education

Post-compulsory educational provision has always been a difficult matter for LEAs, and has now become highly controversial. How is a sufficient choice of subjects and levels to be offered to sixth formers even where the number of students is small? How justified are the traditionally rigid boundaries between 'education' and 'training', the 'academic' and the 'vocational', and between full-time and part-time students? Perennially difficult questions about the educational and economic viability of what is provided have been further complicated by the fact that the number of 16–19 year olds will fall nationally by one third between the early 1980s and the mid-1990s. LEAs certainly needed no urging from the MacFarlane Committee (DES, 1981) to 'reconsider the institutional basis of their provision' when falling rolls were already concentrating their attention on how to combine greater diversity of courses with lower costs at a time of increasing pressure to reduce expenditure from the rates. As was noted in the MacFarlane Committee's Report, rolls were falling especially fast in some urban areas. In South Tyneside, for example, the expected decline in the 15-year-old population from peak to trough (roughly 1979 and 1992) is over 40%; in Newcastle it is estimated as being between 36% and 40%, and in Gateshead and North Tyneside as between 31% and 35%.

Whether they were acting mainly on the logistics of rationalisation or following what they see as the logical conclusion of comprehensive reorganisation, LEAs in some parts of the country have opted for tertiary colleges in which all forms of post-sixteen provision, from A-levels to the educational components of the MSC's Youth Training Scheme, are located. Far more LEAs have chosen to create sixth form colleges by removing sixth forms from schools and concentrating them in 16–18 institutions. Tyneside has no tertiary college, though they exist in County Durham at Peterlee and Consett. North Tyneside has a sixth form college (with 600 students) at Tynemouth, although since it also has an FE (Further Education) college, 11–16 high schools, 13–18 high schools and two (Roman Catholic) 11–18 comprehensives, it represents an interesting medley of almost everything available. South Tyneside has some comprehensives which retain pupils to 18, and others from which pupils wishing to stay on have to move at 16 either to a school with a sixth form or to the FE College (which is being turned into a tertiary college catering for all post-16 students in that LEA except for one Roman Catholic 11–18 secondary school). Gateshead and Newcastle have so far retained their sixth form pupils within their comprehensive schools, but have done so with increasing difficulty. In 1979–80 Newcastle considered, and eventually rejected, plans for either sixth form colleges or for absorbing sixth form provision within the College of Arts and Technology, and alleviated the viability problem temporarily by merging four comprehensives into two. More recently, it has tried the 'clustering' solution in which groups of schools collaborate so as to provide a wide range of subjects and levels of study between them rather than struggling to do so independently. Gateshead's recent plan to remove sixth forms from all its comprehensive schools and create a tertiary college on two sites (based on the existing FE College) has been at least temporarily checked by a High Court ruling following protests by parents' groups at the lack of adequate consultation.

It is at the post-compulsory stage of education that the contrasts with the situation as Mess described it are perhaps most marked. In 1926, staying on rates in schools were very low, and no secondary school except the Royal Grammar School had more than a handful of sixth formers. Newcastle had the Rutherford Technical College (in buildings which were demolished while this chapter was being prepared), and there was a Marine School and an Art School in South Shields. A few schools, notably the two junior technical schools in Newcastle, gave some preparation for engineering. Commercial training was available in Jarrow Central School, the Tynemouth High School, and in various private 'colleges'.

By contrast, the scope of present-day provision is very substantial indeed. All four LEAs have Colleges of Further Education, those in South Tyneside and Newcastle being among the largest in the country.The Newcastle College of Arts and Technology had over 14,000 students in 1985–6, including more than 2,000 who were studying full-time. South Tyneside's College has a similar number of students, including over 6,000 full-time—a larger proportion partly explained by the presence of A-level and other students from high schools without sixth forms. Gateshead's

College had 5,680 students in 1986/7, 756 full-time. North Tyneside's figure for 1986/7 of 6,900 includes 1,763 full-time, the much larger numbers of non full-time students consisting of a mixture of part-time day, part-time evening, block release, sandwich course, evening only and 'open learning' (or 'flexistudy') students. Further Education has traditionally been marked by very diverse modes of participation in study, while schools have insisted on full-time attendance for all except the growing trickle of 'mature' adults joining school sixth-forms for subjects at A-level. This diversity of participation has been increased still further by the wide range of courses funded by the Manpower Services Commission for trainees on the Youth Training Scheme (YTS). The North Tyneside College, for example, has 1,605 such students in 1986/7, most of them YTS trainees whose non-work experience training is at least partly based there.

Another major expansion in provision has been in higher education. Indeed, the total number of higher education students in Newcastle in 1987 is not far short of the *national* UK total in 1926. At that time, the Armstrong College had 700 full-time degree students, two thirds of them coming from Tyneside itself and the College of Medicine had another 300. Both colleges were then part of the University of Durham; they combined as the King's College in 1937, and became the independent University of Newcastle upon Tyne in 1963. Of the University's 8,389 students in 1985/6, only 20% were recruited from the North East region; 11% came from overseas, and the University as a whole is national and international in its interests and achievements. The Newcastle Polytechnic that year had more than 10,000 students, 6,567 studying either full-time or on 'sandwich' type degree courses. Like most Polytechnics, it has outgrown its initial technological base to provide a wide range of courses; indeed, the largest faculty by far is now Social Studies. Although the Polytechnic offers training in several of the professions 'ancillary to medicine', it has nothing equivalent to the University's Medical School. But in other respects, its courses cover similar areas of study and illustrate the large overlap in provision and function across the 'binary line'. The more significant differences have been the much greater emphasis on research in the University, and the presence in the Polytechnic of many students of a kind still rare in universities except in their Education Departments—those on day-release or attending only in the evening.

The only area of contraction, certainly in the number of institutions, has been in teacher training. In the 1920s, there were training colleges at Kenton Lodge and Fenham in Newcastle (the latter a Catholic college), and a Northern Counties College specialising in cookery and domestic science which was supported by the three authorities of Newcastle, Northumberland and Durham. The post-war and 1960s expansions in teacher training brought larger numbers and new colleges, only for falling

Newcastle University – a 'redbrick' University situated in the city centre. The University has over 8,000 students, while the Polytechnic nearby caters for a further 10,000 students in higher education. (*Newcastle City Engineer's Department*).

rolls and rationalisation to produce an equally rapid period of contraction. There are now no free-standing colleges left in Tyneside, teacher training being concentrated in the University and Polytechnic.

Achievements and School Leavers

Rates of staying on for further full-time education after the age of compulsory schooling have long been, and remain, lower in Tyneside than in most other parts of the country. Sixty years ago, Mess suggested that the relatively low proportions attending grant-aided secondary schools was not surprising in an area 'which contains an unusually small middle-class stratum'. Variations of this explanation are still being offered to explain the relatively low staying on rates. In a region which traditionally has had high levels of recruitment into 'heavy' industries not normally requiring 'academic' credentials, and far fewer opportunities in professional, managerial and other white-collar employment than in (for example) the south east of England, the material benefits of prolonged education have perhaps been less visible than elsewhere. The outcome is likely to be less parental pressure for achieving occupational success through acquiring educational qualifications.

The statistics indicate a continuing difference in staying on rates which certainly cannot be accounted for by a higher proportion of pupils leaving school without the examination successes to 'justify' staying on. For example, the proportion of school leavers in the Northern Region with 'no academic qualifications' (no passes of any kind at 0-level or CSE) during the period 1982–1985 was actually lower than in Yorkshire and Humberside, the North West, the West Midlands and Greater London. The proportions leaving with five or more 0-level passes or their equivalent was also higher than in all those regions except the North West, and also higher than in the East Midlands. Yet the proportion of youngsters in the Northern Region leaving school at the minimum age was still the highest of all the English regions, while the proportion staying on in full-time further education was the lowest. The figures for the four Tyneside LEAs 1982–5 are shown below in Table 4.2.

TABLE 4.2. MINIMUM AGE SCHOOL LEAVERS AND THOSE GOING TO FULL-TIME FURTHER EDUCATION: TYNESIDE, NORTHERN REGION AND ENGLAND, 1982–85

Local Education Authority	% leaving at school leaving age (16)	% going to full-time further education
Gateshead	53.5	14.7
Newcastle	46.3	15.8
North Tyneside	46.5	20.0
South Tyneside	50.8	14.6
Northern Region[1]	49.5	19.0
England	45.7	25.5

Source : DES Statistics of Education, 1985.

Note: 1. The Northern Region comprises the counties of Tyne and Wear, Northumberland, Co. Durham, Cleveland and Cumbria.

How much credit or discredit can be attributed to secondary schools or LEAs for the achievements of their school leavers has long been a matter of (often uninformed) controversy. Ignorance has been especially marked when comparisons are made between examination results in different LEAs—for example, in relation to their levels of expenditure, or their retention or abandonment of academic selection—without taking account of the kinds of social background from which their pupils are predominantly drawn. Earlier we described the relatively high levels of spending by the four Tyneside LEAs. They also 'score' relatively highly on the 'index of special needs' used by the government to calculate Rate Support Grant, an index which takes account of the proportion of children with parents in semi-skilled and unskilled employment. Given all that is known about the close association between examination achievements and the socio-economic status of pupils, it is clearly unfair to expect better results of high spending LEAs if their level of spending is a consequence of relatively high levels of social disadvantage.

Straight comparisons of examinations results between schools or LEAs with very different intakes cannot therefore be treated as a fair test based on 'hard facts'. But how to make 'due allowance' for the social characteristics of an intake is a complex matter on which much more work needs to be done. Doing so by treating the proportion of manual workers' children as a proxy measure for social class, which is a common method, is inadequate because it ignores the social diversity of cities. A high proportion of 'working-class' families in some areas may be accompanied by a high proportion of the kinds of professional/managerial families with which 'academic success' at 16+ and 18+ is strongly associated. For example, one analysis of statistics for all English LEAs showed a very high correlation (of 0.84) between the proportion of school leavers with five or more 'good' 0-level passes (that is, grades A-C or CSE Grade 1) and the proportion of children from professional/managerial homes (Gray *et al.*, 1984). In addition we have already commented on the rather small 'middle-class stratum' in parts of Tyneside, and also on the 'creaming' effects of independent schools which largely recruit from that stratum.

This long preamble is necessary if Table 4.3 is to be interpreted with a proper sense of caution.

TABLE 4.3. PUPILS' EXAMINATION PASSES: TYNESIDE, NORTHERN REGION AND ENGLAND, 1982–5.

Local Education Authority	% leaving with no graded results	% leaving with 1 to 4 'good grades' at 16+	% leaving with 5 or more 'good grades' at 16+	% leaving with 1 or more 'A' levels
Gateshead	15.8	26.1	19.9	11.1
Newcastle	12.1	26.8	18.9	13.0
North Tyneside	8.7	26.9	24.0	14.2
South Tyneside	8.6	29.3	19.7	10.3
Northern Region	10.6	N/A	21.9	N/A
England	10.0	N/A	23.6	N/A

Source : DES Statistics of Education, 1985.

It was on the basis of figures like those in Table 4.3, and of their comparison with national averages, that the four Tyneside LEAs have been identified as 'under-achieving' and that Newcastle especially has been criticised as failing its abler pupils. There are, of course, general objections to relying too heavily on examination results as performance indicators; many of the objectives contained in the curriculum policy statements referred to earlier cannot be measured in this way, nor are they necessarily achieved through the formal academic work of the schools. It nevertheless has to be recognised that at a time of rising youth unemployment and also of growing pressure on local authorities to give 'value for money', such comparisons will certainly be made. It is important that they be made fairly. Thus, ignoring any information *except* pupils' results in public examinations at 16+ produces a 'league table' of English LEAs in which nine of the top ten are in socially favoured areas of southern England. But combining examination performance with information on social disadvantages and data on the proportion of parents in professional/managerial occupations, takes North Tyneside into the 'top ten'; while in the most recent and complex calculation of results in relation to those predicted from data on the social composition of all 96 English LEAs, Newcastle appeared in the 'top ten', while both North and South Tyneside were in the top third of the national table (Jesson and Gray, 1986).

Destinations of School Leavers

Even sixty years ago, Mess was drawing attention to the 'harrowing basis of prosperity' in Tyneside as traditional industries declined without being replaced. During the Depression, Tyneside was one of the worst-hit areas of the country, with particularly high rates of unemployment in places like Jarrow and Gateshead. That relative disadvantage is no less apparent in the 1980s; as is noted in chapter 3, the official unemployment figures in 1988 are around 50% above the national average. It is the deterioration in employment prospects over the last twenty years which is especially disturbing. As engineering and other manufacturing industries have continued to decline, so the proportion of school leavers entering industry has fallen rapidly. In Gateshead, for example, it fell from 47% to 16% between 1966 and 1986. An apparently compensating rise from 38% to 58% in the proportions entering clerical, sales, distribution and catering jobs is misleading without reference to the sharp drop in the *total* number of job vacancies available. In 1966, almost all 18-year-olds were in employment; in 1986, that figure was already down to 60%, and was still falling.

If unemployment is now the most important problem facing Tyneside then it is especially acute for those aged 16–25. During a period when national unemployment figures have risen to over three million (and to substantially more by some calculations), with particularly high rates in Tyneside and other 'old' industrial conurbations, it is the young who have been especially vulnerable. Contrary to the views of some commentators, it is not because they are more often lacking in 'employable' skills than were their predecessors, but because employers with many fewer jobs to offer are likely to favour older, 'steadier' recruits unless subsidised from public funds to do otherwise. Among the 400,000 unemployed school-leavers in England in 1983, (a figure which has to be compared with the 4,000 ten years earlier), were large numbers who would have been considered eminently employable even a few years before. It trivialises their problems to argue otherwise. But the startling pace at which their job prospects have declined is more vividly illustrated on a smaller scale. In 1977, 8 out of 255 pupils leaving a Jarrow comprehensive school at sixteen failed to find employment; of the 168 leaving in 1982, 134 failed to do so. It is the MSC's Youth Training Scheme which has effectively replaced the job market for 16-plus school leavers. Over the five years 1981–86, the proportion of Newcastle school leavers registered as unemployed fell from 42% to 29% while the proportions involved in Youth Training rose from 34% to 43%. During that period, the city's Careers Service placed 1,947 young people in jobs and 17,811 on government schemes. In South Tyneside, 49% of pupils completing their period of compulsory schooling in the summer of 1986 went on YTS, compared with only 10% entering employment directly (and 28% staying on in school or college).

Chapter 3 indicates the present scale of MSC training programmes on Tyneside, in the context of what has become the largest national youth training scheme in any non-communist country (Roberts, 1984). As is noted in that chapter, the MSC is now one of Tyneside's largest 'employers', spending over £50 million a year on Youth Training Schemes and the Community Programme for some 19,000 people. Criticisms of the quality of training offered in many placements have abounded, especially those provided by small employers most tempted to use trainees as substitute (or at least heavily subsidised) labour. Particular comparisons are made with the kinds of apprenticeship training which were still widely available in Tyneside in the 1960s and which produced genuinely 'skilled' workers. A counter-argument is that apprenticeships were not only unnecessarily long, but were also inefficiently focused on traditional skills in declining industries and heavily biassed against girls; YTS is very wide-ranging in its occupational scope and at least officially committed to equal opportunities.

However, the main criterion of success for the trainees themselves is whether their scheme leads directly into employment. Nationally, that success rate has been between 60% and 70%, but there is now extensive evidence that the rate is falling, that it is significantly lower in some parts

of the country (including Tyneside), and that it is significantly higher for
trainees who were relatively well-qualified educationally before they began
training. If training does *not* lead to employment for a large minority of
trainees, then it is merely shifting the age of officially-recognised
unemployment upwards. The age group beyond YTS, the 18-25 year olds,
experiences very high levels of unemployment in Tyneside: 23.1% were
unemployed at January 1988, while the rate for young men was even
higher, at 28.0%.

It might be expected that these facts, which are well understood among
potential victims, would enhance the value of educational qualifications as
a defence against unemployment and so increase rates of staying on in
full-time education. Improving your 'market value' as an employee in this
way might seem a particularly obvious tactic when opportunities in service
sector employment, including public services, are declining much more
slowly, when 'white-collar' unemployment is still relatively uncommon,
and when employers may be even more tempted in a 'buyers' market' to
use educational qualifications as a preliminary sieve when dealing with
large numbers of applicants. In fact, staying on rates have either remained
fairly static or varied erratically from year to year in all the Tyneside
LEAs, and they have remained lower than in most parts of the country.
There may well be a time-lag in the region as old attitudes unfavourable to
prolonged schooling are only gradually replaced in response to changing
economic circumstances. But it can also be argued that the characteristics
of vocational relevance claimed by YTS, and increasingly by new courses
in both the schools and further education, are not immediately persuasive
when unemployment remains such a formidable risk. It may also be
necessary to consider closely how far the strong sense of regional identity
traditionally associated with Tyneside focuses the attention of a high
proportion of young people on the *local* job market, rather than considering
the relevance of qualifications to prospects in a wider, national context
(Coffield *et al.*, 1986).

Education for a New Economy or for Unemployment?

Looking to the future, two contrasting scenarios can be drawn. In the
first, Tyneside manages to establish a technologically-based economy,
perhaps with the emergence of high value-added manufacturing activities
or through the export of sophisticated services to other parts of the UK
and overseas. In the second, the economy stagnates through failure to
adapt to changing circumstances and government refusal to intervene;
unemployment continues to grow, particularly among the unskilled and
under-qualified; those with marketable skills migrate; and reliance on
welfare becomes a predominant mode of existence. In practice, neither

extreme is likely. The chances of Tyneside being transformed in the foreseeable future into a fast-growth economy, either through its own effort or by some combination of public and private investment, are poor. Conversely, provided the UK economy sustains reasonable growth, some benefits, if not a fair share, should accrue to Tyneside, as disposable incomes rise. A steady drift of talent to more prosperous regions seems inevitable, but the problem of youth unemployment will reduce because there will be one-third fewer sixteen-year-olds entering the labour market. A core of unemployed lacking the expertise and skills needed for permanent employment may well be a feature of Tyneside for years ahead, but alongside this would be the growth of new jobs in the service sector and skill shortages in certain areas. Geographically, some districts and estates will continue to decline, but close to neighbourhoods with relative prosperity.

It would be easiest to plan educational provision for either of the extreme scenarios. For the former, education programmes would try to satisfy emergent technological requirements, while if under-employment were to dominate, children ought to be offered education that would prepare them for a life of non-work on the assumption that cultural ties to the region would inhibit migration. In fact, the school curriculum must reflect the requirements of children who represent the extremes. Pupils leaving a Tyneside comprehensive school will include potential graduates in electrical engineering and business studies alongside youngsters going on YTS or the dole who will rarely find regular work. From about the age of thirteen, the two groups will have been offered different curricula. Examples of special programmes like the LAPP, designed particularly for the latter group, have already been described. These two groups, though, still represent the extremes. Between are the majority of children, each with unique but largely indeterminate needs. The great challenge to the school is to try to satisfy these needs in the context of an adult life stretching many years ahead. Even with a more modest time-scale, teachers have no way of predicting the requirements of work or the possible life-style of their pupils in precise terms. It is this which makes the needs so indeterminate.

One solution to the problem is to concentrate on short-term objectives—hence the current thrust towards vocationalism in secondary schools. The labour market is tight, therefore children should be better prepared for work. Nearly twenty years ago there was evidence (Schools Council Enquiry, 1968), given little attention at the time, that teachers were much less concerned about preparing children for work than either parents or pupils. Undoubtedly, these concerns of parents have increased recently, particularly in an area like Tyneside. It would benefit no-one, however, if schools felt driven by a coalition of parents, government and employers to over-react. It is one thing to assist children to prepare for adult life—the dominant element of which is the capacity for self-support through work. That ought to be the business of schools. But it is highly inappropriate for them to train for the specific requirements of particular jobs. Such a strategy may result in a short-term reduction in youth unemployment, although in Tyneside this is doubtful, but it overlooks both the needs of the individual and the rapid changes likely to occur in the job market.

Children leaving Tyneside secondary schools must have the capacity to learn the sorts of skills which will be usable in a range of job situations. There can be no certainty about specific job circumstances ten or twenty years ahead. New materials, innovative processes, different machines, alternative kinds of services, will all be developed. Self-employment may become an even more important aspect of the job scene. While we do not know precisely which skills and knowledge will be most appropriate we are certain that individuals who prove self-reliant and possess sufficient confidence will be best suited to this environment. Therefore, the most significant contribution that schools and further education colleges can make in this context is the provision of a broad, general education up to the age of sixteen and beyond. Such an education, if good, does not ignore the workplace. It would include work experience, consideration of the importance of wealth creation, discussion of the role of management and trade unions, and some study of the skills, attitudes and behaviour demanded of workers in highly competitive world markets. In relation to work this general education has three aims. First, to provide pupils with a base of knowledge and skills which will assist their future development; second, to give the confidence and assurance needed to organise this personal development; and third, to raise awareness levels so that individuals are well-placed to respond, adapt and to some extent shape changing job circumstances.

Often it is difficult for schools in Tyneside to take a broad view of vocationalism. Jobs for school-leavers have become extremely scarce; central government and local authorities have decided they must act. Many of the resultant actions are more tactical than strategic. Therefore anything that schools try to do, and even more so specific programmes such as YTS, are too easily viewed by pupils and parents as immediate responses or short-term palliatives, rather than a planned initiative to deal with long-term training and education needs. In many parts of Tyneside a young person is under immense pressure to find any job, whatever it lacks in long-term prospects and further training opportunities. High levels of unemployment even during times of comparative prosperity, and the predominance of jobs which have little satisfaction and few opportunities for advancement, have served to guarantee that such pressures will be transmitted from one generation to the next. In these circumstances the problem for the school is to make the curriculum meaningful to the pupils according to *their* perceptions of what they want from school. A broad, general education, no matter how well designed, will fail the recipient if they do not appreciate its significance. Meeting this criterion makes formidable demands upon schools. By far the single greatest contribution of the new curricular initiatives, such as TVEI and LAPP, has been to promote new styles of teaching and learning. This seems the most promising way ahead. If successful pupils stand a chance of becoming more involved in their own education the habit may persist into their adult lives.

Conclusion

In every way the education of the young people of Tyneside is very different from that described by Mess sixty years ago. Many of the worst problems he outlined, like crowded schools and non-qualified teachers, have been overcome. There now exist support services and other activities to assist education which were never even discussed in the 1920s; and opportunities in further and higher education are much greater. In many schools, though, evidence of considerable pupil deprivation continues, and over the last ten years especially, problems associated with youth unemployment have had a substantial effect, particularly on secondary schools and further education.

Mostly the issues that confront education in Tyneside are those that affect urban areas in the UK. Often the solution of the four Tyneside LEAs since their establishment in 1974 has been to spend above the national average on education. However, evidence about the success of this 'high spending' is far from clear, although some achievements, particularly those associated with pupil examination results, have been notable. Whether the Tyneside LEAs are being successful overall, in terms of achieving value for money, is far too complex a question to attempt to answer here. What is clear, though, is the sustained pressure on them since the mid-1970s to restrict educational spending and the likelihood that this pressure will continue, and perhaps grow. Financial retrenchment at a time of falling rolls will lead to some difficult decisions about school closures and reorganisations, and priorities as between buildings, teaching materials and the employment of staff.

One peculiarity of the Tyneside LEAs is their continuity of political control[3]. Since the reorganisation of 1974 all have had a substantial Labour majority. There are advantages in such continuity, particularly when difficult decisions must be made, as short-term electoral popularity may be less important to councillors. There is also the danger of complacency, and a shortage of new ideas from politicians. There is no consensus of opinion as to whether political stability attracts or repels particular types of senior professional staff, who have to work most closely with elected members. An outcome of continuing Labour control has been a heightened antipathy towards central government since 1979. All authorities, whatever their political complexion, have felt steadily more deprived of freedom as expenditure controls have tightened, but as a group the Tyneside LEAs feel particularly aggrieved. They question government claims about support for education being at historically high levels, particularly if factors such as inflation, shortage of books and equipment, and the deterioration of buildings are considered (Crispen and Marslen-Wilson, 1987). Their view of extra educational spending as one means to compensate for pupil deprivation, particularly in some localities, seems to be in jeopardy. Although some additional monies are available from the government and the European Community, targeted on areas like Tyneside, it is insufficient to launch major initiatives in (say) community education, which many Councils would find attractive.

The sixtieth anniversary of the publication of Mess's book sees a major Education Act whose effects may well be as sustained as those of the 1944 Education Act. Among the main items, government will impose a national curriculum. The Tyneside LEAs will have to ensure its organisation in all their schools. The relationship between LEA and school is likely to change decisively as the monitoring function of the LEA grows. In primary schools the curriculum will probably not be very different to that offered at the present time, with emphasis on Maths, Language and Environmental Studies. In secondary schools the process of squeezing out minority subjects (such as Music, Art, a Second Foreign Language), already started by financial retrenchment and falling rolls, will continue, with pupils up to the age of 16 having to spend between 30% and 40% of their time on English, Maths and Science and a further 50% to 60% on other foundation subjects such as Technology, a Modern Foreign Language, History/ Geography. Undoubtedly the staffing of this curriculum will cause substantial problems for the four Tyneside LEAs.

As part of the curriculum all LEAs will have to arrange for the testing of pupils against attainment at the ages of 7, 11 and 14 in English, Maths and Science. There is a high probability that statistical tables will be constructed and published, comparing the performances of such schools using raw test scores. Yet, as discussed earlier, there are major problems with interpreting raw scores, not least through the influences of the children's socio-economic backgrounds. The overall scores of a school may not reflect its achievement, especially if it has a large proportion of its children from working-class backgrounds, a particular feature in Tyneside. Yet the government intends that one outcome from publishing results will be more likelihood of parents choosing one school rather than another. There will also be an increase in the choices available to them through a system of open enrolment. 'Popular' schools will be able to expand to take as many children as buildings permit.

On the financial side, all secondary schools and primary schools with more than 200 pupils will have substantial freedom in deciding how to spend their budgets. The LEA will need to publish how much money it is giving to each school (and the formula for funding). Simultaneously, the direct involvement of the LEA in school governing bodies will diminish, with more parental, community, teacher and business involvement. More significantly, schools will be able to opt out of LEA control, and receive grant direct from central government, if a majority of parents choose this arrangement. It is likely that such a drastic step will have little impact in Tyneside, but possibly a number of schools, through their governors, will threaten to 'opt-out' to achieve their way in the new school-LEA relationship. In further education also, college governing bodies will be much freer of LEA controls in curricular, budgetary and organisational terms. Indeed, the Polytechnic will move outside the LEA completely as it attains corporate status. In total these developments seem certain to dominate the evolution of education in Tyneside for the first part, at least, of the *next* sixty years.

NOTES

1. For example, during 1984–85, Newcastle spent nearly £40 per secondary pupil on the Careers Service, and Gateshead over £30, while the average figure for all LEAs was nearer £20 per pupil. Net spending per child on meals and milk in Newcastle was just under £100, and in North Tyneside over £70, compared with mean expenditure for all LEAs of less than £60.
2. *Report of the Consultative Committee of the Board of Education on the Education of the Adolescent* (1926) and *Report of the Consultative Committee of the Board of Education on the Primary Schools* (1931).
3. However, following a dispute in the local Labour Party, North Tyneside was controlled by a coalition of Labour and non-Labour councillors for a short period in the mid-1980s.

REFERENCES

Batley, R., O'Brien, O. and Parris, H. (1970) *Going Comprehensive: Educational Policy-making in Two County Boroughs*. London: Routledge & Kegan Paul.

Benn, C., and Simon, B. (1970) *Half Way There: Report on the British Comprehensive School Reform*. McGraw-Hill.

Chartered Institute of Public Finance and Accountancy (CIPFA) (1987) *Education Statistics Actuals, 1984–5*. London: CIPFA.

Coffield, F., Borrill, C. and Marshall, S. (1986) *Growing up at the Margins: Young Adults in the North East*. Open University Press.

Crispen, A. and Marslen-Wilson, F. (1987) *Local Education Authority Expenditure Variations: Trends, Causes and Implications*. Research Report for ESRC.

Department of Education and Science (DES) (1981) *Education for 16–19 Year Olds: A Review undertaken for the Government and the Local Authority Association*. London: HMSO.

Department of Education and Science (DES) (1986) *Report by Her Majesty's Inspectors on the Effects of Local Authority Expenditure on the Education Service in England 1985*. London: HMSO.

Gray, K., Jesson, D. and Jones, B. (1984) Predicting Differences in Examination Results between Local Education Authorities. *Oxford Review of Education*, 10 (1), 45–68.

Jesson, D. and Gray, J. (1986) Examination Results and Local Authority League Tables *in* J. Gretton and A. Harrison (eds.), *Education Audit 1986*. London: Public Money.

Jesson, D. Gray, J., Ranson, S. and Jones, B. (1986) Some Determinants of Variations in Expenditure on Secondary Education, *Policy and Politics*, 13 (4), 359–391.

Parkinson, M. (1970) *The Labour Party and the Organisation of Secondary Education, 1918–65*. London: Routledge & Kegan Paul.

Roberts, K. (1984) *School leavers and their Prospects*. Open University Press.

Royal Institute of Public Administration Operational Research Unit (RIPA) (1968) *Performance and Size of Local Education Authorities*. Research Studies, 4, of the Royal Commission on Local Government in England. London: HMSO.

Schools Council Enquiry 1 (1968) *Young School Leavers*. London: HMSO.

5

HOUSING

Stuart Cameron and Paul Crompton

In the 1920s housing conditions in Tyneside were, in some respects, the worst in England and Wales. Looking at the effects on housing in Tyneside of 'the great expansion of industry and population in the last century', Mess considered the character of the existing towns and of the new industrial communities: 'In the former case the oldest streets have often become narrow and congested slums, and constitute a serious and intractable problem; but these towns have some compensation in the dignity and picturesqueness which come from a long history. The newer industrial towns have nothing so bad, but they have nothing so good, and they are often distressingly featureless'. (Mess, 1928, p.75).

The housing problems of the 1920s identified by Mess were seen mainly as problems of overcrowding. Mess applied 'three simple tests' to judge the standard of housing in Tyneside: the ratio of dwellings to families; the number of persons per room; and the density of persons per acre. On the first test, the extent to which families shared dwellings, Tyneside compared favourably with the national picture. There was a shortage of dwellings, with more families than separate dwellings available, but the ratio of families to occupied dwellings of 1.075 was better than the national average of 1.13, and can be compared with a London average of 1.60.

It was the second test which revealed what was for Mess the root of the problem in Tyneside: the very small size of dwellings, particularly the large number of dwellings with only one or two rooms. This was the case throughout Tyneside. For example, in Newcastle 36.8% of homes had only one or two rooms, in Gateshead it was 38.9%, compared to only 14.1% for England and Wales. The result of families living in this accommodation was severe overcrowding, with 34.9% of Tyneside families living at a density of more than two persons per room.

This exceptionally high degree of overcrowding was found not only in Tyneside but throughout Northumberland and Durham, and was virtually unparalleled anywhere in England and Wales. Mess speculated on the reasons for this. One aspect was the dominant local industries. The free colliery housing provided by the mine-owners had established a standard of very small and poor quality houses. The housing built rapidly and at high density around the shipyards, where incomes were highly uncertain, had reinforced this standard; this latter was built largely in the form of

Slum housing – Pipewellgate, on the banks of the Tyne in Gateshead, c.1930. (*Newcastle City Libraries*).

Slum housing at Catherine Street, South Shields in 1937; subsequently demolished. (*South Tyneside Libraries*).

Tyneside flats[1], 'a form of housing not allowing much variety and setting a somewhat low standard of house-room' (Mess, 1928, p.83). Mess suggested, though, that an additional factor was local custom and tradition—it reflected the long history of backwardness and poverty of the Border counties, and also the influence of Scotland where housing standards were, and remained, lower than in England and Wales.

On the third 'test', the density of houses per acre, Mess also found the residential areas of Tyneside inadequate; there were rows of Tyneside flats packed together with tiny yards and back lanes, and with even the areas of middle-class housing lacking gardens. He noted the paradox of houses crowded together, yet surrounded by large areas of underused open land, which was characteristic of industrial Tyneside.

In comparison with the problem of overcrowding, Mess saw the problems associated with the standards of building and amenities as less serious. The worst conditions were in the ancient slum houses on the steep river banks of the old towns in Newcastle, Gateshead and the Shields, the 'picturesque' but ruinous areas which were mostly to be swept away in the early slum clearance schemes of the 1930s. For the rest, the rows of Tyneside flats, although small, cramped and monotonous, were by the standards of the time 'moderately well built' and 'fairly convenient'.

National housing policies in the inter-war years can be divided roughly into two phases. In the 1920s the major concern nationwide was to increase the housing stock to overcome the shortage of housing experienced after the First World War. In the 1930s, attention increasingly turned to slum clearance and the replacement of the worst housing in the existing housing stock. When Mess was writing little had, as yet, been done to remedy the existing housing problems of Tyneside. At that time, housing policies were still mostly concerned with the 'post-war housing shortage'. Mess noted that, overall, Tyneside was lagging behind in achieving the targets set nationally for the construction of working-class housing, with the one exception of the City of Newcastle.

In this housing drive a crucial difference, which set the pattern for much of the recent past, was that on Tyneside the contribution of the local authorities was much greater, and of the private sector much smaller, than in the rest of England and Wales. The private sector, by way of subsidised and unsubsidised house-building, had contributed 62% of all new housing in England and Wales in the years between 1919 and 1927, but in Tyneside only 40%. Government subsidy had also done more in Tyneside than elsewhere to create a new and higher standard of housing, and Mess suggested that 'municipal effort' was not a temporary expedient to tackle a post-war housing shortage, but would be needed for a considerable time for the 'colossal task' of remedying the existing deficiencies in housing standards.

Applying Mess's 'three simple tests' to a comparison of the housing situation of Tyneside in the 1920s with the position today indicates the extent of the transformation of housing standards and the degree to which the 'colossal task' has been completed.

By 1971 (comparable figures are not given in the 1981 Census), there was a crude, though small, surplus of housing, with a ratio of households to occupied dwellings of 0.99 compared to 1.075 in 1921.

A direct comparison of overcrowding in terms of persons per room is difficult because of changes in standards. For Mess, overcrowding was living at more than two persons per room. Present standards regard a density of occupation of more than 1 person per room as overcrowding, and more than 1.5 persons per room as severe overcrowding. Even on these revised standards, the incidence of overcrowding has fallen dramatically. By 1981, the proportion of Tyneside households living at more than 1 person per room was 4.4%, and at more than 1.5 persons per room was only 0.6%, compared with the situation in 1921 quoted above where 34.9% of Tyneside households lived at a density of more than *two* persons per room.

In discussing the dense layout of housing areas and the density of population per acre which resulted, Mess did not provide comprehensive data for Tyneside since 'statements as to density of population per acre are likely to be misleading, because there are few acres which are entirely devoted to residential purposes' (Mess, 1928, p.91). He did, however, provide examples of particularly densely-packed wards. In Newcastle, Westgate ward had a density of 172.1 persons per acre and Byker 126.0; in Gateshead, East Central had 152.6 persons per acre; and in South Shields, Rekendyke had 184.7 and Laygate no less than 206.8 persons per acre. By comparison, the most densely populated Tyneside ward in 1981, at Bensham in Gateshead, had a density of just 49 persons per acre.

These comparisons, and particularly the figures on persons per room, show the enormous improvement in housing conditions which has been achieved since the 1920s. Moreover, the task of remedying the problems of the older housing stock since that time has included the virtual elimination of other deficiencies, such as dwellings lacking baths and hot water systems, which had scarcely even been recognised as problems in the 1920s. We now look at how this improvement was undertaken and show how much has been achieved in Tyneside.

Changes in Housing Conditions in Tyneside to 1981

Looked at in the national context, the progress in removing the housing problems inherited from the 19th century has been particularly impressive in Tyneside. By 1981, the position with regard to the problems of overcrowding and lack of amenities was as good, if not better, than in England and Wales as a whole.

TABLE 5.1. HOUSING CONDITIONS, TYNESIDE AND ENGLAND & WALES, 1951–1981

Overcrowding: proportion of households with more than 1 or 1.5 persons per room.

	Tyneside		England & Wales	
	1 to 1.5 per room % of households	More than 1.5 per room % of households	1 to 1.5 per room % of households	More than 1.5 per room % of households
1951	16.2	11.7	10.9	5.1
1961	12.7	6.1	7.5	2.8
1971	7.1	2.1	4.5	4.5
1981	3.8	0.6	3.9	3.9

Amenities: Proportion of households with/without basic amenities.

	Tyneside			England & Wales		
	share bath %	lack bath %	have all amenities[1] %	share bath %	lack bath %	have all amenities[1] %
1951	4.0	38.0	56.0	8.0	37.0	52.0
1961	1.7	24.9	71.7	4.6	22.0	69.3
1971	1.2	12.2	81.1	3.4	5.8	82.1
1981	0.4	1.1	97.6	1.3	1.9	95.4

Source : Census of Population, 1951, 1961, 1971, 1981.

Note: 1. In 1981 'all amenities' referred to bath/shower and inside WC. In 1951 it included piped water, a cooking stove, a kitchen sink, a WC and a fixed bath. Definitions have changed with improvements in housing standards.

As can be seen from Table 5.1, overcrowding, which was the characteristic Tyneside problem identified by Mess, was still substantially more prevalent in Tyneside in 1971, but by 1981 was just below the national average. The number of dwellings lacking amenities such as a bath was, by 1981, substantially below the national average, and, overall, a higher proportion of Tyneside dwellings had all modern amenities.

In fact, Tyneside shares this relative improvement with regard to the 'traditional' measures of poor housing conditions[2] with other English conurbations outside of London. Problems of this kind are no longer concentrated in the great Northern industrial cities; progress in these cities has been such that there are, for example, now many areas of the outer South East with a greater proportion of households lacking amenities than in Newcastle or Manchester. Even in comparison with other conurbations, though, the progress in Tyneside has been particularly marked.

Two processes have produced this transformation in housing conditions. The first process is the building of new housing to broadly modern standards. Since the First World War, and especially since the Second World War, almost all of this new house building has been done either by the private sector for owner-occupation, or by the public sector for local authority renting, with almost no building for private renting. Compared to the rest of England, in Tyneside the public sector has played a much greater role and the private sector a much smaller role in the production of housing. As a result, the tenure structure is different, and the high level of local authority housing makes the tenure pattern of Tyneside more similar to that of Scotland (Table 5.2).

TABLE 5.2. HOUSING TENURE, TYNESIDE, ENGLAND & WALES, AND SCOTLAND, 1981.

Tenure	Tyneside	England & Wales	Scotland
Owner-occupied %	38.9	58.0	35.0
Council rented %	47.2	28.9	54.6
Housing Association %	3.2	2.0	1.6
Private rented %	10.7	11.1	8.8

Source : Census of Population, 1981.

The second process has been the renewal of older housing areas, either through slum clearance or though grant-aided improvement of older housing. Like the other major conurbations, Tyneside has experienced large-scale slum clearance programmes; but, in addition, especially in the 1970s, an unusually successful housing improvement programme seems also to have made a particular contribution to the great amelioration of housing conditions.

These two processes will now be examined in turn, and the respective roles of the public and private sectors considered.

Housing construction

Data on housing construction in Tyneside reinforces the picture of the dominant role of the public sector in Tyneside's housing. In the mid-1950s, when the national post-war boom in private housebuilding for owner-occupation began, Tyneside shared in it to some extent, and building for owner-occupation played a substantial part in the provision of modern housing. Even so, until the 1980s the public sector remained dominant.

TABLE 5.3. AVERAGE ANNUAL HOUSING COMPLETIONS IN TYNESIDE BY SECTOR, 1945–86.

	Public Sector		Private Sector	Total	% Public Sector
	Council	Housing Association			
1945–55		3360	539	3899	86.2
1956–60		3376	1710	5086	66.4
1961–65		2684	1480	4241	63.4
1966–70		3989	1345	5334	74.8
1971–75	2414	142	1573	4129	61.9
1976–80	2472	530	1072	4074	73.7
1981–86	484	357	1442	2283	36.8

Sources: 1945–55 Housing Returns for England and Wales.
1956–66 Ministry of Housing and Local Government, Housing Statistics.
1967–86 DoE Local Housing Statistics

Note: Tyneside figures prior to 1974 are aggregated from those local authority districts which were wholly included in the four new Metropolitan Districts created in 1974.

In the 1980s the previously established pattern of housebuilding changed dramatically (Table 5.3). This was a result of the enormous fall in the levels of local authority housebuilding which resulted from spending constraints placed on local authorities by the Conservative government (TUSIU, 1987). The ratio of public to private sector building has been more or less reversed. Within the public sector there has been a further change with the growing significance of building by housing associations[3]. Before the 1970s, building by housing associations was quite insignificant and housebuilding for rent was dominated by the local authorities. Housing association construction did increase in the 1970s, but remained subsidiary to the building of council houses. In the 1980s, housing associations have become as important as local authorities in house building. It should be noted, though, that this is a relative growth in importance since the actual numbers of houses built by housing associations has declined since the latter half of the 1970s—but this decline has been much less severe than the massive reduction in council building. The level of housebuilding in the private sector has increased in the 1980s, but only to return to the levels of the 1960s and early 1970s, and not enough to offset the decline in the public sector. As a result, the overall production of housing has fallen substantially, and is now less than half that of the late 1960s.

There is some variation between the Tyneside Districts in the relative importance of the public and private sectors. Newcastle and Gateshead are close to the Tyneside average. South Tyneside has a rather higher proportion of local authority housing (56.3% in 1981), and a correspondingly lower level of owner-occupation. In contrast, North Tyneside has more owner-occupation, with 44.9% of housing owner-occupied in 1981. This is because North Tyneside includes what is effectively a part of the commuter belt of Newcastle in the seaside areas of Whitley Bay, Tynemouth and Monkseaton—areas with relatively high levels of owner-occupation. In contrast, North Tyneside's riverside areas between North Shields and Wallsend follow the more usual Tyneside pattern with large amounts of council housing.

In the following two sections the characteristics of housing which has been built in the public and private sectors are considered in more detail.

The Public Sector. Local authority housebuilding on Tyneside began in Newcastle in 1904, and the local authority sector now displays an enormous variety of types of housing, reflecting changing priorities and fashions both at national and local levels.

One feature of local authority housebuilding in Tyneside is that much of it has been linked to slum clearance, providing new housing for people from slum clearance areas. Nationally, central government housing policy has fluctuated in the prominence it has given to slum clearance. After the First World War there was a period of building council housing to add to the stock of housing to meet 'general needs', followed by a period when council housing was built mainly to rehouse people from slum clearance areas. A similar sequence can be seen in the first 20 years after the Second World War. In both periods, there was a tendency for the switch to housing for slum clearance purposes to be accompanied by a reduction in levels of subsidy, and consequently a reduction in standards of space and housing quality.

This pattern can be seen reflected in the council housing stock of Tyneside. Some of the most attractive council housing is in the cottage estates built in the 1920s, such as at Pendower in Newcastle and Balkwell in North Tyneside. In contrast, one of the most notoriously problematic Tyneside council estates is the South Meadowell in North Tyneside, an estate of mostly flats, built to reduced standards in the 1930s to rehouse the population of the riverside slums of North Shields (North Tyneside CDP, 1976).

In the 1950s, too, the switch of housing policy to slum clearance brought both reductions in housing quality in the public sector, and also an emphasis on building at higher densities to conserve the national stock of agricultural land. Newcastle provides two classic examples, Noble Street and North Kenton. In the inner city, the five-storey 'walk-up' flats built in 1958 in the Noble Street area of Benwell to replace cleared 19th century housing were of such poor quality that by 1977 these 'slums on the drawing board' (Benwell CDP, 1978) had themselves been demolished. At

High Heaton estate – a 'cottage estate' built by Newcastle Corporation in the mid-1920s. (*Newcastle upon Tyne City Libraries and Arts*).

North Kenton, a 1950s' suburban council housing development, the local authority was obliged by central government to increase the density of development by incorporating, into what was intended as an estate of conventional houses with gardens, numbers of poor-quality 3- and 5-storey flats and maisonettes, which have again become a serious problem in recent years.

In fact, although it is the 'utopian' Modernist architecture of the 1960s which is most often associated with current problems in local authority housing (Coleman, 1985), in Tyneside the cheap slum clearance housing of the 1950s, particularly the very common blocks of maisonettes[4] of up to five storeys, pose a more extensive problem.

Tyneside does, of course, have its monuments to the large-scale 'utopian' local authority architecture of the 1960s and early 1970s. Indeed, nowhere was the rhetoric of the need for large-scale, futuristic transformation of the urban environment stronger than in the Newcastle of the early 1960s, when T. Dan Smith was the leader of the Council and Wilf Burns the City Planning Officer. In that era, the objectives of clearance and redevelopment went beyond a concern with poor physical housing conditions. It involved a rejection of the whole environment of the rows of Tyneside flats inherited from the 19th century, and the desire to create a housing environment that was a visual symbol of modernity.

'Tyneside flats' at Noble Street in Newcastle's west end, 1955, shortly before demolition. (*TUSIU*).

Noble Street was redeveloped with poor quality 'walk up' council flats. This photograph, taken in 1978, shows these 'slums on the drawing board' just before they, in turn, were demolished. (*Newcastle City Engineer's Department*).

As in other conurbations there are high-rise point blocks, particularly in Newcastle which has over 4,000 dwellings in high flats. In fact, many of the point blocks are reasonably popular; more problematic has been a number of large-scale developments of slab blocks with deck or corridor access such as at Church Walk, Walker; Killingworth Towers in North Tyneside and St Cuthbert's Village, Gateshead.

The 'Byker Wall' – an innovative linear block of council flats built in the 1970s and Tyneside's best-known contribution to new housing architecture. The 'Wall' serves to enclose an area of attractive and well-landscaped low-rise housing. (*Newcastle upon Tyne City Libraries and Arts*).

In the 1970s, council house building in Tyneside followed the national trend of a return to low-rise and more traditional building, for the most part in inner city redevelopment areas, and usually on fairly small sites. One remarkable exception to this is the redevelopment between 1970 and 1982 of the Byker area of Newcastle, which produced a quite unique housing area (Futagawa, 1980). Designed by the Swedish-based architect Ralph Erskine, with 2,000 dwellings combining tight-knit low-rise housing with the linear high-rise 'Byker Wall', it attempted a humane approach to large-scale redevelopment, both in the colourful architecture and landscaping, and in the development process which rehoused the local community in its old area and involved them in the design process.

The Private Sector. In contrast to the great variety of types of housing produced at different periods by the public sector, the production of housing in the private sector for owner-occupation in Tyneside has been much more uniform. In the 1930s, and again after 1955, it has consisted almost entirely of conventional low-rise housing in suburban locations. Only in the 1980s has this begun to change, as will be discussed below. At the same time, there has been a second process of growth in owner-occupation arising from the transfer from private landlords to owner-occupation of older housing.

Data from building society records (Nationwide Building Society, 1987) provides a useful comparison of owner-occupied housing in Tyne and Wear[5] and nationally. The age profile of the housing stock is almost identical to that of the UK with, for example, the same proportion (26%) of pre-1919 houses. Owner-occupied dwellings in Tyne and Wear are, however, both larger (averaging 964 sq.ft. compared to 932 sq.ft. for the UK) and better equipped—for example, 81% of the area's private sector dwellings have central heating compared with 75% nationally, and 68% have car parking facilities compared with a national figure of 59%. This again reinforces the picture of the enormous progress in the improvement of housing conditions in this area.

In comparing the type of private sector housing, one feature of Tyne and Wear is a greater proportion of semi-detached and terraced houses and fewer detached houses (11% are detached in Tyne and Wear compared with 17% for the UK). This perhaps provides some confirmation for the oft-repeated claim that there is a lack of high-quality 'executive' housing in the area which, it is also claimed, inhibits the attraction of new industry. Of course, many of those seeking executive housing will look beyond the boundaries of the Tyneside conurbation itself—and to the north and west of the conurbation in particular these needs may be met in Northumberland which has a comparatively high proportion (20%) of detached houses in its housing stock, and has many attractive rural locations favoured for such housing. There may be more of a problem to the south of the conurbation. Indeed, South Tyneside has noted (South Tyneside MBC, 1985) that the price of detached houses there is relatively high and that 'there are very few sites within the Borough's built-up area where demand for very high-priced housing can be met'.

The most notable feature of the owner-occupied sector in Tyne and Wear, however, is the very low level of house prices. The Nationwide data for the year ending March 1987 showed an average price of £27,519, only two thirds of the national average price of £41,724. Clearly the low average price reflects lower than average incomes, but it also permits people with lower incomes to enter owner-occupation. For example, the data showed an average income of first-time buyers in Tyne and Wear of £12,600, compared to a UK average of £14,436. Entry into owner-occupation in Tyne and Wear was also made easier by the fact that the average deposit required was only 52% of the national average, and the building society loan covered a higher proportion (74.9% compared to 68.5%) of the

Leafy suburbia at Jesmond Park West, adjacent to Jesmond Dene, Newcastle. (*Newcastle City Engineer's Department*).

purchase price. First-time buyers in Tyne and Wear bought houses at an average price of only £18,780 with loans which covered 91% of the purchase price.

The Nationwide sums up the situation in the North East as a whole like this:

> 'Within the North East of England there is a wide variety of property available to meet the needs of most borrower types. Large detached houses are available in all counties to meet the needs of the wealthier former owner-occupiers who can pay prices in the £45,000—£60,000 range. At the other end of the market small, often older terraced properties are available to first time buyers wishing to move into owner-occupation. These properties can frequently be obtained at prices well below £20,000'. (Nationwide Building Society, 1987).

Housing renewal

By the beginning of the 1980s, the renewal of the housing stock in Tyneside had removed much of the legacy of inadequate 19th century housing. Tyneside has seen a massive and sustained housing clearance programme, beginning in the 1930s and continuing after the Second World War from the early 1950s to the beginning of the 1980s.

TABLE 5.4. ANNUAL AVERAGE SLUM CLEARANCE AND HOUSING IMPROVEMENT IN TYNESIDE, 1967–1986

	Slum Clearance	Renovation		Improvement Grants to Private Sector
		Council	Housing Association	
1967–70	1716	1697	6	1458
1971–75[1]	2034	4817	211	4084
1976–80	1682	673	444	1618
1981–86	321	1702	609	2684

Source: DoE Local Housing Statistics.
*Note:*1. Before 1973 improvement grants given to Housing Associations on the same basis as private owners were not separately identified in Local Housing Statistics and were included in the totals for the private sector. This may apply to a small number of grants to Housing Associations in Tyneside.

Nationally, the 1970s saw a marked curtailment of slum clearance programmes, and a major shift to housing improvement as a means of overcoming the remaining problems of pre-1919 housing. In Tyneside, though, a substantial level of slum clearance and redevelopment was sustained through the 1970s. Comparing the period 1968–1971, when slum clearance was in full swing, with the period 1978–1981, the rate of slum clearance in England and Wales fell by 52% but the corresponding fall in Tyneside was only 18%. Only in the 1980s did slum clearance substantially decline, and that decline was dramatic; by 1985 slum clearance in Tyneside had virtually ceased.

Despite the importance of slum clearance, housing improvement has also made a major contribution to housing renewal in Tyneside. In Tyneside, as nationally, this has mostly taken the form of *ad hoc* grants to individual house owners. These grants peaked in the early 1970s, with no less than 8,143 private sector improvement grants in 1973. This was particularly associated with the 1971 Housing Act which provided for higher grant levels (75% of costs compared to the current standard of 50%) in the Development Areas, which included the whole of Tyneside, a provision which lasted until April 1974.

Compared to the provision of individual grants, the inclusion of older housing in housing improvement areas has been on a small scale. In fact, the provision in the 1969 Housing Act for the declaration of General Improvement Areas (GIAs) was mostly used by Tyneside local authorities during the early 1970s for the modernisation of estates of older council housing, and was an element in the very high levels of council house renovation in that period—reaching a peak of 8,045 dwellings modernised in 1972. This contrasts with the falling away of renovation of council housing in the late 1970s, down as low as 238 properties renovated in 1978.

Nevertheless, the declaration of older housing areas as GIAs was an important and successful element of housing policy in Tyneside in the early 1970s. By 1980, some 42 GIAs had been declared in the four Tyneside Districts. This was followed in the second half of the 1970s with a very successful use in Tyneside of the powers in the 1974 Housing Act to declare Housing Action Areas (HAAs), which were used along with GIAs and also non-statutory improvement area designations such as Newcastle's 'Special Improvement Areas'. By April 1980 there were 23 declared HAAs in Tyneside with about 6,300 dwellings. The largest programme was in Newcastle, with almost 3,000 dwellings in 8 HAAs and including two HAAs, at Arthurs Hill and Lower Heaton, which each had over 800 dwellings and were among the biggest in the country.

The importance of these area programmes went beyond the relatively small number of houses included in the improvement areas, in that they effectively defined the limits of the redevelopment programme. This is particularly true of the HAAs. In Newcastle, for example, the houses in almost all of the HAAs were, prior to 1975, scheduled for early clearance. They were, in effect, included in HAAs as the poorest housing for which improvement was an option. Remaining old housing of poorer quality continued to be demolished, and this process was virtually completed by the early 1980s. What was initially better housing continued to be improved in GIAs or non-statutory improvement areas.

The improvement areas in Tyneside are marked by a high rate of success in improving dwellings within the areas. This is particularly notable in the case of the HAAs, which presented the greatest challenge. HAA programmes were very much less successful in many other parts of the country but, by contrast, in Newcastle by March 1980 some 84% of dwellings in the 8 HAAs declared in 1975 had been successfully improved (Newcastle City Council, 1980) and similar rates of improvement were achieved elsewhere in Tyneside. This success seems to be attributable partly to the high level of local authority intervention in implementing the programmes, and partly to the nature of the local housing stock.

Here again, the Tyneside flat is a significant factor. Most of the HAAs, in particular, consisted of Tyneside flats. Usually a 'pair' of flats (i.e. upper and lower) are improved together. Only one roof has to be renewed, only one damp-proof course installed, and a two-storey extension in the back yard can provide a new kitchen and bathroom for each flat. Moreover, two improvement grants are available, one for each flat. Thus, compared to other housing forms, Tyneside flats can be renovated economically and within the financial ceilings of the improvement grant system.

Even so, the improvement of these areas required intensive efforts by the local authorities. One important contribution to the success of HAAs in Tyneside was the creation of special teams of local authority officers to implement the policies. South Tyneside, for example, based its improvement teams within the improvement areas (Bradley, 1980). This was backed up by a willingness to serve compulsory repair or improvement notices on landlords, and, if necessary, Councils would acquire and improve dwellings themselves. Most of the dwellings in these areas were owned by private landlords, and persuading private landlords to invest in improvement has always been the most difficult aspect of housing improvement policy. Some of the dwellings acquired were transferred to housing associations, most notably in Arthurs Hill HAA where North Housing Association took over and renovated over 400 dwellings (Cameron and Stewart, 1982). Despite this element of municipalisation in HAAs, private landlords were persuaded to retain and improve a substantial proportion of the houses. In the case of Newcastle, landlords still owned 39% of dwellings in HAAs in 1980, almost all of them improved, compared to 60% at the beginning of the improvement programme.

The policy in the 1970s of retaining and improving large sections of the 19th century housing stock completed the virtual elimination of the problem of housing lacking amenities, but stands in sharp contrast to the ambitions of the 1960s and involves an acceptance of the old, cramped pattern of terraced houses and Tyneside flats criticised by Mess. However, the density of occupation of such areas is now much lower, principally because the old inner area housing tends nowadays not to house families, but rather to provide for the growing number of small, non-family households, both young and old.

In the 1980s the number of improvement grants given to private owners, and also the level of council house renovation, have increased substantially, although still well below the levels attained in the early 1970s. In the case of grants to private owners, one feature of the 1980s has been a pattern of very wide fluctuations in the availability of grants. In 1983/84, 90% repair and intermediate grants were, for a time, quite widely available since at that time central government boosted grants to private owners in an effort to stimulate the economy. In 1984 as many as 4,635 grants, mostly repair grants, were given in Tyneside. Subsequent reductions in finance cut the availability of grants and by 1986 the number of grants provided had fallen back to 1,558. There has also been a return to an emphasis on *ad hoc* grants to owner-occupiers. Major programmes of area improvement and targeting on priority areas, approaches which were characteristic of the late 1970s, are for the most part not possible because of the reductions in the resources available to local authorities.

Reviewing the processes which produced the enormous improvements in housing conditions in Tyneside since the 1920s, it is evident that the 'spadework' was done before the 1970s by the local authorities—an effort on a massive scale but sometimes rather crude in its approach, concerned sometimes more with quantity rather than quality. In the 1970s the job of solving the old housing problems was 'finished off' in a more sensitive way, through housing improvement areas, small-scale redevelopment and the increasing involvement of the housing associations. All the while, the private sector made its own contribution to providing a modern housing stock through new building for owner-occupation and the rehabilitation of old properties by the improvement of the better-quality older housing transferred into owner-occupation. For the most part, though, the activities of the public and private sectors remained fairly separate and distinct.

New Problems in the 1980s

Although many of the problems of the past have been overcome, some problems remain, and new housing problems are emerging. Some of these arise out of past policies, notably the concern to produce as many new houses as quickly and as cheaply as possible and the social division of the population resulting from past housing policies. Others arise from the failure to sustain the levels of investment in the creation of better housing conditions.

Disrepair in the private sector

During the 1970s—and nowhere more than on Tyneside—the problems of old housing which lacked modern amenities largely disappeared, but by the end of the 1970s a new concern was arising: that the housing stock was increasingly falling into disrepair. This problem was identified in the 1977 Green Paper on housing policy (DoE, 1977), and was the main finding of the 1981 English House Condition Survey. This revealed that there had been a 68% reduction in dwellings lacking amenities between 1971 and 1981, but an 18% *increase* in dwellings in serious disrepair. The problem of disrepair also seems to be more widespread throughout the housing stock. It remains much more common in pre-1919 housing, but serious disrepair is also increasingly apparent in more modern housing, particularly inter-war housing. Moreover, while it used to be assumed that poor housing conditions were concentrated in housing rented from private landlords, the majority of housing in disrepair is now in the owner-occupied sector (although it remains the case that a higher *proportion* of houses in the declining private rented stock are in disrepair or lack amenities). The reflection of this trend in Tyneside was illustrated by a survey carried out in 1985 by Newcastle City Environmental Services Department of areas of pre-1939 private housing (Newcastle City Council, 1986). This revealed that about 13% of these dwellings were probably unfit, another 8% required substantial repairs and 2% lacked at least one amenity. While the highest proportion of unfit housing was in the pre-1919 stock, the survey revealed the 'particularly disturbing feature' that about 20% of the inter-war properties surveyed were unfit or in substantial disrepair. The report suggested that this represented a steady deterioration in standards, and it would seem that some of the progress of the past is being lost due to the inadequate level of maintenance and renewal of the housing stock.

Disrepair in Council housing

The housing issue which is probably causing most concern in the 1980s is the emergence of serious problems in the council housing stock. Reports by the Department of the Environment (DoE) and by the Association of Metropolitan Authorities (AMA) have agreed on an estimated cost of about £20 billion to rectify the problems of the local authority sector nationally (DoE, 1985a; AMA, 1983a, 1983b, 1984). In 1985 the DoE considered that a total of 145,000 council houses in Tyne and Wear were in need of repair and estimated that it would cost the four Tyneside authorities £414 million to repair their housing stock (NCHA, 1987).

There are a number of different aspects to disrepair in council housing. Firstly, although council housing is mostly 'modern' in the sense of being built after 1919, some council housing is now over 60 years old, and a large part of the problem reflects a falling behind in the 'normal' process of repairing and modernising such housing. The AMA estimates that the national backlog of repairs of this kind represents about £9 billion (AMA 1983b). A further problem is presented by the half-million dwellings built by local authorities between 1945 and 1955 using pre-cast concrete system building techniques. Most of these are houses with gardens built to good standards which are in themselves popular with tenants, but the building systems were largely experimental and untried and of the several dozen separate systems used almost all are now under suspicion of suffering from severe structural defects and decay. The AMA estimated the national cost of remedying these defects at about £5 billion (AMA, 1983a). Such dwellings were built extensively in Tyneside; in Tyne and Wear as a whole there are 16,000 of them (NCHA, 1987), and South Tyneside, for example, has a particular problem with an extensive stock of system-built housing of this period. Gateshead has found the problems associated with such housing 'both extensive and expensive to remedy' (Gateshead MBC, 1985). The work to 348 'Airey' houses in Gateshead was costing £7.22 million, and this level of spending applied to other known and potentially defective post-war housing in Gateshead would imply a cost of over £40 million.

The other problem area is the stock of 'non-traditional' housing of the 1960s and 1970s, also built using pre-cast, system building methods, and often also 'non-traditional' forms such as high-rise and slab block flats. Again, serious structural problems have emerged in housing of this kind, and the cost of remedying these nationally is put at a further £5 billion

(AMA 1984). In this housing in particular, though, the problems are not only structural, they are also often problems arising from the fact that these estates are unpopular, stigmatised and 'difficult-to-let'. Indeed, in the case of Killingworth Towers, which is discussed in more detail below, the deck-access flats less than 20 years old which are being demolished are well-built and structurally sound, but are so unpopular that people will not live in them. In such housing, unpopular design features are usually combined with a history of housing allocation which has concentrated the most disadvantaged in certain housing areas (Cameron, 1987). In each of the Tyneside Districts there are examples of problems of this kind.

The process of social polarisation which concentrates the disadvantaged in certain council housing areas must also be seen in the general context of the social polarisation in our housing system as a whole. The local authority is increasingly becoming the provider of homes to the poorest in society. One reflection of this is the high proportion of council tenants with incomes low enough to receive Housing Benefit: in an area of high unemployment such as Tyneside this proportion is particularly high—in 1986 between 68% and 70% of council tenants in each of the Tyneside Districts were recipients of Housing Benefit (CIPFA, 1986a).

Housing needs and shortage

Overall, Tyneside has a larger and better quality stock of housing than ever before. There is now a small crude surplus of dwellings over households and the population of the area is declining. In this situation it would seem illogical to talk of housing shortages. There are, nevertheless, some 37,000 people on local authority waiting lists for housing in Tyneside, and waiting lists have been growing in recent years. In 1985/86 there were 5,834 people presenting themselves to Tyneside local authorities as homeless, of whom only 25% were given permanent housing (CIPFA, 1986b). There are indeed new pressures creating new housing needs for the future. The main source of pressure for additional housing is demographic changes which are producing more smaller households. These consist of three main categories: the elderly, young adults and those whose existing household has been divided by marital breakdown. The most obvious aspect of the housing demand generated by these groups is the need for small dwellings near to urban services. The other feature of these groups is that they are generally likely to have relatively low incomes, especially in an area such as Tyneside where, for example, many young adults are unemployed. In reviewing the implications of its population projections on housing need, North Tyneside Council suggests that:

'These changes in household composition will affect the demand for differing house types and tenures. For example, pensioners, young persons and lone parents are likely to be more dependent upon the public sector than the private sector for housing as they will have more limited incomes. In the past they have also relied on privately rented housing. As this declines it reinforces their dependence upon council and housing association provision. Some people's needs could, however, be met through the various low cost home ownership initiatives supported by the council. This will depend upon the general level of prosperity' (North Tyneside MBC, 1987a).

There has been some specific provision for the elderly and young adults by both the private sector and housing associations. In the local authority sector the building of sheltered accommodation for the elderly has been the one area to be sustained, to some extent, during the 1980s but has nevertheless been quite limited. Between 1980 and 1985 Tyneside councils built 477 units for the elderly, while housing associations built 437 (DoE Local Housing Statistics). In practice, local authorities have mainly met the need for housing for these groups by adapting the use of their existing stock. In the local authority sector there is a substantial 'mismatch' between the supply of existing housing, which consists mainly of family sized houses, and the demand, which is mainly from one- and two-person households. Of course, there is a similar 'mismatch' in the owner-occupied sector, but here there is less concern to match dwelling and household size.

In the local authority sector this pressure from small households often coincides with a situation where the local authority has 'non-traditional housing'—flats and maisonettes of various kinds, which were originally built for families but which are now seen as unsuitable for children. Often, the demand for housing from small households is met by allocating them such housing. Sometimes this has been converted for the purpose, but more usually it is simply 'under-occupied'. This may, of course, lead to the concentration of certain types of households—notably single parents and young adults—in the least popular council housing.

The decline in resources

In the 1980s there has been a massive reduction in direct public spending on housing, which is reflected in Tyneside by the fact that the Housing Investment Programme (HIP) allocations for capital spending on housing from central government to the Tyneside Districts fell, in cash terms, by 64% between 1979/80 and 1987/88 (NCHA, 1987). Resources from the Housing Corporation for investment by housing associations have also been reduced, although less so than the resources of local authorities. Overall, as has been seen above, this has resulted in a fall in levels of activity in housing in Tyneside, particularly in the number of new houses being built.

Policies in the 1980s

The beginning of the 1980s marked a major watershed in housing, partly because of the emergence of new housing problems as old ones were largely solved, but partly also because of a major change in the whole direction of housing policy. This change derives from the policies of the Conservative Government from 1979, with their overwhelming emphasis on the private sector. Nowhere have the implications of this change in policy been more profound than in Tyneside, with its tradition of large-scale public sector action to meet housing needs.

Generally, the response in Tyneside to these changes has been positive. During the 1980s the whole of Tyneside has been under the control of Labour local authorities, but these authorities have generally adopted a fairly pragmatic approach to housing policies, accommodating to, rather than confronting, central government and seeking out whatever new opportunities arise for meeting local housing needs.

As a result, a review of housing policies in Tyneside in the 1980s reveals a considerable number of examples of new and exciting ways of providing and renewing housing, many of which involve partnerships between different agencies: private sector builders, building societies, local authorities, housing associations and central government. Some of these are described below, but the question which must also be raised about these innovations is whether, in the context of Tyneside, they can effectively replace the policies of the past and offer solutions to match the scale and nature of today's housing problems.

The growth of owner-occupation

In the first half of the 1980s central government housing policies were dominated by the objective of increasing the level of owner-occupation. House-building for owner-occupation in Tyneside has increased sharply in the 1980s. The increase has been quite rapid, reaching a peak in 1983 when 1,862 private sector dwellings were completed, the highest post-war number, but then falling away again to 1,142 in 1986. The comparative increase has been most marked in South Tyneside, which previously had very low levels of private sector building and which effectively 'caught up' with the other districts in this period. In fact, though, the late 1970s was a period of very low levels of private housebuilding in Tyneside and the increase in the 1980s really only meant a return to the scale of private sector building of the early 1970s. What is new is the fact that building in the private sector now represents the largest element of new building, within a much reduced overall total.

Nevertheless, in comparison with the country as a whole, Tyneside remains an area of low levels of owner-occupation, but even more markedly, as outlined above, it is an area of very low house prices. This picture of low house prices is reflected in the Northern Region as a whole. Only one region in the UK, Yorkshire and Humberside, has average prices which are slightly lower (Halifax Building Society, 1987). Comparisons between the North and the South East sharply reflect the 'North-South divide' in house prices. Prices in the South East average 2.2 times those of the North and in Greater London prices are 2.4 times higher. Moreover, the rate of increase of house prices in the North has been the lowest of any region. Between 1983 and 1987, prices have risen by only 20.2% in the North, compared to a rise of 40.6% for the UK, 65.1% for the South East and 82.9% for Greater London (Halifax Building Society, 1987).

From the point of view of the consumer in Tyneside the owner-occupied housing market provides better than average housing at a very much lower than average price. However, the low level of house prices may be a double-edged sword, in as much as it implies comparatively low levels of returns to housebuilders which could inhibit the private sector in investing in new forms of housing provision.

Council house sales

In addition to the increased level of building of new housing for owner-occupation the other main element in the growth in owner-occupation, nationally and in Tyneside, has been the sale of council housing to sitting tenants under the 'Right-to-Buy' provisions of the 1980 Housing Act. By March 1986 there had been 16,000 'Right-to-Buy' sales in Tyneside (DoE Local Housing Statistics), amounting to 10.7% of the council stock in 1981. Following the national pattern, sales have declined in the most recent years, from a peak of 5,740 in 1982/83 down to 1,483 in 1985/86. In view of the very large local authority sector in Tyneside this level of sales may not represent a major problem in terms of the availability of rented housing. However, it is clear in Tyneside that, as elsewhere in the country, the pattern of sales is very uneven, concentrated in the outer estates of traditional houses. Thus, in Newcastle, sales by 1984 had accounted for more than 10% of 3-bedroomed council houses and bungalows, but less than 1% of flats (Newcastle City Council, 1984). Sales accounted for between 15% and 20% of the council stock in outer wards such as Castle, Westerhope and Denton, but less than 2% in inner city wards such as West City, Benwell and Byker. This has affected the characteristics of the remaining council stock; thus Gateshead noted that 'the sale of 3,199 council houses over the past 5 years has increased the proportion of high density flats and maisonettes in relation to traditional housing' (Gateshead MBC, 1985).

The proposals outlined in the Government's Housing White Paper in September 1987 (HMSO, 1987), and now incorporated in what is currently (mid-1988) the Housing Bill, will offer council tenants a 'Tenants Choice' to opt out of local authority control, and find or accept a new landlord. This marks a major new phase in the attempt by the government to reduce the local authority sector. Its likely effects on Tyneside are difficult to assess. The proposals in the Housing Bill to deregulate rents in both the private rented and housing association sector do suggest that rent levels would be substantially higher with 'independent sector' landlords[6], although proposals in the Bill to remove all subsidies to general rent levels in council housing will also reinforce the rapid increase in rents in the council sector.

The private sector in inner-city housing renewal

Until the 1980s the private developer in Tyneside, building housing for owner-occupation, had concentrated mainly on green field sites in the outer areas of the conurbation with the exception, perhaps, of high-priced infill development in high status established residential areas such as Gosforth in Newcastle. A major theme of housing policy in recent years has been to involve the private sector in housing renewal in the inner city, something which had previously been almost entirely left to the public sector.

The Tyne and Wear County Council Structure Plan, submitted in 1979, attempted to encourage this aim through land allocation policies by restricting land allocation for housing in outer areas to 'force' development to inner city locations. However, this strategy was diluted in the Plan as adopted in 1981 because of modifications by the Secretary of State for the Environment which increased housing land allocations by 25% by adding land in the outer areas in response to the representations made by housebuilders. Despite the abolition of the County Council in 1986, the Structure Plan remains in operation until the new Unitary Development Plans for each District are prepared. Overall, though, the housing land allocations to 1996 in the Structure Plan seem to be adequate. The main exception is South Tyneside, where it is felt that existing allocations are inadequate given the rapid increase in private sector development (South Tyneside MBC, 1986).

Although the strategy of restricting outer area housing development has not really been effectively pursued there has, nevertheless, been a major increase in private sector building activity in the inner areas throughout Tyneside. This may be partly due to a preference by developers and purchasers for new housing on infill sites in established environments, particularly in the more desirable older housing areas. It is also due to the development of new ways of encouraging private developers into the more difficult renewal areas of the inner city by way of partnerships between the public and private sectors.

Public-private sector partnerships in new house-building have taken a variety of forms in Tyneside. The simplest is the direct sale of former local authority land to private developers. Local authorities have been required by central government to dispose of surplus land to private developers (DoE, 1980a), and of course the reduction in local authority construction has left them with land—in former clearance areas, for example—which they are unable to develop themselves. Local Housing Statistics record sales of local authority land to the private sector between 1980/81 and 1985/86 totalling 26 hectares, largely in North Tyneside and Newcastle.

Local authorities in Tyneside have also used more complex arrangements with private developers. One such arrangement is to make land available to developers under a building licence, with the ownership of the land then being conveyed direct to the individual house purchaser. The licence agreement may allow the local authority to specify the type of development, and may also reserve 'nomination rights' so that the houses are offered initially to council tenants or applicants on the housing waiting list. In the early 1980s North Tyneside and Newcastle in particular developed a number of such schemes (9 in North Tyneside, 6 in Newcastle). Two schemes in the Byker area of Newcastle produced by the volume housebuilding firms Leech and Bowey between 1981 and 1983 provide good examples (Cameron and Thornton, 1986). They utilised sites which had been part of the Byker redevelopment scheme mentioned above, but which the council were unable to build on because of cuts in their housing investment allocations. Instead, the local authority quite successfully used a licence agreement to control the nature of the development to meet housing needs. Thus, all of the dwellings in one scheme, and 75% in the other, were purchased by council nominees— either council tenants or people on the housing waiting list. To assist larger families to purchase the bigger, 3-bedroom units, the local authority financed an 'equity-sharing' scheme on about a third of the units, allowing a mix of purchase and renting which is less expensive initially than outright purchase. As a result, the housing was bought mostly by local people, with 67% of purchasers from Byker or the surrounding areas (Cameron and Thornton, 1986).

This degree of local authority influence on the nature of the purchasers is perhaps exceptional. Even so, compared to the population in the local authority housing in Byker, these owner-occupied housing schemes fulfilled only a part of the whole spectrum of local housing needs: the new owner-occupiers were mostly young families, but the most striking difference was that most of them had a head of household in work (this applied to 88% in the owner-occupied schemes, but only 38% of local authority tenants in Byker).

Attracting private housing to the 'inner city' has, in fact, involved action in a number of rather different 'arenas'. The building licence schemes described above were, for the most part, within the areas of 19th century working-class housing which formed a ring around the central areas of the main towns, and which have been subject to recent slum clearance and redevelopment policies. Two other, rather different, kinds of inner city housing development have also involved attracting the private sector: housing development in the town centre itself, especially the city centre of Newcastle and in older riverside areas, and the involvement of the private sector in renewing former local authority housing.

Recently in Tyneside attention seems to have shifted towards private investment in these latter two kinds of inner city housing, and involving a further important incentive attracting private developers into the inner cities: the Urban Development Grants, which have been available since 1983 from the DoE. These grants provide a cash incentive to 'lever-in' private sector investment to more difficult development sites. In Newcastle city centre and Quayside five schemes of this kind had been supported by Urban Development Grant up to 1987 and there are a number of similar schemes in the pipeline involving both new building and the conversion of existing buildings to housing use.

Clearly, these schemes are not meeting 'local housing need', since these are areas which have had no significant local resident population for many years. They are catering for a rather specialised market of households wanting to buy housing in the city centre, and at the same time are contributing to the renewal of the fabric and the life of run-down areas. In some cases the housing is fairly expensive; its contribution to inner city policy is in terms of physical renewal, rather than in meeting the housing needs of an existing inner city population. There is, however, every indication that housing development of this kind will continue to grow, particularly under the auspices of the new Tyne and Wear Urban Development Corporation. It is not only private housebuilding firms that have been involved in such developments; this has also become a new field of activity for housing associations, as will be discussed below. In addition, there is the beginning of what may prove to be a major involvement by building societies. For example, at Leazes Court, in the centre of Newcastle, the Abbey Housing Association, a subsidiary of the Abbey National, has built flats and houses for sale. Also, in a pioneering scheme at Mill Dam in South Tyneside, Northern Rock Building Society has been directly involved in building houses. In these two cases an Urban Development Grant has not been necessary but, given the low prices of housing in Tyneside compared to similar housing elsewhere, it seems likely that many schemes will continue to rely on a subsidy through UDG or something similar such as the 'improvement-for-sale' subsidy.

Renewing and managing council housing

In the local authority sector construction has virtually stopped; attention has now turned to maintaining, renewing and improving the management of existing council housing. These issues are particularly acute in those areas of council housing which are unpopular, stigmatised and difficult to let.

The history of council housing in Tyneside has produced a legacy of large amounts of good housing, but also some housing which is unpopular and unsatisfactory. The problems of these areas are often complex, stemming partly from the physical design of housing, but partly from the social processes of housing allocation and household movement which can lead to the concentration of the most disadvantaged in certain estates. The response to these problems has likewise been varied and complex but three main strands can be identified: physical improvement and redesign; improved management; and tenure change—although action on particular estates usually involves some combination of these.

At the extreme, local authorities throughout Tyneside have found it necessary to demolish modern council housing which people will no longer live in. The largest recent example is the demolition of Killingworth Towers in North Tyneside. This estate of 700 flats in a complex of grey concrete slab blocks, with external deck access and linked by overhead walkways, was built as the visual centrepiece of the new township of Killingworth. It was meant to recreate the image of a medieval hill village, but became a blight on the township and a place where only those most desperate for housing would live (Taylor, 1978; Cameron, 1987). After several attempts to improve the situation these flats—which were completed only in the early 1970s—are now being demolished.

In some cases, however, it has been possible to remodel and re-use council housing of unacceptable design. The North Kenton estate in Newcastle provides a range of examples of how, since the late 1970s, the maisonette blocks built in the 1950s have been remodelled. The basic problem of these blocks was their mixing of family and non-family accommodation. In the case of five-storey blocks this was approached by conversion of whole blocks to flats to house single young people. Some of the three-storey maisonette blocks, on the other hand, have been converted to terraces of individual houses. Others have been converted to flats, while some have remained as maisonettes, but have been remodelled to give private gardens and individual access (Cameron, 1987). However, the cuts in resources have made it difficult for local authorities to revitalise their own rented housing. In North Kenton, for example, this has led to some transfer of tenure of housing. Some of the conversion of maisonettes to town houses was done on an 'improvement-for-sale' basis by the local authority (DoE, 1980b), and other blocks are being improved for sale by a housing association.

Of course, another possibility is to transfer difficult-to-let council housing to a private sector developer for refurbishment for sale. There have been a small number of schemes of this kind in Tyneside. Probably

Demolition of Killingworth Towers, 1987. These deck access flats, built in the 1970s, became stigmatised and 'difficult-to-let'; demolition eventually proved to be the only realistic option. (*Newcastle Chronicle & Journal*).

the most notable is a scheme known as St John's Green in Percy Main, North Tyneside. Here, a linear development of 18 five-storey maisonette blocks had become 'difficult-to-let' and in 1982 nine of the blocks were sold to the housebuilding firm of C M Yuill Ltd for conversion for sale. What is most striking about the refurbishment of these blocks is the transformation of their appearance, with the use of red-pantile roofs, wooden balconies, and the creation of courtyards around the blocks. By comparison, the changes *within* the blocks have been quite limited. The overwhelming emphasis in the refurbishment by the private developer has been in changing the image of the blocks. This has succeeded to the point that they were used to provide the illustration on the front cover of the introductory brochure (DoE, 1985b) for the DoE's 'Estate Action' agency (this agency, known originally as the Urban Housing Renewal Unit, was established in 1984 to encourage the revitalisation of run-down estates). A survey in 1985 (Cameron, 1987) allowed a comparison between the new purchasers of the refurbished flats and maisonettes, and the remaining tenants of the nine blocks which stayed in council ownership. It showed a sharp contrast: the new owners were drawn from outside the local area and were predominantly white-collar workers, whereas the tenants of the council blocks were a very deprived population, with 77% of those heads of households who were interviewed being unemployed.

Before rehabilitation – block of vandalised council flats at Percy Main, near North Shields, built in 1958. (*Newcastle Chronicle & Journal*).

After rehabilitation – private developer Yuill's took over the flats and modernised them, helped by a government Urban Development Grant subsidy. Pitched roofs and balconies were added and, internally, new kitchens and bathrooms installed. The scheme – comprising nine such blocks – was completed in 1984 and re-named St John's Green. (*Newcastle Chronicle & Journal*).

So far, the number of examples of private sector renovation of former local authority dwellings is small, no more than one or two schemes in each District. Invariably, too, the attraction of a private developer has required a substantial subsidy in the form of an Urban Development Grant. In the case of St John's Green, for example, the Urban Development Grant amounted to about £8,000 per dwelling and represented about 36% of the cost of the project (Munday and Mallinson, 1983). One obvious reason for this is that, given the generally low level of house prices in Tyneside, and the difficulty of attracting purchasers to former council estates, the prices of these refurbished dwellings are, by most standards, very low (in St John's Green, prices were between £10,000 and £18,000). This is a general problem when involving the private sector in housing renewal in Tyneside: the 'valuation gap' between the cost of building or renovation and the likely prices in the local housing market, a gap which must often be met by a substantial subsidy. In fact, there are several examples in Tyneside where it has not proved possible to find a 'private sector solution' to problem council housing. For example, in the case of Killingworth Towers, private sector refurbishment schemes were invited, and some were submitted, but after consideration it was decided that demolition was the only viable course. The remaining council blocks at Percy Main are also now being demolished; no developer could be found to undertake a similar scheme with these.

In some cases where involving the private sector has not proved viable the local authority has gone ahead with rehabilitation. The largest recent example is St Cuthbert's Village in Gateshead. Here a scheme of selective demolition and remodelling of a complex of deck access blocks is being carried out with a major financial allocation from Estate Action. Following the political priorities of central government, Estate Action usually look for an element of privatisation in the schemes they support, but in this case a wholly public sector project is being supported, perhaps indicating a recognition of the limitations of the involvement of the private sector in an area like Tyneside.

Another option open to local authorities is to involve housing associations in rehabilitating council estates. The Tyneside local authorities seem to be turning increasingly to this approach, as at the Rochester Estate in Newcastle where a partnership between the City Council and North British Housing Association is remodelling old council tenements to produce a mixture of flats and houses for sale and to rent. One reason why local authorities may prefer a partnership with housing associations is a degree of concern over the rather poor quality of refurbishment of some examples of conversion of former council housing by private developers.

Nationally, local authorities are being encouraged to look not only at privatisation but also at more sensitive and decentralised housing management to improve local authority estates. This is an essential element of most of the schemes supported by Estate Action, drawing heavily on the experience of the DoE's Priority Estates Project (Power, 1984). Management of housing by local authorities has often been bureaucratic and insensitive, but styles of housing management are now changing. Tyneside has a number of long-standing estate-based management projects, such as those at Cowgate in Newcastle and Springwell in Gateshead (Cameron, 1987). Significantly, perhaps, both of these projects are on 'cottage estates'—estates of conventional houses which have, nonetheless, become stigmatised and difficult-to-let. In fact, estate-based management has not always proved capable, in itself, of overcoming the problems of run-down estates. There are several examples, including Killingworth Towers and St Cuthbert's Village, where a local management project combined with small-scale environmental improvements has failed to halt the decline and more radical measures have proved necessary.

Most of these examples of local area housing management on problem estates have been special projects, often financed through the DoE Inner City Programme. Now, however, local authorities are extending this principle to their normal housing management system. A decentralisation to estate-level housing management in Newcastle is nearing completion, and North Tyneside are planning an ambitious programme involving the combined decentralisation of a range of services, including housing management (North Tyneside MBC, 1987b).

The proposals in the current Housing Bill introduce an entirely new mechanism for the renovation of local authority housing estates, the declaration by the Secretary of State for the Environment of a Housing Action Trust. Again, this reinforces the trend of removing responsibility from local authorities; a Housing Action Trust will involve the transfer of housing to an independent trust who will, after initiating a rehabilitation programme, be expected to transfer the housing to owner-occupation or to renting in the independent sector.

The role of housing associations

There is a substantial housing association sector in Tyneside, which has played an increasing role in local housing policies. As well as a variety of smaller local housing associations, there are a number of major housing associations which are very active in the area.

The main role of housing associations in the 1970s was building housing for rent. This included general family housing, but housing associations also played a particular role in providing housing to meet the needs of groups such as the elderly and young single people, (eg. the Bewick Court

Crown Hotel scheme at Clayton Street West, Newcastle city centre. The listed Crown Hotel facade was incorporated into this sensitive development of 216 flats, completed by North British Housing Association in 1982. The central landscaped courtyard, shown here, provides communal tennis courts and car parking. (*Newcastle City Engineer's Department*).

and Crown Hotel developments by North British Housing Association, providing housing for single young people in Newcastle City Centre). To this was added an increasing involvement in the improvement for rent of older housing, and involvement in improvement area policies.

It has already been suggested that the growing importance of housing associations in the 1980s is partly a reflection of the decline in local authority investment in housing. Construction by housing associations has actually declined somewhat. Renovations by housing associations in Tyneside reached a peak of 1,098 in 1982, but had by 1986 fallen to 372. Nevertheless, housing associations have been asked to fill some of the gaps left by the cuts in local authority housing investment, and have changed and expanded the scope of their operations.

Housing associations are now playing a major role in inner city renewal schemes, such as in the Quayside area of Newcastle. There have also been some examples of housing associations taking on the role of organising area housing improvement, as with the involvement of North Housing Association in the rehabilitation of the Northbourne Street area of Newcastle, and in the scheme in the Avenues area of Gateshead which involves a partnership with Northern Rock Building Society and Gateshead Borough Council in a joint Avenues Agency to rehabilitate 1,800 houses.

For housing associations too, the influence of central government policy has reduced the resources available to them to provide housing for rent, and they have been encouraged instead to provide housing for sale. The improvement or conversion of housing for sale has become an important part of their operations. In Tyneside this has included the sale of some of the 19th century housing acquired and improved in housing improvement areas. It has also included the conversion of large older houses for sale, the conversion of city centre buildings for housing use, and the improvement for sale of former council housing.

In view of the declining resources available from the government's Housing Corporation, housing associations are now looking increasingly to partnership with the private financial sector to provide investment. In 1987, North Housing Association negotiated a pioneering scheme whereby £100 million from private financial institutions is being invested by them in dwellings for 'Assured Tenancy' renting at rents above the normal Fair Rent levels, and some of the schemes being financed in this way are to be in Tyneside. This type of scheme has set the pattern for the reorganisation of housing association finance proposed in the current Housing Bill. This will involve primary reliance on finance from the private sector, and the abolition of Fair Rents for new tenancies. The housing association movement has expressed fears that this financial regime will prevent housing associations from continuing to fulfil their role of meeting the housing needs of low-income groups (Best, 1987).

Conclusions

Housing problems do not disappear, they simply change their nature. Progress in housing in Tyneside since the 1920s has probably been as great as anywhere in the country and Tyneside now has a housing stock which is generally of good quality and of low cost. Some of the problems of the past have been virtually eliminated, but new problems arise. For the future, the main issues would seem to be: maintaining an adequate level of repair and replacement of the existing stock and tackling the problem of difficult-to-let council housing; and meeting the needs for more housing arising from the growth of small households, young and old, many of them likely to be households with low incomes.

In the 1980s there has been a fundamental change in the context within which housing policies can be developed to meet these needs. The housing policies of the Conservative Government have precluded the local authority sector from playing the major role which has characterised housing in Tyneside, and current central government proposals seek to further reduce this role by transferring existing housing out of local authority ownership. The intention is that the housing policies of the future should look to the private sector and to housing associations acting as channels for private sector investment.

What does the future hold for Tyneside in this situation? On the one hand there are reasons for optimism. In particular, there is a range of agencies, many of them locally based, which have demonstrated their willingness to become involved in innovative housing schemes. These include major housebuilding companies, such as Leech, Bowey and Yuill; housing associations such as North Housing and North British; and building societies such as Northern Rock. The local authorities, too, have demonstrated their ability to work in new ways in partnership with these other agencies. On the other hand, there must be doubts for the future on a number of counts.

The first, and perhaps the most important issue, concerns the scale of investment. So far, the total impact of new policy initiatives, interesting as they are, has been very small in comparison with the output of the policies of the past. All the schemes of new building and conversion in inner areas involving partnerships between local authorities, private developers and housing associations have probably produced no more than 2,000 new dwellings over the past five years or so. This is the equivalent of *four months* of local authority building at the rates achieved back in 1968. The massive reduction in investment by local authorities has not been compensated by growth elsewhere. As a result there has been a large overall reduction in the production, improvement and renewal of housing in Tyneside.

The second, and related, area of doubt, is whether a reliance on the private sector is viable in the economic conditions of Tyneside. As has been said, the low level of housing costs in all sectors is a two-edged sword. It benefits the consumer and is, perhaps, a tribute to the success of past policies. At the same time it discourages new private investment by offering low potential returns from both selling and renting, and suggests that there is likely to be a continuing need for large-scale subsidies to attract private sector investment into the more difficult aspects of housing renewal.

The final question is how the private sector, through owner-occupation or new forms of renting, can meet the housing needs of those on low incomes, given the possibility that a large element of the growth in housing need in Tyneside may be from these households.

NOTES

1. 'Tyneside flats' were the characteristic form of working-class housing in Tyneside in the 19th century, and they are found virtually nowhere else in Britain. They consist of rows of what appear to be conventional terraced houses but, in fact, each 'house' is divided into an upper and lower flat, each with its own front door onto the street.
2. For most of the post-war years inadequate housing has been seen mainly in terms of 'lack of space' and 'lack of plumbing'—bath, inside WC, hot water system. These have been the focus of statistics on housing conditions, for example in the Census, and the main criteria for establishing priorities in slum clearance and housing improvement programmes.
3. Housing associations are private, non-profit-making bodies established to provide housing. They vary enormously in size and in the focus of their activities. Since the 1960s, most have been supervised and supported by a central government body, the Housing Corporation, and have been encouraged by successive governments as a 'third arm' of housing policy, filling the gap between owner-occupation and council renting. For the most part they provide housing for rent, and since 1974 this has been on a 'Fair Rent' basis, not very different from local authority renting.
4. The term 'maisonette' refers here to a dwelling which, in its basic form, consists of a flat on the ground floor and a two-storey apartment above this. The term is also used to refer to the two-storey unit itself (the term 'duplex' is sometimes used to refer to the same type of dwelling). As well as the basic three-storey units, 'maisonette blocks' can refer to units which combine these elements in buildings of various heights. Thus a common building form in Tyneside in the 1950s was a five-storey block with a flat on the ground floor and two layers of maisonettes above.
5. The Nationwide Building Society statistics refer to the whole of Tyne and Wear, including Sunderland, rather than to Tyneside alone.
6. The term 'independent rented sector' is used in the 1987 Housing White Paper (HMSO, 1987) and in the current (1988) Housing Bill to denote housing owned by both private landlords and by housing associations. It is used to distinguish these from local authority rented housing, and to indicate that housing associations are to be regarded as part of the private, not the public, sector.

REFERENCES

Association of Metropolitan Authorities (AMA) (1983a) *Defects in Housing: Part 1, Non-Traditional Dwellings of the 1940s and 1950s*. London: AMA.
Association of Metropolitan Authorities (AMA) (1983b) *Defects in Housing: Part 3, Repairs and Modernisation of Traditionally Built Dwellings*. London: AMA.
Association of Metropolitan Authorities (AMA) (1984) *Defects in Housing: Part 2, Industrialised and System-Built Dwellings of the 1960s and 1970s*. London: AMA.
Audit Commission (1986) *Managing the Crisis in Council Housing: A Report by the Audit Commission for Local Authorities in England and Wales*. London: HMSO.

Benwell Community Development Project (CDP) (1978) *Slums on the Drawing Board: Benwell CDP Final Report, No.4.* Newcastle: Benwell CDP.

Best, R. (1987) Statement from National Federation of Housing Associations. *The Guardian, 18 November 1987.*

Bradley, J. (1980) The HAA Approach: Monitoring & Evaluation of the Charles Street HAA, South Tyneside. *CURS Research Memo.,* 77. Birmingham: Birmingham University Centre for Urban and Regional Studies.

Cameron, S. and Thornton, G. (1986) Build for Sale Partnerships in Byker. *Housing Review, 35,* 2.

Cameron, S. (1987) *Recent Approaches to Problem Council Housing in Tyneside; DTCP Working Paper 3.* Newcastle upon Tyne: Department of Town and Country Planning, Newcastle University.

Cameron, S. and Stewart, R. (1982) Area Housing Improvement in Newcastle—Past and Present. *Housing Review, 21.*

Chartered Institute of Public Finance and Accounting (CIPFA) (1986a) *Housing Rent Statistics.* London: CIPFA.

Chartered Institute of Public Finance and Accounting (CIPFA) (1986b) *Homelessness Statistics, 1985/86.* London: CIPFA.

Coleman, A. (1985) *Utopia on Trial: Vision and Reality in Planned Housing.* London: Hilary Shipman.

Department of the Environment (DoE) (1977) *Housing Policy: a consultation document.* Cmnd 6851. London: HMSO.

Department of the Environment (DoE) (1980a) *Land for Private Housebuilding, Circular 9/80.* London: HMSO.

Department of the Environment (DoE) (1980b) *Local Authority Improvement for Sale and Homesteading. Circular 20/80.* London: HMSO.

Department of the Environment (DoE) (1985a) *An Enquiry into the Condition of the Local Authority Housing Stock in England, 1985.* London: DoE.

Department of the Environment (DoE) (1986) *Urban Housing Renewal Unit Annual Report, 1985–86.* London: DoE.

Futagawa, Y. (1980) *Byker Redevelopment: Byker area of Newcastle upon Tyne 1969–82/ Ralph Erskine.* Tokyo: A.D.A. Edita

Gateshead Metropolitan Borough Council (1985) *Repair and Improvement of Local Authority Housing Stock: Returns to DoE Regional Office.*

Halifax Building Society (1987) *The Halifax House Price Index: Regional Bulletin, No.13.*

HMSO (1987) *Housing: The Government's Proposals.* Cmnd 214. London: HMSO.

Munday, N. and Mallison, H. (1983) Urban Development Grant in Action. *Public Finance and Accounting, December 1983.*

Nationwide Building Society (1987) *Nationwide Regional Profiles: The North East.*

Newcastle City Council (1980) *Report on Area Improvement Progress to Housing Committee, 5th July 1980.*

Newcastle City Council (1984) *Report by Director of Policy Services on Council House Sales to Housing Committee, 22nd March 1984.*

Newcastle City Council (1986) *Report by Director of Environmental Services on Enforcement Activities in Private Sector, Housing Committee 10th September 1986.*

Northern Consortium of Housing Authorities (NCHA) (1987) *Housing in Tyne and Wear: The Case for Investment.* NCHA.

North Tyneside Metropolitan Borough Council (1987a) *Towards a Housing Strategy.* North Shields: North Tyneside MBC Housing Services Department.

North Tyneside Metropolitan Borough Council (1987b) *Going Local in North Tyneside.* North Shields: North Tyneside MBC Housing Services Department.

North Tyneside Community Development Project (CDP) (1976) *Some Housing and Town Planning Issues in North Tyneside: An Overview.* North Shields: North Tyneside CDP.

Power, A. (1984) *Local Housing Management: A Priority Estates Project Survey.* London: DoE.

South Tyneside Metropolitan Borough Council (1985) *Ten Years of Progress in South Tyneside.* South Shields: South Tyneside MBC.

South Tyneside Metropolitan Borough Council (1986) The Housing Market in South Tyneside. *Quarterly Industrial Review,* 4. South Shields: South Tyneside MBC Planning Department.

Taylor, P. (1978) Difficult-to-Let, Difficult-to-Live-In, and Sometimes Difficult-to-Get-Out-Of: An Essay on the Provision of Council Housing with Special Reference to Killingworth. *Centre for Urban and Regional Development Studies, Discussion Paper 16.* Newcastle: CURDS.

Trade Union Studies Information Unit (TUSIU) (1987) *Homes and Jobs: A Report on Housing Need and Job Potential.* Newcastle: TUSIU.

6

HEALTH AND HEALTH PROVISION

Ann Holohan, Gordon Pledger and David Wilson

Henry Mess considered that ill health resulted from many factors. On the one hand, he referred to 'ignorance and carelessness in the rearing of children', and mentioned also intemperance and negligence. On the other hand, he referred to the effect on health of 'social and industrial conditions on Tyneside', citing overcrowding, smoke, and poor sanitary conditions as well as poor wages, high unemployment, and the precariousness of jobs in shipbuilding. Explanations of ill health which emphasise the first set of factors have been called 'victim-blaming theories', and those which emphasise the second set, 'system-blaming theories' (Graham, 1985). Mess was an early pioneer in suggesting that both sets of factors must be taken into account.

The debate on their relative importance continues today and is of central concern, since each approach leads to very different types of remedy—either encouraging people to change their style of life, or else mounting a radical attack on social and economic conditions. But whichever perspective is adopted, health care provision also undoubtedly has a major influence on patterns of illness and mortality.

Since the 1920s, there have been radical changes both in lifestyles and in social conditions, and the formation of the National Health Service (NHS) in 1948 revolutionised health care services almost overnight. There have also been major new developments in treatment and medical technology—the advent of antibiotics, use of blood transfusions, better treatment of trauma and sepsis, developments in the treatment of mental illness. All these changes have led to marked improvements in health and reductions in mortality rates in all parts of the country. In the 1920s, Tyneside was well below the national average on most health and social indicators. Has Tyneside fully shared in the improvements? Have the gaps widened, narrowed, or been eliminated or reversed? And whatever the answers, why?

An Overview: Inequalities in Health in the Northern Region

Professor Peter Townsend and his colleagues have recently undertaken a research study of the Northern Region examining health and deprivation (Townsend *et. al.*, 1988). The main purpose of the study, carried out in conjunction with the Northern Regional Health Authority, was to highlight the considerable differences in health within the Northern Region, acknowledging also that the Region as a whole experiences poor health in relation to most parts of the country. This research built on the earlier 'Black Report', *Inequalities in Health* (DHSS, 1980), and is also closely related to the Health Education Council's recent study, *The Health Divide* (Whitehead, 1987).

Townsend and his colleagues constructed an *index for health* comprising three indicators: data on deaths (mortality); data on birth weights and rates of sickness and disablement (morbidity). He suggests that these three measures focus on an area's health quality in different ways: mortality relates to the past experience of individuals; birth weight serves as an index of future child development and also maternal health; and sickness and disablement serves as an intermediary between the two. In addition, four indicators from the 1981 Census of Population were used to construct an overall *deprivation index*. These indicators—unemployment rates, car and home ownership and rates of household overcrowding—represent surrogate measures for income and living conditions.

These measures of health and deprivation were calculated for the 678 local authority wards in the Northern Region. A close correlation was found between deprivation and standards of health. The study also showed that differences in health between local populations are very wide—indeed, much greater than had previously been assumed.

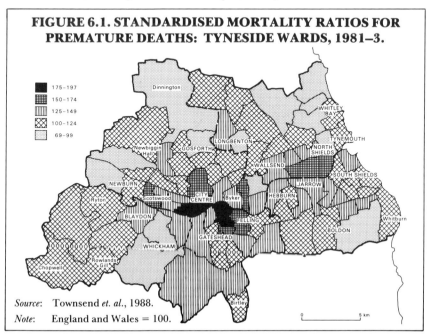

FIGURE 6.1. STANDARDISED MORTALITY RATIOS FOR PREMATURE DEATHS: TYNESIDE WARDS, 1981–3.

175–197
150–174
125–149
100–124
69–99

Source: Townsend *et. al.*, 1988.
Note: England and Wales = 100.

Tyneside was found to have a particularly high incidence of premature death—even higher than for the Northern Region as a whole. Of Tyneside's 88 wards, 73 had mortality rates higher than those for England and Wales for deaths under the age of 65 (see Figure 6.1). The worst were Bede ward in inner Gateshead and the West City ward of inner Newcastle; in these areas, the rate of premature mortality is nearly twice the national rate. West City also has the highest rate of unemployment in Tyneside. The lowest rates were found in the coastal suburb of Monkseaton—there, the premature mortality rate is just over two thirds of the national level.

There is very little available data on the incidence of ill health and Townsend's study had to rely on figures for the permanently sick from the 1981 Census. Here, 'permanent sickness' is defined as the proportion of all residents of 16 and over in private households who classed themselves economically inactive as a result of permanent sickness. As with mortality, Tyneside records rates of permanent sickness above the average for the Region and England & Wales. North Tyneside, with its more affluent suburbs, has lower rates of permanent sickness and mortality than the

TABLE 6.1. HEALTH INDICATORS, TYNESIDE, NORTHERN REGION AND ENGLAND & WALES

Health Districts/ Local Authority Districts[1]	Premature deaths (at under 65 years) (1981–3)		Permanently sick (1981)		Low birth weights[3] (< 2800 gm) (1982–4)	
	Index[2] (E&W=100)	(No.)	%	(No.)	%	(No.)
Gateshead	125	(2160)	3.0	(5011)	15.3	(1171)
Newcastle	118	(2609)	2.7	(5854)	15.9	(1641)
North Tyneside	112	(1879)	2.4	(3780)	16.2	(1111)
South Tyneside	119	(1636)	2.7	(3377)	14.5	(819)
Northern Region[4]	115	(28142)	2.5	(59493)	14.8	(17392)
England & Wales	100	—	1.8	—	N/A	—

Source: Townsend et.al., 1988, Table 6.3.
Notes: 1. Health Districts are coterminous with local authority districts in Tyneside.
2. The mortality ratio/index has been calculated to take account of age structure by comparing death rates for Tyneside and England & Wales for five-year age groups. The age-standardised number of excess deaths is thus given relative to national mortality rates.
3. Percentage of live births under 2800 gms. The standard measure of low birth weight is live births under 2500 gms; consequently there is no data for under 2800 gms available for England and Wales.
4. The Northern Region comprises the counties of Tyne and Wear, Northumberland, Co. Durham, Cleveland and Cumbria.

other Tyneside Districts, while the worst of the Districts is Gateshead (Table 6.1.). As with mortality rates, West City had the highest incidence of permanent sickness, while the lowest incidence was in Monkseaton and South Gosforth.

In contrast with mortality and permanent sickness, the Northern Region as a whole has a much better record on birth weight. The worst District is North Tyneside—though it also has Tyneside's worst wards (Collingwood and Riverside) and best wards (Whitley Bay and Monkseaton) on this indicator. In contrast, South Tyneside has a relatively favourable position on low birth weight.

Mortality

In view of Townsend's findings, can we provide further data to sharpen the focus on premature death and also on infant mortality in Tyneside?

Perinatal and infant mortality

Perinatal mortality refers to still-births plus deaths in the first week of life per 1000 live and still-births; infant mortality refers to deaths (excluding still-births) from the moment of birth through to one year old. Both these measures, especially perinatal mortality, are used nationally and internationally as measures of the 'effectiveness' of health care, although many would suggest an extension of their significance to include a link with the social and economic circumstances of a region.

Perinatal Mortality. In 1985, 6,463 babies were still-born or died in the first week of life in England & Wales, a rate of 9.8 for every 1,000 live births. This rate varied according to the social class of the father (in the case of 'legitimate' births) and the size of the family. For example, the rate for women with husbands in unskilled manual jobs who already had three or more children was 19.5 per 1,000; for women whose husbands were in professional jobs and who were having their second child the rate was 6.6 per 1,000. Illegitimate children were more likely to suffer early death: the perinatal mortality rate for illegitimate births in 1985 was 12.1 per 1000 live births, compared with 9.2 per 1000 for legitimate births (OPCS, 1987a).

Perinatal mortality has been falling steadily and substantially for many years, both in the country as a whole and in Tyneside. The position in Tyneside is, in general, encouraging, with two Districts (Newcastle and North Tyneside) recording perinatal mortality rates well below the rate for England & Wales in 1985—and indeed among the lowest in the country.

Nationally, perinatal mortality has been halved between 1975 and 1985 and Tyneside has shared in this improvement (Table 6.2). Despite the general fall in perinatal mortality rates there remains, however, a stubborn class difference in the risk of death in the perinatal period. For example, in the Northern Region, the perinatal death rate for babies born to professional parents was 5.2 per 1000 in 1984 compared to 11.1 per 1000 for babies born to unskilled manual workers (OPCS, 1987a).

TABLE 6.2. PERINATAL MORTALITY RATES, TYNESIDE, NORTHERN REGION AND ENGLAND AND WALES, 1975 AND 1985

Health Districts/ Local Authority Districts	Perinatal mortality: no. of still-births and deaths in first week of life per 1000 live and still-births	
	1975	1985
Gateshead	24	11.2
Newcastle	15	7.0
North Tyneside	15	5.7
South Tyneside	20	13.9
Northern Region	20	9.8
England & Wales	19	9.8

Sources: OPCS Vital Statistics, Series V.S., Nos.2 (1977) and 12 (1987).

Most recent studies demonstrate the importance of low birth weight as a major factor in perinatal death and, indeed, later handicap (Northern Regional Health Authority, 1986). In Newcastle, the perinatal mortality rate for babies weighing less than 2500 gms. at birth was as high as 69 per 1000 in 1984, as compared with a rate of only 5 per 1000 for babies weighing more than 2500 gms. There are two numerically important categories of low birth weight—spontaneous onset of labour with early delivery, and babies born small but of normal gestational age. The women who suddenly and unexpectedly go into labour are more likely to be young, unmarried, to smoke cigarettes and to be of low weight prior to conception. Tragically, they are also more likely to have had previous perinatal deaths and previous low-birth-weight babies. Low birth weight at term does not vary appreciably with the age of the mother, but it is more likely to occur in first pregnancies, among the wives of the unskilled, those under-weight at the start of pregnancy and those who smoke. As there is no proven palliative medical treatment the main hope of reducing low-birth-weight infants must lie in primary prevention.

Regular antenatal care has played a part in the long-term fall in UK perinatal mortality. However, other factors have also helped to reduce perinatal mortality—in particular, better medical care during labour; better housing and sanitation; improved nutrition; the decline of infectious diseases and increased availability of abortions.

There is probably some scope for further reducing the level of perinatal mortality. More accessible antenatal services need to be developed, within general practice, for example. There is a need, too, for greater encouragement of women to take better care of themselves during pregnancy—to improve their nutrition and stop smoking. However, as in most areas of health care, the wider context also needs to be considered. Economic and social deprivation strongly influence perinatal mortality and the widening gap between the affluent and the poor seems highly likely to exacerbate class differences in mortality and undermine efforts to reduce perinatal mortality.

Infant Mortality. Mess devoted considerable space to analysing the distribution of infant deaths on Tyneside, listing the causes of death and offering some explanations. Mess noted the general downward trend in infant deaths (despite the temporary increase during the Great War) but also pointed out that Tyneside rates were high in comparison with the average for urban areas in England & Wales. Table 6.3 clearly indicates the continuing downward trend, from a rate in Newcastle, for example, of 80 per 1,000 births in 1933–35 to only 8.8 per 1,000 births in 1983–85. In addition, Tyneside's infant mortality rates are now nearer those of England & Wales then ever before—and in three of the four Tyneside districts are actually *below* the national rate.

TABLE 6.3. INFANT MORTALITY RATES, TYNESIDE, 1933–85

Health Districts/ Local Authority Districts[1]	Infant Mortality[2]					
	1933–1935		1958–60		1983–85	
	Rate/ 1000	(No.)	Rate/ 1000	(No.)	Rate/ 1000	(No.)
Newcastle	80	(425)	26	(159)	8.8	(31)
Gateshead	81	(331)	26	(102)	10.3	(26)
North Tyneside	71	(172)	24	(87)	7.7	(18)
South Tyneside	90	(266)	24	(87)	8.1	(16)
England & Wales	60	—	22	—	9.7	—

Sources: OPCS Vital Statistics, Series V.S and Reports of the Registrar General.
Notes: 1. Health Districts are coterminous with Local Authority Districts in Tyneside. Data for 1933–35 and 1958–60 computed by amalgamating former local authority areas to current administrative areas.
2. Rate per 1000 live births and the average number of deaths each year.

In the 1920s, approximately one third of infant deaths were due to debility, one fifth died of diarrhoea, and bronchitis and pneumonia accounted for about a sixth. A considerable number died of infectious diseases such as whooping cough and measles. In 1986, most deaths were due to congenital abnormalities and prematurity. The great reduction in deaths due to infection has resulted from a combination of several factors, including improvements in general living conditions, better infant care and nutrition, chemotherapy, antibiotics and immunisation, and better antenatal care. In 1930, 102 Tyneside children aged 1–14 died of infectious diseases; by 1986, the figure was down to 4.

The infant mortality rate in the children of unskilled workers in Britain today is a lot less than that of professional families in the early 1930s. This represents an enormous improvement in the health of the disadvantaged in contemporary society and it is an improvement which has been shared and sustained in Tyneside. Great progress has been made, particularly since the last war; the incidence and severity of childhood major infections, for example, has reduced considerably since the pioneering study of a thousand families in Newcastle was undertaken in the late 1940s (Spence *et.al.*, 1954)[1]. However, there has been little alteration in the pattern of inequalities—post-neonatal deaths (deaths of infants aged from one month to under a year) in unskilled families still remain much higher than in professional families. Despite the overall decline there is a persisting social class gradient—from birth (and even before), life chances are strongly affected by class (Whitehead, 1987).

Finally, it is worth pointing out that there has also been a dramatic fall in maternal deaths in or after childbirth in Tyneside, from 67 women dying from conditions associated with childbirth in 1930 down to 1 in 1986. The main reasons for this fall include general improvements in women's health, smaller families, blood transfusions, obstetric flying squads in the earlier years, the introduction of antibiotics, better pre-eclampsia treatment and safer operations. A further significant and related issue here is the availability of legal abortions; in the past, 'back street abortions' resulted in some serious illness, even death, of pregnant women. The rate of pregnancy termination in Tyneside is, in fact, below the national average. In 1985, termination as a proportion of all registered pregnancies ranged from 11.7% in Gateshead and North Tyneside to 16.3% in Newcastle—below the 17.7% figure for England and Wales (OPCS, 1986).

Adult mortality

Mess devoted his discussion on adult mortality mainly to tuberculosis, which in the 1920s was 'still to be reckoned as one of the most formidable enemies of man', even though there had been a substantial fall in the number of cases and deaths from the disease since the mid-19th century.

Although the scale of the problem in the 1920s and 1930s was considerably smaller than a century before, tuberculosis was still a common disease with a high level of associated mortality. In 1920, 1922 and 1924, Gateshead had the highest tuberculosis death rate of any County Borough in England and Wales, and in 1923 and 1925 this unenviable distinction was held by South Shields. The rates were even higher in Tyneside's smaller towns such as Blaydon and Newburn[2]. Again, the relative importance of various factors which contributed to the disease caused considerable debate. What role did malnutrition, overcrowding, ventilation, water supplies and housing play in the aetiology of the disease? 'It cannot be doubted', commented Mess, 'that the greater part of these deaths, nearly half of which are those of young persons under the age of twenty-five, are unnecessary deaths'—avoidable with prompt and adequate treatment. In 1930, 822 people died from tuberculosis in Tyneside, compared to only 13 deaths from this disease in 1986. The few deaths today on Tyneside are mainly in the elderly, and in certain ethnic groups, and the disease can now be effectively treated on an outpatient basis. This decline, as with infant mortality, is due to innoculation, improved social conditions, better nutrition and specific therapies. The amelioration of conditions such as malnutrition and overcrowding (which

TABLE 6.4. STANDARDISED MORTALITY RATIOS (SMRs) FOR SELECTED CAUSES OF DEATH, TYNESIDE 1981–5 (INCLUSIVE)

Cause of Death	Health Districts/Local Authority Districts				Tyneside (4 Districts) Total No. of deaths (No.)
	Gateshead	Newcastle	North Tyneside	South Tyneside	
	SMR	SMR	SMR	SMR	
Neoplasms (cancers)[1]	116	121	117	117	(14,075)
Diseases of circulatory system[2]	117	105	112	111	(26,868)
Diseases of respiratory system[3]	118	105	113	120	(7,224)
(ENGLAND & WALES – 100)					

Source: OPCS Mortality Statistics-Area, Series DH5.
Notes: 1. Principally lung cancer, breast cancer and stomach cancer.
2. Half these deaths were from ischaemic heart disease and a quarter from cerebrovascular disease.
3. Principally pneumonia, bronchitis, emphysema.

led to heavy exposure to the disease) greatly reduced the prevalence of tuberculosis, a reduction accelerated by the introduction of effective clinical intervention.

But a combination of deprivation and lifestyle factors produce relatively high death rates from certain major diseases in Tyneside. 'Standardised Mortality Ratios' (SMRs) may be calculated to take into account, or standardise for, differences between the local and national age/sex composition. Comparisons on this basis show that death rates for neoplasms and diseases of the circulatory and respiratory systems are high in Tyneside, around 15% to 20% above national rates (Table 6.4).

The three causes of death listed in Table 6.4 are the three most important causes of mortality in Tyneside. Diseases of the circulatory system account for about half the deaths, neoplasms account for nearly a quarter and diseases of the respiratory system represent about an eighth of deaths.

In 1986 the main causes of death in those aged 1–34 years, both in Tyneside and nationally, were accidents (especially for males); for those aged 35–54 the most important causes were neoplasms (cancers of the stomach, lung and breast) and ischaemic (coronary) heart disease; for those aged 55–74, neoplasms (especially lung and breast cancer) and ischaemic heart disease; and for those aged over 75, neoplasms, heart disease, stroke and pneumonia.

Infectious diseases have become far less important as a cause of death since the 1930s and accidents, cancer and coronary heart disease have become more significant. Life expectancy has, of course, increased: life expectancy at birth in England and Wales in 1930–2 was 58.7 years for males and 62.9 for females, and by 1983–5 life expectancy had risen to 71.8 for males, 77.7 for females. Today, nearly 16% of the population of Tyneside are aged over 65, compared with only 6% in 1930. Most deaths now occur after the age of 65. In 1930 nearly two-thirds of deaths in Tyneside were of people *under* 65 while in 1985 less than a quarter of deaths were accounted for by the under 65s (Table 6.5).

TABLE 6.5. PROPORTION OF TOTAL DEATHS AT VARIOUS AGES, TYNESIDE, 1930 AND 1986

	Age distribution of deaths				
	Pre-school children	School children	Aged 15–44	Aged 44–65	Aged 65+
1930[1]	17.5%	3.4%	17.8%	26.2%	35.1%
1985	1.3%	0.1%	2.3%	19.0%	77.3%

Source: OPCS Mortality Statistics-Area, Series DH5 (1987)
Note: 1. Data for 1930 computed by amalgamating former local authority areas to current administrative areas.

Table 6.6 below examines the age/sex mortality rates of Tyneside and England & Wales in 1985. At all ages under 45 the local rates are similar or better than national rates; it is only in those aged over 45 that local rates are higher than the national average. The higher relative mortality of the older groups may, to an extent, reflect the harsh conditions of the past in Tyneside—in their youth, there was high unemployment and substantial air pollution, infections were much more common and there was no National Health Service. It may be that, as the present younger cohorts (with low relative mortality rates) reach middle age, the mortality rates for the older age groups in Tyneside will move closer to the national average. This will probably depend very much on behavioural factors such as smoking, diet and stress which link to the major killer diseases of middle and old age. On the other hand, it may be that, as the younger cohorts reach middle age, the familiar excessive death rates will appear once again, the effects of earlier life circumstances only becoming manifest in mortality after the age of 45.

TABLE 6.6. AGE/SEX MORTALITY RATES, TYNESIDE AND ENGLAND & WALES, 1985

	Annual death rates per 1,000 in each age group							
	All ages	1–14	15–34	35–44	45–64	65–74	75–84	85+
Males								
Tyneside	13.4	0.6	0.12	1.5	27.7	50.8	110.9	229.5
England & Wales	12.0	0.7	0.15	1.7	22.5	44.3	104.1	223.5
Females								
Tyneside	13.0	0.5	0.7	1.1	14.7	29.0	67.8	177.1
England & Wales	11.7	0.6	0.7	1.1	13.0	24.1	64.1	178.0

Source: OPCS Mortality Statistics—Area, Series DH5 (1987).

At the beginning of the 1980s coronary heart disease appeared to be 'Britain's disease of the decade', and there were calls for urgent action to meet a most substantial health care problem. In 1985 coronary heart disease accounted for nearly 28% of all deaths, and it is a major cause of *premature* mortality (deaths before the age of 65), especially for males (even though four fifths of the deaths occur in persons aged 65 years or over). In Tyneside, mortality rates for coronary heart disease are high in comparison with rates for England & Wales (Table 6.7) and the national rate is itself high in comparison with many other developed countries.

TABLE 6.7. MORTALITY RATES FOR CORONARY HEART DISEASE, TYNESIDE AND ENGLAND AND WALES, 1985

| | Annual death rates per 1000 in selected age groups | | | |
	All ages	45–54	55–64	65–74
Males				
Tyneside	4.2	2.4	7.8	16.8
England & Wales	3.8	2.2	6.7	15.6
Females				
Tyneside	3.3	0.5	2.5	8.9
England & Wales	2.8	0.4	2.0	6.8

Source: OPCS Mortality Statistics—Area, Series DH5 No.12 (1987).

Amongst the under 65s, deaths from coronary heart disease in Tyneside are more than three times higher for males than females. It is, however, a fallacy to suggest that coronary heart disease is predominantly a male disease, since 44% of those who die from the disease are women—though the overwhelming majority of these female deaths occur after the age of 65. Coronary heart disease is thus an important cause of death amongst women, being responsible for a total of 1429 female deaths in Tyneside in 1985 (compared with 1694 male deaths). Yet it generates little comment, either regionally or nationally; by contrast, cancer of the cervix— accounting for the deaths of 37 women in Tyneside in 1985—receives massive media exposure, especially concerning the provision of screening facilities.

In view of the decline in deaths from tuberculosis since the 1920s, are there such predictions for a decline in deaths from coronary heart disease? This question leads to the role of prevention in reducing risk factors associated with this disease.

Smoking cigarettes is considered to be one of the principal risk factors: the evidence suggests that the overall risk for smokers of death from coronary heart disease is about twice that for non-smokers. The incidence of smoking, and smoking-related diseases such as lung cancer, is certainly higher in Tyneside than in the country as a whole, primarily because the area has an above-average proportion of people in those social groups (manual workers) which have a high incidence of smoking (in 1984, in England & Wales, 17% of professional people smoked cigarettes, compared with 49% of unskilled manual workers). Households in the Northern Region spend more on cigarettes than the national average despite the fact that household incomes in this Region are well below average[3]. It has been calculated that over 1700 deaths a year in Tyneside can be attributed to smoking; in Newcastle alone, the estimated annual death rate from smoking is 295 per 100,000 population for males and 118 per 100,000 for females, compared with national rates of 230 per 100,000 for males, 90 for females (Northern RHA and Northern ASH, 1984).

Nutrition—especially fat (and particularly the saturated fat) content of habitual diets, and its relationship with cholesterol levels—has also been considered a risk factor in relation to heart disease. But with household incomes in the North the lowest of all regions in England & Wales, the ability to change diets—especially if this involves extra expense—may be limited. A series of national surveys have indicated that falling income leads to the consumption of an increasing proportion of carbohydrates and poor diets are often associated with obesity, which in turn is considered another risk factor in coronary heart disease. South Tyneside Community Health Council has noted that convenience foods form a larger part of weekly food expenditure than in the country as a whole and that the consumption of fruit was the lowest in the country (South Tyneside CHC, 1984).

Excessive consumption of *alcohol* is also related to the area's high incidence of heart disease. Household expenditure on alcohol is well above average in the Region[4] and this contributes not only to heart disease but also to a wide range of other problems—such as a high rate of alcohol-related illnesses, alcohol psychosis and drinking and driving accidents—all of which put demands on the health services (Regional Working Party on Problem Drinking, 1983). Finally, *stress* can be added to this list of risk factors in heart disease, and stress is, without doubt, commonly associated with the anxieties of poverty, unemployment, and low income—conditions well known to many Tyneside families.

Morbidity

Undue emphasis on mortality rates can leave unstated the problems of chronic illness and incapacitating conditions. But morbidity (ill health) is difficult to define and measure. One popular assumption is that people who experience distressing symptoms invariably consult a doctor. Many studies have indicated that this is not so and indeed it had been calculated that only 1 in 37 'symptom episodes' lead to a patient-initiated consultation with a family doctor (Calnan, 1987; Patrick and Scambler, 1982). There exists what has been called a significant 'clinical iceberg', where self-care, self-medication and the use of alternative medicine play a major role. Other factors such as the nature of the symptoms, the perceived severity, the degree of disruption and the pressure from others to consult, mediate in the decision to seek medical care.

There are three most commonly used methods of measuring morbidity: measuring the use of health services (such as the numbers of people admitted to hospital or consulting their general practitioner); screening, in which a whole population or a sample are investigated to see if they have a particular disease or set of symptoms; and self-assessment surveys in which people are asked about their own state of health. It is the first of these measures that is most often used, but such patient studies will not reveal a full picture of illness behaviour or the social characteristics of those who experience symptoms and do not consult. On the other hand, screening (for high blood pressure, for example) is not national policy and such studies have not been widely undertaken.

Some helpful information on the extent of sickness in the country, as assessed by people themselves, is provided by the *General Household Survey (GHS)*. This survey, conducted with a sample of households, provides an important supplement to official health records as it shows how sickness affects people with different kinds of employment, housing and so on. But of major interest is that the GHS gives an indication of those who are sick, but who do not consult a doctor or visit a hospital.

In the GHS, questions are asked about chronic and acute illness. Respondents are asked if they have any long-standing illness, disability or infirmity, and the manner in which their activities may be limited by these conditions. In the 1985 GHS, 29% of males and 31% of females in the country as a whole reported having a chronic condition (OPCS, 1987c). Acute illness was defined as an illness or injury which restricted normal activities in the two weeks preceding the interview, and in 1985, 11% of men and 14% of women reported acute illness. The prevalence of chronic conditions increases with decreasing socio-economic status; thus, males in unskilled jobs were found to be 1.5 times as likely as professional men to report a long-standing illness and the variation was even greater for women. These differences were at their greatest after the age of 45. In addition, employed men and women, in all age groups, have a lower incidence of limiting long-standing illness than those who are unemployed or economically inactive. In view of these findings it may be expected that incapacity and illness in Tyneside would be above-average on account of the area's relatively high proportion of people in manual occupations and also its high level of unemployment.

Local information on the incidence of ill health is limited. The 1981 Census does show, however, that the proportion of economically active people off work as a result of temporary sickness is higher for Tyneside (at 2.5%) than for England & Wales as a whole (at 1%). The proportion of people rendered economically inactive through permanent sickness in Tyneside is also above the national average and, indeed, also above the regional average (Table 6.1).

A detailed local survey of the handicapped in the community, undertaken in Newcastle in 1983/4, sheds some light on the prevalence and pattern of ill health in the city (Newcastle District Health Authority and Newcastle City Council, 1984). This study estimated that there were

20,500 handicapped men, women and children in Newcastle, living in 18,000 private households (8% of the population and 17% of all households). Over a third (7,000) were aged over 74 and the highest proportions of handicapped people were mainly found in the least affluent areas of the city. Over the 10 years since a similar survey was conducted, the number of significantly handicapped people had increased by 7%, despite a reduction in the total population of about 10%. This trend is related in part to the increasing numbers of the elderly population in the city during this period—the number of people aged 75 and over increased by 19% between 1971 and 1981.

The main cause of handicap was found to be diseases of the bones and organs of movement, in particular arthritis, which accounted for over half of this group. 34% of the handicapped were disabled because of these diseases and altogether over half of the handicapped suffered restricted movement to some degree. It was estimated that 3,700 women over the age of 60 suffer from arthritis in Newcastle. Men in their 50s and 60s in particular suffered from heart disease and other diseases of the circulatory system, and it is estimated that 2,000 men between 50 and 75 are affected in this manner in Newcastle. The survey indicated that about 400 people were mentally handicapped in the City, but over twice as many were mentally ill or suffering from personality disorders.

The report on this survey of the disabled and handicapped in the community concluded by raising a number of important issues concerning the future of social and health care in Newcastle:

- An increase in the numbers of handicapped people in the community is to be expected, mainly due to the increase of the elderly population aged 75 and over. The proportionate increase is likely to be greatest amongst the more highly dependent groups, partly as a result of care in the community policies and also because of the growing number of very elderly people.
- Informal carers, relatives, neighbours and friends make a significant contribution to the care of the handicapped. It was noted that this contribution *far outweighs that of either statutory or voluntary services*. Most of these informal carers are women.
- If projections for increasing numbers of highly dependent handicapped people living on their own are correct, there are major implications for service provision—district nurses, home helps, meals on wheels, social workers, and aids and adaptations. The provision of care in the community should involve careful co-ordination of a range of services, together with sensitive support for informal carers.

This survey thus revealed the considerable needs which have to be met to ensure that 'care in the community' is effective. About 8% of Newcastle's population—a figure thought to be similar to the national average—regard themselves as handicapped to some degree, and this proportion is rising, adding to the demands on statutory and voluntary services, and above all, on the informal carers.

Deprivation and Health

In their recent work on inequalities in health, Townsend and his colleagues selected four indicators to represent material deprivation in the Northern Region: unemployment, car ownership, house ownership and overcrowding. On all these measures, the North clearly emerges as relatively deprived in comparison with national averages, and Tyneside itself is even more deprived than the Region (Table 6.8).

TABLE 6.8. SELECTED MEASURES OF DEPRIVATION, TYNESIDE, NORTHERN REGION AND ENGLAND & WALES

Local Authority	unempl.	houshlds witht. car	houshlds overcrowd.[1]	Houshlds not owner occupied	Class IV & V houshlds[2]
	%	%	%	%	%
Gateshead	14.2	57.2	4.9	61.4	26.8
Newcastle	14.5	58.8	4.6	61.1	23.5
North Tyneside	12.6	52.9	3.3	55.1	22.1
South Tyneside	17.0	59.5	4.6	68.5	26.8
Northern Region	13.5	48.3	3.8	52.9	25.2
England & Wales	9.8	38.5	3.4	42.2	21.7

Source: Townsend *et.al.*, 1988, Table 6.3; from 1981 Census of Population.
Notes: 1. Overcrowded households defined as living at a density of more than one person per room.
2. Class IV and V households: with semi or unskilled manual head of household.

Townsend found a clear statistical correlation between material deprivation and poor health in the North. However, links between the two do need elucidation, and here we look specifically at two factors—housing and unemployment—and their relationship with health.

Housing and health

Mess regarded overcrowding as a crucial factor in relation to ill health, contributing to the spread of infection and linked particularly to disease amongst children. Without doubt, overcrowding was a severe problem in Tyneside, much more serious than in most other parts of the country because of the preponderance of small houses (and Tyneside flats) and large families. Since Mess's time, much progress has, of course, been made in tackling this problem—to the point where, by 1981, the incidence of overcrowding in Tyneside was below the national average (see Chapter 5).

Nevertheless, overcrowding is still a problem in some parts of Tyneside, notably in the inner areas along the river. In Scotswood, the worst ward in Newcastle for overcrowding, 12.3% of households lived at densities of more than 1 person per room in 1981, compared to only 0.8% in South Gosforth, the least overcrowded ward.

Very considerable improvements have also been made in the provision of basic household amenities, such that today nearly all Tyneside's households have an inside WC and a bath. However, overcrowding and the provision of amenities are only part of the picture; there are still people throughout Tyneside living in poor or unsuitable housing, perhaps not overcrowded or lacking amenities but characterised by such problems as condensation and damp penetration, structural faults, disrepair, excessive noise and inaccessibility to basic services.

Local studies provide some confirmation of the continuing importance of the link between poor housing and poor health. In a survey of 360 children admitted to a paediatric unit in Gateshead, for example, 19% of children suffering respiratory disease (a major cause of admission) lived in overcrowded conditions—houses with an average of more than 1.5 persons per room—a proportion well above the 6% of overcrowded households in the area (Holohan, 1978). In addition, the study revealed that two Gateshead wards, Bensham and Riverside , had disproportionately large numbers of sick children and both had a high percentage of households lacking basic amenities and also had high levels of unemployment.

Another local study (Byrne *et al.*, 1986) examined the relationship between housing and health in Council-built accommodation in Gateshead. Comparing self-reported illness with the national *General Household Survey*, this sample was found to be in considerably worse health. The differences were most marked in relation to acute illness. In 1982, the GHS reported 10% of females and 13% of males suffering from illness restricting normal activity. The corresponding figures in this Gateshead study were 34% for females and 24% for males. In an interesting innovation, respondents' perceptions of the relationship between housing and health were elicited. 31% of households reported structural defects which they directly associated with health problems among household members; and for 'difficult-to-let' estates this rose to 51%. One of the factors mentioned in the Black Report (DHSS, 1980) as a cause of ill health was inadequate heating; as many as 42% of households in this Gateshead study said they were unable, due to costs, to keep warm in the winter, and the diseases they associated with such conditions were respiratory diseases, rheumatism and arthritis. Data on the health of children, as assessed by the mother, revealed disturbing differences between housing areas. Again, in 'difficult-to-let' areas children were more likely than those in better areas to have experienced recent illness, in particular, frequent chesty coughs and wheezy chests. As the writers comment: 'bad housing has a harmful effect from an early age, and causes children in 'bad' housing areas to have more health problems than those in 'good' areas'. Indeed, they concluded their report by suggesting that 'mass housing has proved to be an expensive social disaster, not least in health terms'.

A recent study of housing conditions and health in Edinburgh (Martin *et.al.*, 1987) confirms that children living in damp houses, especially where fungal mould is present, had higher rates of respiratory disease (which were unrelated to smoking in the household), and higher rates of symptoms of infection and stress. It is clear from such studies that housing should remain an important public health issue. In addition, it should also be borne in mind that early exposure to an adverse living environment is likely to increase vulnerability to illness in later life—particularly to chronic respiratory disease, which continues to be a main cause of mortality and morbidity in Tyneside.

Unemployment and health

There is quite widespread agreement that unemployment has deleterious effects upon health. But this is a contentious issue and one which has, in the past, received remarkably little attention; indeed, as Smith (1987, p.183) points out, 'health authorities and health workers have been slow to wake up to the considerable health implications of mass unemployment'. The whole subject of unemployment and health is under-researched, especially the effects of unemployment on the family.

Unemployment undoubtedly has significant psychological effects, including stress and worry, loss of self-esteem, rejection, hopelessness and despair. It also has material consequences, with reduced income affecting patterns of consumption and the use of leisure. Both these factors appear to influence mortality and morbidity though the links remain to be established in detail: the epidemiology of unemployment is very complicated, not least because of the wide range of conditions associated with unemployment and the difficulty of testing hypotheses with often weak data and a variety of confounding variables (Smith, 1987, p.110). There may, in addition, be factors involved which have a positive influence, such as removal from exposure to health hazards at work— though this may be offset by more time spent in a damp house.

Brenner (1979) has argued that unemployment is positively correlated with trends in mortality, regarding unemployment as a threatening 'life event' which increases morbidity and, eventually, mortality (see also Moser *et. al.*, 1987). The children of unemployed people also appear to experience much higher levels of morbidity (MacLure and Stewart, 1984).

A local study undertaken in North Tyneside pointed to links between unemployment, deprivation and poor health (Colledge, 1981) and connections between deprivation and health in the North have been explored by Townsend *et.al.* (1988). Probably the most *clear-cut* relationship emerging from the research on the issue is the link between unemployment and poor mental health (Platt, 1984). Certainly, suicide and parasuicide have been found to be more common among the unemployed, and stress and resulting family tension are frequently associated with unemployment. There is some limited local evidence, from North Tyneside, of a direct link between rising unemployment and increased psychiatric admissions (Kenny, 1980).

The relationship between unemployment and health remains unclear and needs further study, especially at the local level. Most would agree, however, that high unemployment exacerbates health problems in Tyneside.

The Provision of Health Services in Tyneside

Hospitals

Mess's description of hospitals serving Tyneside in the 1920s suggests a somewhat complicated and inadequate provision. The largest general hospital at that time was the Royal Victoria Infirmary (RVI) in Newcastle, with 572 beds, which served the whole of the four Northern Counties. Tyneside's other general hospitals included the Ingham Infirmary at South Shields and Tynemouth Jubilee Infirmary, as well as several smaller hospitals. There were special hospitals, too—for children, for eye treatments and skin diseases, for example. In addition, there were the Poor Law Hospitals, which Mess described as good, despite their age, and the municipal isolation hospitals. Mess felt that the most serious deficiency lay with these isolation hospitals, some of which were 'very bad indeed', had poor sanitation, old premises, insufficient accommodation and where patients sometimes caught other infections. Mess concluded with a plea for a permanent hospital council for Tyneside to review provision, secure co-ordination, eliminate waste and fill gaps in provision.

Since the formation of the NHS in 1948, hospital provision has been greatly improved. There has also been a major growth in the numbers of medical, nursing and auxiliary staff and a large increase in skills and specialised work.Old fever hospitals and TB sanatoria have been closed and remaining hospitals substantially upgraded. The RVI, for example, has seen a great deal of new development, and new hospitals, such as the Freeman, have been built. The three general hospitals in Newcastle have many regional speciality units such as those for cancer treatment, kidney failure, transplantation and neurosurgery and benefit, too, from direct links with the Medical School at Newcastle University. The new Freeman

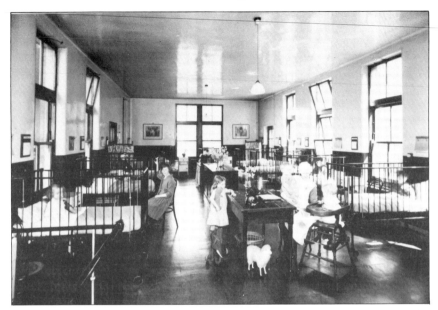

A children's ward at the Fleming Memorial Hospital for Sick Children in the 1930s. (*Newcastle upon Tyne City Libraries and Arts*).

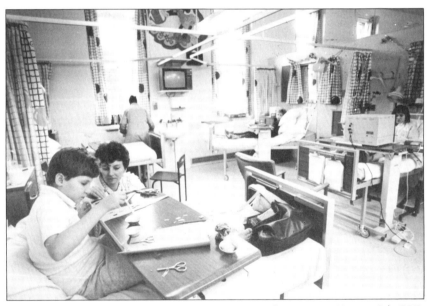

Making Christmas decorations in the new children's wards at Newcastle's RVI, 1987. These wards have been opened to replace accommodation at the Fleming which was closed in Autumn 1987. The new wards have mother and baby rooms, with facilities for treatment, play and relaxation. (*Newcastle Chronicle & Journal*).

Hospital, opened in 1978, has a purpose-built Regional Cardiothoracic Centre which was the third in the country to be recognised for special funding for heart transplantation. In addition, the care of mentally ill and handicapped persons is moving from institutions, originally custodial but later more therapeutic, to a range of community-based resources backed up by small units in general hospitals. This will eventually lead to the profound change, if not the demise, of the original 'asylums' of St. Mary's, St. George's, and St. Nicholas Hospitals.

Hospital provision has been rationalised, concentrated at a smaller number of larger hospitals. Just before the War, in 1938, Tyneside had a total of 38 hospitals, providing altogether 4,993 beds.By 1985, Tyneside had 29 hospitals, though the number of beds has stayed much the same (5,053 in 1985). The throughput of inpatients has, however, almost quadrupled over the past fifty years as the length of stays in hospital has shortened. Nationally, the average length of stay for acute cases has fallen from 11 days in 1975 to less than 8 days in 1985; moreover, while the number of beds decreased slightly over the period 1975–85, the number of inpatients treated rose by 27%. It is expected that inpatient stay will shorten still further and admissions will increase; alongside this, a further reduction in the number of hospitals in Tyneside is forecast.

If we examine the common causes of admission to general hospitals in Tyneside in 1985, malignant disease, especially of the lung, breast, stomach, colon and rectum, top the list, followed by diabetes, 'glue ear' (an ear infection in children), coronary heart disease, heart failure, stroke, varicose veins, and tonsils and adenoids. In contrast with the 1920s, very few beds are now for infectious disease, and considerably more are in use for geriatric patients.

Hospital services are by far the largest sector of the NHS, absorbing around 60% of the overall health care resources and involving expenditure equivalent to an annual average of £325 per person (1985 figures). One of the main factors contributing to the financial expansion of the NHS has been the growing numbers of the old or very old in the population; not only is their episodic demand for health care higher, but each period of treatment tends to last longer than for younger patients. Average expenditure on health care for the over 75s is more than ten times greater than the average outlay on people of working age and the growth of the 'elderly elderly' puts increasing pressure on NHS resources. In addition, advances in technology add to the pressure in terms of investment, staffing requirement and costs arising from higher rates of survival (for example, the heart transplant programme at the Freeman Hospital treated around 50 people in 1987 at a cost of £1 million).

In Tyneside—as in many other areas—NHS resources are being stretched to the limit and there are staff shortages, particularly affecting nursing provision. The severity of the financial crisis became particularly

The Freeman Hospital, opened in 1978. (*Newcastle City Engineer's Department*).

apparent in 1986 when the Newcastle District Health Authority, faced with a shortfall of £3.5 milion, found it necessary to save money by carrying out a number of ward closures (TUSIU, 1986). Despite such efforts to reduce expenditure there remains a shortfall in funding, especially for medical and surgical equipment. Newcastle District Health Authority has commented that:

> 'Essentially the Authority is spending every penny which it has to maintain patient services at current levels and there are no reserves to protect it against the vagaries of fortune... The cracks in the Newcastle service are widening and the paper [to conceal them] is growing increasingly thin' (Newcastle DHA, 1987).

Such comments could serve also for Tyneside's other District Health Authorities. The service is under pressure, especially in the hospitals, and it remains to be seen whether more government finance or new private sector arrangements will bring an alleviation of these problems.

Family practitioner services

The Family Practitioner Services include the General Medical, General Dental, Pharmaceutical and Ophthalmic Services. These services, administered by Family Practitioner Committees, are provided by professionals who are independent contractors and are funded directly by central government rather than local health authorities. Expenditure on these services in the UK as a whole in 1986 amounted to £4,484 million, representing an average of £79 per person (Office of Health Economics, 1987). In real terms, expenditure on Family Practitioner Services has doubled since 1949 while the hospital sector has seen a fourfold increase over that period.

In 1985 there were some 32,355 General Practitioners ('GPs' or family doctors) in the UK, providing free medical care under the NHS. Practically everyone in the population is registered as an NHS patient. For most, the family doctor is the first point of contact with primary health care facilities and it is usually through the family doctor that access to hospital and specialist treatment is obtained. The number of GPs has been growing both regionally and nationally; the Northern Region had 1,656 GPs in 1985, an 18% increase on 1975, which compares with a 20% increase for England as a whole. It is worth noting however, that the numbers of hospital doctors have grown even faster to respond to new demands on hospital services, including those brought about by an ageing population and technological developments.

The level of provision of GPs in Tyneside is very close to the national average (Newcastle FPC, 1986). But there is evidence that the more deprived groups in disadvantaged areas of Tyneside have difficulties in obtaining access to GPs and related services. Local surveys seem to indicate that a key problem with GP services in Tyneside is accessibility. This appears to be especially difficult in some inner city areas and also in some large peripheral estates (Knox, 1979). A study by the Gateshead Community Health Council in 1983 on the needs and problems of the Saltmeadows Estate pointed to the absence of health services on the estate itself, while visits for antenatal care, in particular, involved lengthy and expensive bus journeys to the town centre. There are similar problems with access to dental services—with the highest provision in affluent areas and the lowest in the more deprived areas (Carmichael, 1985). Lack of a car and a telephone add to the problems faced by disadvantaged groups in gaining access to GPs and other services.

The number of prescriptions issued by GPs has steadily increased and certainly has grown enormously since the 1920s. In Mess's time, many ailments were treated not with drugs but with homely remedies. For rheumatism, for example, sufferers were advised to 'avoid wet and wear flannel, and take no malt, sugar or pastry': by contrast, in 1985, 22 million rheumatic preparations a year were prescribed by GPs. The total NHS drugs bill is now very substantial, at over £2,000 million a year.

Despite some problems of access to GP services, the higher incidence of ill health in the region does seem to be borne out by statistics on prescription rates and GP consultation rates. In the Northern Region, an average of 7.5 prescriptions per head were issued in 1985, compared with the average for England of 6.8 (Office of Health Economics, 1987). This provides a crude measure of morbidity; only the North West area (with 8.5 prescriptions per head) and the Mersey area (8.1 per head) exceeded the figure for the Northern Region. This pattern is repeated for GP consultations per head of the population, with the North recording a figure of 4.7 consultations per head a year compared with a national figure of 4.3. Again, this was only exceeded by the North West and Mersey areas.

Community services

Mess made no mention of care for the mentally ill, the mentally handicapped or the elderly. Today, these groups represent a major part of the demand for health care. The increasing survival of the very old and greater recognition of mental illness have meant that some 60% of hospital inpatients are now in the geriatric and psychiatric sectors.

In recent years, a prime concern of policy has been to try to reduce the numbers of such patients in institutional care and instead provide community-based services. In reality, however, this often shifts the burden of care onto relatives, normally the nearest female relative. Care *in* the community seems often to result in care *by* the community, with little support from the state. This can place considerable pressure on carers. Without doubt, care in the community can provide a better quality of life for many people who are now in institutional care, but this should not be at the excessive cost of the quality of life experienced by carers (Newcastle District Health Authority and Newcastle City Council, 1987).

In respect of provision for the mentally ill, it is clear that in Tyneside the shift from hospital care to community care has been slow. There is a considerable shortfall in residential accommodation and day care places; provision has been growing but is well below the number of places required to meet guidelines drawn up by the DHSS. In 1986 there were 128 residential places (hostel and long-stay residential places) for the mentally ill in Tyneside while DHSS guidelines suggest a need for 253 places. Tyneside had 225 day care places for the mentally ill in 1986, compared with DHSS guidelines of 505 places.

Newcastle stands out as providing a much higher level of provision than the other Tyneside districts—indeed, it is among the biggest spenders on mental health care in the country. The Audit Commission (1986) has estimated that a gross expenditure of at least £2 per head of population by Social Services Departments is necessary to provide *basic* care for mentally ill people in the community. In the whole Northern Region, only Newcastle reached this minimum (gross expenditure of £2.25 per head in

1985–6), while North Tyneside spent £1.26, Gateshead £0.97, and South Tyneside only £0.86 per head (Richardson, 1988). There is also a considerable shortfall in staff needed to implement community care: in Tyneside there are only 44 community psychiatric nurses, well below the DHSS guideline figure of 81. A recent report on mental health care in the North by MIND pointed out that there was not just the need to spend more, but also argued for the faster implementation of community care, greater service integration and a more accessible, sensitive and innovative approach (Richardson, 1988). The report—strongly criticised by the Northern RHA—concluded that 'the Northern Region is arguably the worst place in England to become mentally ill'; patients here are more likely to be hospitalised, be treated with ECT (electroconvulsive therapy) and psychotropic drugs, rather than receive alternatives like psychotherapy and remain in the community.

More encouragingly, however, some new community-based initiatives are being implemented in parts of Tyneside. In North Tyneside, for instance, the Health Authority is developing a new community psychiatric nursing service and a Day Hospital for the mentally ill. The voluntary sector is also increasingly active: for example, the Northern Schizophrenia Fellowship, a registered charity, is supporting Day Centres, clubs and sheltered workshops and is planning a hostel in conjunction with Newcastle Health Authority.

Mental health care in the community at Rosehill Day Centre, Howdon. This Centre, run by the Northern Schizophrenia Fellowship, offers a range of activities and assistance for those with practical and emotional problems. (*Mark Pinder*).

Increasing awareness of the burden placed on those caring for the mentally ill and the elderly has led to the development of support schemes to give some respite to families. Newcastle's carers support schemes provide surrogate carers who will carry out any task done by an informal carer such as basic nursing, personal care, providing food and drink, escorting, advice and general support. Such services do not replace home helps but complement them (Newcastle City Council, 1986). In addition, Newcastle has a District Nursing Service offering round-the-clock care and a mental handicap nursing scheme which supports severely handicapped people in their own homes. Alongside this service, several small homes, with care staff, have been developed in the Newcastle area to help children and young adults returning to the community from long-stay institutions; here the aim is to provide a non-institutionalised 'home for life', encouraging independence and integration. For the elderly, a particularly successful and popular initiative is the formation of care teams comprising community nurses (Macleod and Main, 1985). These teams offer a health assessment service on an 'outreach' basis, identifying and screening elderly people in the community and encouraging clinic attendance or home visits; they provide a service which many GP's practices could not offer themselves.

Preventive medicine

Traditionally, preventive medicine has largely concerned public health legislation. In Tyneside, the 1956 Clean Air Act has undoubtedly had an impact, especially in reducing respiratory disease. Subsequent legislation in such areas as consumer protection and health and safety at work have also reduced some health hazards, preventing accidents and ill health. But both nationally and locally, increasing attention has recently been focussed on a broader conception of preventive approaches to health. Over the last ten years there has been a substantial increase in lobby groups (against smoking, for example); greater public interest and awareness of the relationship between health and lifestyle; and the growth and development of self-help groups and local projects. At the same time, there has been mounting concern that preventive medicine is under-resourced and a growing recognition that this field of medicine needs to be accorded greater priority (HMSO, 1988).

Preventive medicine embraces a number of interrelated issues. First, it ties in to a recognition of the need for social and economic change, notably to improve housing conditions and reduce unemployment—factors which have a substantial impact on health. Here the call has been for greater social justice, a need emphasised in the Health Education Council's controversial report *The Health Divide* (Whitehead, 1987). A second issue is that of education, promoting an increased awareness of health care and the availability of health services. Related to this is the need to ensure that services are more accessible and are tailored to the needs of clients. Thus, in their report on *Deprivation and Health*, the British Medical Association points out that traditional methods of health education have not always been successful in reaching less advantaged members of society, and new methods, including community initiatives, should be explored (BMA, 1987). This report commented that antenatal care, child health surveillance, immunisation and cervical screening services are all underused by disadvantaged groups and there is a clear need for more—and more effective—health education and service delivery.

In Tyneside there are certainly indications of an increasing emphasis on prevention and new initiatives are being explored. The District Health Authorities have set up health promotion and disease prevention groups to produce policies and stimulate discussion on topics such as smoking, accident prevention, alcohol, heart disease and diet. Newcastle has developed a call and recall scheme for cervical screening, and breast screening is planned to start in 1989/90. But resource problems are holding back such initiatives; Tyneside's health authorities have reported, for example, that new schemes to detect cervical cancer are being hampered by insufficient computer facilities. The Community Health Councils are also actively pursuing preventive approaches. In addition, there is a range of other initiatives such as 'Look After Your Heart' campaigns; a health education caravan at festivals and public events in the region; the provision of health education material in other languages; and the encouragement of self-help groups and community projects.

The Walker Health Project – a seriously underfunded health initiative based in one of Tyneside's most deprived areas. This group meets regularly at the Project to learn about, prepare, and share healthy meals in a friendly environment which offers mutual support and company. (*Walker Health Project*).

Among the local projects is the Walker Health Project set up in Newcastle in 1982 to look at ways of giving people greater opportunities for better health. Regular sessions at the Walker Centre include a Women's Group, a Food Group and a Health Project shop. A community worker is also available to give advice and a new Health Discussion Group is being formed. Another local project is the Riverside Centre in Newcastle which provides help with child care, runs support and discussion groups and offers information on various health topics ranging from stopping smoking to sexually-transmitted diseases. In North Tyneside the Community Health Council is developing a Well Woman Centre to provide help and support specifically for women. In North Shields, South Shields and Gateshead, Alcohol and Drug Advisory Services have been set up. A Tranquilliser Advice and Support Project—one of only three in the country—has also been established in Newcastle in conjunction with the recently-formed North East Council on Addictions. And the need for preventive medicine has been recognised by the local press, with Newcastle's *Evening Chronicle* running a campaign to encourage the immunisation of children to protect them from whooping cough and measles—the take-up rate for immunisation was, until recently, low in the area.

Present Dilemmas and Future Strategies

AIDS

The most serious *new* threat to public health, now receiving a great deal of publicity, is AIDS (Acquired Immune Deficiency Syndrome). By 1986 it was estimated that, world-wide, 10 million people had become infected with the human immunodeficiency virus since its discovery at the beginning of the decade. By December 1987, 1,227 cases had been recorded in the UK, 697 of which had resulted in death, but the number of those infected was estimated at up to 30,000. It is thought that there could be between 5,000 and 40,000 deaths a year in the UK in the mid-1990s, mainly of young people. The number will depend entirely on whether sexual practices and the use of intravenous drugs change. The vast majority of AIDS cases and deaths have been in the South East (935 [76%] of the 1,227 cases recorded in the UK by December 1987 were in the four Thames health areas). At present the majority of cases are in haemophiliacs, male homosexuals, and intravenous drug users. The Northern Region had recorded 31 cases, including 22 deaths, the third highest total for areas outside the South East.

A number of clinical departments in Newcastle, including the Haemophilia Centre, the Sexually Transmitted Diseases Clinic, the Infectious Diseases Unit, and the laboratory services, have rapidly introduced services. Liaison between these departments, the Health

Authority's Health Education Unit, voluntary organisations such as AIDS North, and the local authority services have been developed. In addition, a unique care scheme for AIDS sufferers, their relatives and friends, is being set up in Newcastle. This involves collaboration between the Northern RHA, the City Council's social services department and voluntary organisations. Direct patient care will be provided at home and in hospital by team members, who will work alongside existing community staff. The Region's recently appointed AIDS Service Co-ordinator has stressed the value of this multi-disciplinary strategy to support sufferers and their families, and it is expected to provide a model for the rest of the country.

The resource implications of AIDS are considerable since expenditure per patient is currently estimated at around £18,000; by mid-1987 over a quarter of a million pounds had been spent in the North helping victims who subsequently died and a similar amount will be spent on current sufferers. The government has provided 'new' money to help the health authorities cope with the problem but it is unlikely to be enough: Regional Health Authorities and Social Services Departments could well face increasingly difficult resource priority decisions in the future.

AIDS raises a wide variety of difficult issues[5] which need attention and action, including: the confidentiality of screening and whether it is to be compulsory; the role of the social services in providing community support; the choice of hospice or hospital care; dispelling fear of the disease, especially for those providing care in the community; the issue of free needles to drug addicts to reduce transmission of the disease; and an end to victimisation in access to insurance, housing and jobs. Finally, research into the disease process itself, treatment, and possible prevention and cure, and the best methods of changing sexual behaviour, are essential priorities in the years ahead.

The NHS and the future

By 1986/7, total NHS expenditure in England reached £16 billion a year. NHS expenditure has been continually increasing and the Northern Region has shared in this growth, with a 12% real increase in NHS resources between 1974 and 1984. This growth in resources has meant more patients being treated and a significant increase in the numbers of doctors and nurses. The North has been helped by efforts to re-allocate NHS resources more fairly between the regions and has benefited from new innovations—for example, the establishment of the heart transplant unit at Newcastle's Freeman Hospital.

However, the increase in NHS spending has not matched growth in demand arising from demographic changes and rising expectations. Demand for health care services appears infinite, forever increasing: the more doctors do for patients the greater their rate of survival, resulting in increased demand for treatment of degenerative disease in old age.

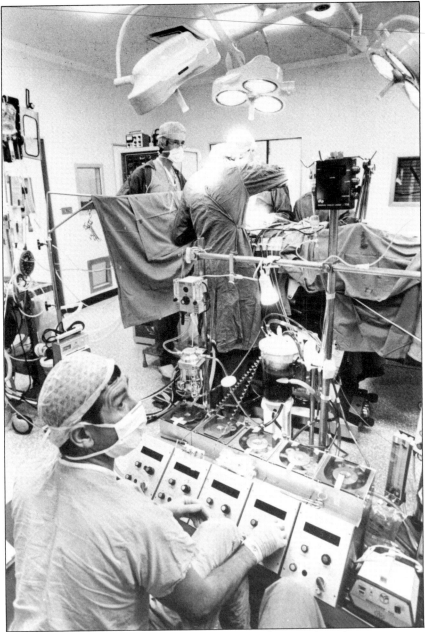

Technological developments such as 'high-tech' cardiothoracic surgery put pressure on NHS resources. This operation at the Freeman in 1988, to replace the heart valve and bypass the coronary artery of a 57-year-old woman, took five hours to perform. 600 bypass operations are performed at the Freeman each year. (*Newcastle Chronicle & Journal*).

The NHS is thus widely seen to be in a state of permanent crisis, with long waiting lists, staff shortages and concern about the quality of care. Moreover, there are still major (and growing) inequalities in provision and the service is criticised for inefficiency and lack of accountability. There are also major ethical issues, notably in relation to pregnancy termination, embryo research and the level of technical care to be given to the elderly.

In recent years there has been a considerable shift towards private sector provision as an alternative to the NHS and pressure for the privatisation of services within the NHS. Nationally, the number of private hospitals and clinics has grown (resulting in a substantial decrease in the number of pay beds within NHS hospitals). A great many elderly people requiring long-term care are now catered for in private residential and nursing homes (Tyneside had as many as 79 private homes for the elderly and physically handicapped by 1987). And private medical insurance is becoming increasingly common in Britain. The next few years will certainly see even greater encouragement and further growth of private health care; there are, for example, calls for more privatisation of a wide range of ancillary services and hospital management, and tax relief schemes to encourage private medical insurance.

Tyneside will clearly continue to be affected by this shift in emphasis to private sector health service provision, though it will undoubtedly remain the case that the overwhelming majority of people will still be wholly dependent on the NHS. Compared with London and the South of England, Tyneside has little private health care: in the North generally only 3% of the population were covered by private health insurance in 1982 compared with 13% in outer London (Laing, 1985). For most Tynesiders there is, therefore, no alternative to the NHS and its maintenance, growth and development is thus of crucial importance to the area.

Conclusion: Health for All?

This chapter has highlighted inequalities in health: on most indices, Tyneside's mortality and morbidity are worse than the national average. Material deprivation is a key underlying factor in generating these inequalities, though lifestyle factors are certainly important as well.

It has long been argued that the medical profession is in a special position to assess the impact of socio-economic circumstances on health; they form a powerful lobby but have remained, apart from some notable exceptions, singularly muted over the past few decades. Thus the publication of the British Medical Association's report, *Deprivation and Health*, can be seen as something of a breakthrough, an important step forward by the profession in speaking out on issues of deprivation and inequalities in health. In the conclusions to that report, the BMA makes it clear that no amount of redistribution of resources within the health and social services sector will resolve the health problems caused by deprivation. Increased resources for housing, employment creation, income support, education, health and social services are needed. Although low-cost initiatives are possible which might alleviate the health problems of some disadvantaged groups, 'the problem as a whole is so great and so entrenched within the structure of society as to be insoluble without significant diversion of public resources' (BMA, 1987). Such statements are of particular relevance to Tyneside.

As far as health care provision is concerned, the late 1980s has witnessed a deepening crisis in the NHS nationally and locally. The big issue is the question of resources. On the one hand, increases in finance have not fully met pay rises and the costs of inflation, while on the other hand, demand and costs are rising as a result of an ageing population and technological developments. New initiatives, such as screening, add to the pressure. Firmer management control has helped—but there were still 9,000 people on waiting lists for inpatient care in Newcastle in March 1987. Inability to meet demand means difficult decisions have to be made about priorities, often involving moral, ethical and political issues. At the same time, there are new challenges and new calls on resources—for funding community care and preventive medicine, for example.

A great deal has been achieved over the last sixty years; people in Tyneside enjoy better health and health care and live longer. It remains to be seen whether advances in health care will be available to all or whether the gap between levels of public and private sector provision will widen, along with a deepening division between the affluent and the deprived. 'Health for All' should be the aim for Tyneside in the future.

NOTES

1. The health and development of a sample of over 1000 children born in Newcastle in 1947 was studied for a period of 15 years. The first report on this study (Spence *et.al.*, 1954) showed that important improvements in health were taking place; even then, however, 10% of children in the sample had whooping cough in the first year of life. The second report (Miller *et.al.*, 1960) looked at the first five years and this was followed by a final report on the sample up to the age of 15 (Miller *et.al*, 1974).
2. Between 1912/13 and 1935/37 mortality rates from tuberculosis fell by almost a half in England and Wales, and in Gateshead and South Shields fell by nearly two-thirds. Blaydon in 1935/37 was Tyneside's 'blackspot' since tuberculosis deaths had fallen by only 20% (see Goodfellow, 1940).
3. Average weekly household expenditure on tobacco in the North was £5.02 in 1985–6, compared with a UK average of £4.49. *Total* average weekly household expenditure in the North was £146.59, while the average for the UK was £173.89 (Department of Employment, 1987).
4. Average weekly household expenditure on alcoholic drink was £8.73 in the North in 1985–6, compared with £8.18 for the UK (Department of Employment, 1987)
5. The issues raised by AIDS are not completely new. Mess noted the reappearance of smallpox—there were as many as 400 cases of the disease in Blaydon alone in 1925—and stressed the importance of vaccination. It is worth recalling (now that smallpox has been eliminated) that vaccination was compulsory within six months of the birth of a child; the public good was regarded as paramount, taking precedence over the rights of the individual. The issue of contact-tracing has been well-established in the case of venereal disease; in fact, Tyneside pioneered tracing, introducing a unique experimental scheme in 1943 to contact and trace the network of people associating with a known case of the disease in order to provide treatment and control infection.

REFERENCES

Audit Commission for Local Authorities in England & Wales (1986) *Making a Reality of Community Care*. London: HMSO.

Brenner, M.H. (1979) Mortality and the National Economy: A Review, and the experience of England and Wales. *Lancet*, 1979; ii: 568–73.

British Medical Association (BMA) (1987) *Deprivation and Ill Health*. BMA Board of Science and Education. London: BMA.

Byrne, D.S., Harrison, S.R., Keithley, J. and McCarthy, P. (1986) *Housing and Health*. Aldershot: Gower.

Calnan, N. (1987) *Health and Illness*. London: Tavistock.

Carmichael, C.L. (1985) Inner-city Britain—A Challenge for the Dental Profession in Inner-city Newcastle. *British Dental Journal*, 159 (1), 24–7.

Colledge, M. (1981) *Unemployment and Health*. North Shields: North Tyneside Community Health Council.

Department of Employment (1987) *Family Expenditure Survey, 1986*. London: HMSO.

Department of Health and Social Security (DHSS) (1980). *Inequalities in Health: Report of a Research Working Group* ('Black Report'). London: DHSS.

Goodfellow, D.M. (1940) *Tyneside: The Social Facts*. Newcastle: Co-operative Printing Society.

Graham, H. (1985) *Health and Welfare*. London: MacMillan.

HMSO (1988) *Public Health in England*. Cmnd. 289. London: HMSO.

Holohan, A. (1978) The Court Report and Acute Illness in Children in a Northern Town. *Health and Social Service Journal*, 88, 23–28.

Kenny, M. (1980) *Effects of Unemployment on Health*. North Shields: North Tyneside Community Health Council.

Knox, P.L. (1979) The Accessibility of Primary Care to Urban Patients. *Journal of the Royal College of General Practitioners*, 29 (220), 160–8.

Laing, W. (1985) *Private Health Care*. London: Office of Health Economics.

Macleod, E. and Main, P. (1985) The Nursing Care Team: A Task Force Approach. *Royal College of General Practitioners, Occasional Paper, 35*.

Maclure, A. and Stewart, G.T. (1984) Admission of Children to Hospital in Glasgow: Relation to Unemployment and other Deprivation Variables. *Lancet*, 1984, ii: 682–5.

Martin, C.J., Platt, S.D. and Hunt, S. (1987) Housing Conditions and Health. *British Medical Journal*, 294, 1125–27.

Miller, F.J.W., Court, S.D.M., Walton, W.S. and Knox, E.G. (1960) *Growing Up in Newcastle upon Tyne*. Oxford University Press.

Miller, F.J.W., Court, S.D.M., Knox, E.G. and Brandon, S. (1974) *The School Years in Newcastle upon Tyne, 1952–62*. Oxford University Press.

Moser, K.A., Goldblatt, P.O., Fox, A.J. and Jones, D.R. (1987) Unemployment and Mortality: Comparison of the 1971 and 1981 Longitudinal Census Samples. *British Medical Journal*, 294, 86–90.

Newcastle City Council (1986) *Respite Family Care and Mental Handicap in Newcastle*. Newcastle: City Council Policy Services and Social Services.

Newcastle District Health Authority (1987) *Budget Setting 1987/88 Papers*. Newcastle: Newcastle DHA.

Newcastle District Health Authority and Newcastle City Council (1984) *Disabled and Handicapped in the Community, 1972–84*. Newcastle DHA and Newcastle City Council.

Newcastle District Health Authority and Newcastle City Council (1987) *Carers' Support: A Review of Carers' Support in Newcastle, 1986–7*. Newcastle DHA and Newcastle City Council.

Newcastle Family Practitioner Committee (1986) *Annual Programme 1985–6*. Newcastle: Newcastle FPC.

Northern Regional Health Authority (1985) *Collaborative Survey of Perinatal and Late Neonatal Mortality*. Newcastle: Northern RHA.

Northern Regional Health Authority and Northern Action on Smoking and Health (ASH) (1984) *Keeping Tabs on the North*. Newcastle: Northern RHA and Northern ASH.

Office of Health Economics (1987) *Compendium of Health Statistics*. London: OHE.

Office of Population Censuses and Surveys (OPCS) (1977, 1987) *Vital Statistics: Local and Health Areas, England and Wales*. Series VS Nos.2 and 12. London ; HMSO.

Office of Population Censuses and Surveys (OPCS) (1986) *Abortion Statistics*. Series AB, No.12. London HMSO.

Office of Population Censuses and Surveys (OPCS) (1987a) *Mortality Statistics—Perinatal and Infant: Social and Biological Factors*. Series DH3 No.18. London: HMSO.

Office of Population Censuses and Surveys (OPCS) (1987b) *Mortality Statistics—Area*. Series DH5 No.12. London: HMSO.

Office of Population Censuses and Surveys (OPCS) (1987c) *General Household Survey 1985* (GHS). London: HMSO.

Patrick, D.L. and Scambler, G. (eds) (1982) *Sociology as Applied to Medicine*. London: Tindall.

Platt, S. (1984) Unemployment and Suicidal Behaviour: A Review of the Literature. *Social Science and Medicine.*, 19, 93–115.

Regional Working Party on Problem Drinking (1983) *Drinking Problems? Current Practice and Policy Guidelines for Industry, Commerce and the Helping Agencies*.

Richardson, K. (1988) *Let's Not Mince Words: The State of Mental Health Care in the Northern Region*. Gateshead: Northern MIND.

Smith, R. (1987) *Unemployment and Health: A Disaster and a Challenge*. Oxford: Oxford University Press.

South Tyneside Community Health Council (1984) *Community Health Services in South Tyneside. A Plan for Marketing*. South Shields: South Tyneside CHC.

Spence, J., Walton, W.S., Miller, F.J.W. and Court, S.D.M. (1954) *A Thousand Families in Newcastle upon Tyne*. Oxford University Press.

Townsend, P., Phillimore, P. and Beattie, A. (1987) *Health and Deprivation: Inequality and the North*. London: Croom Helm.

Trade Union Studies Information Unit (1986) *Cause for Concern: The State of Newcastle's NHS*. Newcastle: TUSIU.

Whitehead, M. (1987) *The Health Divide: Inequalities in Health in the 1980s*. London: Health Education Council.

7

TYNESIDE LIFE
Peter Hetherington and Fred Robinson

Tyneside has retained a strong and distinctive identity, perhaps less marked than in the past but still clearly evident. As Henry Mess pointed out, Tyneside's strong local characteristics and identity spring largely from its physical isolation—Cheviot Hills to the north, Pennines to the west, North Sea to the east and a great swathe of farmland between the north east of England and Yorkshire. This physical isolation has meant that Tyneside has remained 'more independent, more self-centred, more provincial . . . than Lancashire or Yorkshire, or almost any other great industrial area of England' (Mess, 1928, p.25). Both physically and culturally, Tyneside is certainly distinct from the rest of northern England, while there is no doubt that many people in Tyneside regard London and southern England as essentially another country.

The distinctiveness of Tyneside and its relative isolation is emphasised by the Geordie dialect, an adaptation of Northumbrian, characterised by that rolling 'burr', but given a blunter twang by those who moved to Tyneside during the nineteenth century. J.B. Priestley, visiting Tyneside on his 'English Journey' in 1933, called it 'most barbarous, monotonous and irritating'. He found objectionable 'the constant 'ay-ee, mon' or 'ay-ee yer b.....' of the men's talk and the never-ending 'hinnying' of the women'. Yet, nationally, Geordie is undoubtedly a popular dialect and carries with it a certain fierce pride and loyalty to the area. It has survived the onslaught of standardised grammar—and even received a little recognition and promotion in local publications like 'The Geordie Bible' and 'Larn Yersel Geordie'.

The place itself is a mixture of old and new, architectural gems and disasters as well as a great deal that is quite nondescript. The River Tyne is the central feature, giving the conurbation a focus (though a focus often seemingly ignored by Tynesiders) and strong physical features, particularly the steep gorge between Newcastle and Gateshead Newcastle city centre has some fine and gracious streets and buildings as well as some rather uninteresting, even ugly, modern architecture. The blend of old and new has not been wholly successful, but Newcastle is generally regarded as a reasonably pleasant city, probably better than most.

Mess noted that local people had a 'singular blindness to the almost incredible ugliness of a large part of the arca'. Priestley didn't like the look of the place any more than the dialect: 'I have a very distinct recollection of taking a great dislike to the whole district, which seemed to me so ugly that it made the West Riding towns look like inland resorts. The people were not so bad once you got to know them, though even to a Yorkshire lad they appeared uncouth'. He gave credit to Newcastle's 'sombre dignity' but was not favourably impressed by Gateshead: 'the whole town seemed to have been carefully planned by an enemy of the human race . . . no true civilisation could have produced such a town'.

Much has changed since then; the 'ugliness' witnessed by Mess and Priestley has largely disappeared. Housing conditions have been greatly improved and smoke control legislation has made the atmosphere much cleaner—most of the smoke-blackened buildings have been cleaned too. The landscape is now greener, especially along the river, where factories and shipyards have been swept away by the process of deindustrialisation. Without doubt, though, some of the 'sixties' redevelopment was insensitive, in some cases quite disastrous. Newcastle cannot be proud of the partial destruction of old Eldon Square, or the construction of the wholly undistinguished John Dobson Street, or the uncompromising Swan House office block. Likewise, Gateshead cannot be proud of its hideous concrete town centre or the flats at St. Cuthbert's village—once held to be a 'showpiece', now recognised as a damp concrete ghetto.

Although the modernising zeal of the 1960s brought quite considerable physical changes to Tyneside, these changes may in some ways be superficial. In a perceptive and complimentary essay, Austin Mitchell sees Tyneside and the North East as a 'living museum'—'last, loneliest, most loyal to the old ethos', where old-fashioned working-class values and culture survive. A 'way of life, dying in the rest of the country, is here perfectly preserved: its own language, a local culture . . . a real warmth and a built-in sense of superiority based on a clamorous inferiority complex' (Mitchell, 1986). Isolation, as he points out, breeds resentment—of London, the South, the different—yet also breeds local pride and a sense of community. Moreover, Tyneside's parochial conservatism has hardly been challenged by contact with other cultures since the area has such a small ethnic minority population.

But times have surely changed. Extraordinary though it may seem, Tyneside is not now famous for its manufacturing industries, but for its shopping malls, night clubs and flashy cocktail bars. The industries which sustained Tyneside's traditional styles of life have undergone severe contraction. National influences must be taking their toll of local characteristics. What, then, is now left that is distinctive about Tyneside and its 'Geordie' natives apart from the dialect? Has Andy Capp gone the way of the dinosaur and the dodo?

Beamish Museum – award-winning celebration of the past. This 'open-air museum' includes a reconstruction of a North Eastern town in the 1920s, complete with terraced houses, shops, pub, park and trams. (*Beamish Museum*).

Stereotypes, Images and Reality

'. . . the North East still suffers from the popular 'Andy Capp' image—little men in cloth caps struggling through a landscape of pits and back-to-back housing. The image stems from the region's proud industrial heritage . . .'

(Newcastle Chronicle and Journal, 1987, p.5)

Andy Capp—that drooping, cloth-capped, chain-smoking, beer-swilling, sexist, workshy cartoon character—is probably the best-known stereotype of the Geordie. It is a stereotype which has proved remarkably resilient and is popular with the media. Updated and rejuvenated, it reappeared in 'Auf Wiedersehen, Pet', a television series (produced in Birmingham) which followed the exploits of a gang of Tyneside building workers in Germany. In 1988, we even had the appalling re-emergence of Andy Capp himself—in a Thames TV series featuring James Bolam, the Geordie 'likely lad' who lives quietly in West Sussex when not lampooning Tyneside. The 'region's proud industrial heritage' also shows few signs of being forgotten—celebrated over again by Tyneside's new film-makers and sold, with great success, by the 'heritage industry'. Beamish Open Air Museum, along with dozens of smaller-scale attractions, keeps alive images of a Geordie past inhabited by Andy Capp's more respectable neighbours.

But the area's promotional agencies, the local authorities and much of the Labour Movement are anxious to destroy the Andy Capp stereotype and images of pit heaps and rows of terraced houses. They want, instead, to foster an image of a modern, progressive Tyneside of the 1980s—and they are having some success in 'selling' this new image of Tyneside and the wider region. Thus the current 'Great North' promotional campaign is intended to get rid of 'the myth of the downtrodden North' and 'reflect and encourage the positive mood of the region . . . to broadcast our region's strengths to the rest of the UK and overseas as part of the drive to bring new investment and opportunities'. It has increasingly become taboo to talk about problems or negative aspects of the area. Tyneside must now be portrayed in a positive light, since the new conventional wisdom is to talk the area up, not continually do it down, in the interests of encouraging investment and convincing a sceptical City (or preferably an overseas company) that Tyneside is the place to locate that new branch plant or build that new development.

The people that matter in Tyneside—the old industrial class-cum-gentry and the Labour Movement (those twin pillars of the local establishment) and also the newer self-made moguls—are busy promoting the new image. Back in 1986, Mrs Thatcher told them to stop being 'moaning minnies' and her advice has been taken to heart. The 'begging bowl mentality' is no longer acceptable in the area—nor does it cut much ice in Whitehall or Westminster. A new consensus has emerged in which 'problems' are played down, while 'enterprise' and 'opportunity' are the touchstones of the new orthodoxy. Those who persist in being 'moaning minnies' are now labelled disloyal, negative and intent on undermining the efforts to promote the area for new investment.

Certainly it is possible to point to aspects of Tyneside today which lend credence to this modern image. There is the neon shopping extravaganza of Eldon Square and its vast, outwardly anonymous rival, the MetroCentre, across the Tyne in Gateshead, successfully attracting a predominantly car-borne, high-spending, middle class clientele. There is some new Japanese industry—Komatsu at Birtley, Nissan at Washington—and some 'high-tech' businesses. There is apparently money around, though much of it may be credit. The region has, according to the market researchers at Tyne Tees TV, more 'style leaders' per head than any other region in Britain—youngsters who spend heavily on clothing, drink, music and cosmetics. Young people here 'like to express their individuality, they take their appearance seriously . . . like to experiment with new products, keep up with the latest fashions, and to stand out in a crowd' (Tyne Tees TV, 1987). Any observer in Newcastle's Bigg Market/Cloth Market/High Bridge area on a Friday or Saturday night will attest to this consciousness of fashion and high spending power.

'A way of life, dying in the rest of the country, is here perfectly preserved'. Sunday dinner-time at the Northumberland Arms, West Allotment, North Tyneside, 1985. (*Stan Gamester*).

Macey's Bar in the Groat Market, Newcastle, 1988 – a place for the young 'style leaders' of the 1980s. Designer clothes and 'sophisticated' drinks – no cloth caps, brown ale, dominoes or darts. (*George Pope, BBC North East*).

Could we now be witnessing the emergence of the post-Andy Capp stereotype—well-dressed, money to burn and, perhaps, little care for tomorrow? Has Tyneside now really grown affluent and shaken off its traditional ways? Are the old stereotypes now just history, resurrected to haunt us by the mischievous media?

Statistics presented in earlier chapters have highlighted the relative deprivation of Tyneside. Tynesiders are more likely to experience unemployment and less likely to own a house or a car than people in most other parts of the country. People here have a higher chance of dying younger and suffering from cancer or heart disease. More children leave school at the earliest opportunity but they are unlikely to find a permanent job. Moreover, average household income in this region is the lowest of *all* regions in the UK. (Table 7.1). Not surprisingly, a greater proportion of this smaller income is spent on the necessities of food, clothing and fuel: but housing is much cheaper so takes a smaller share of expenditure. The

TABLE 7.1. HOUSEHOLD INCOME AND EXPENDITURE, NORTHERN REGION, UK, AND SOUTH EAST, 1985–6.

	NORTHERN REGION[1]	UK	SOUTH EAST
INCOME			
Average weekly household income	£187.7	£225.4	£269.1
EXPENDITURE			
Average propn. of household expenditure spent on:			
Food, clothing, fuel	37.0%	33.4%	30.6%
Housing	15.0%	16.6%	18.5%
Alcohol & tobacco	9.4%	7.3%	6.2%
Durable household goods	6.6%	7.5%	8.2%
Transport, other goods/ services	32.0%	35.3%	36.6%
DURABLE GOODS			
Proportion of households with:			
Washing machine	85%	80%(GB)	75%
Telephone	73%	80%(GB)	86%
Video	26%	28%(GB)	32%
TRANSPORT			
Cars per 1000 population	214 (Tyne & Wear)	319	356

Source: Regional Trends, 23 (1988)
Note: 1. On account of the sample sizes used in the surveys of income and expenditure, figures are only available for the Northern Region as a whole but this data can be taken as a good indicator of circumstances in Tyneside. (The Northern Region comprises Tyne and Wear, Northumberland, Co. Durham, Cleveland and Cumbria).

chain-smoking and beer-swilling Andy Capp figure cannot be totally fictitious since we spend a greater proportion of our (smaller) income on alcohol and tobacco than in *all* other regions. The 'average' household is more likely to have a washing machine, less likely to have a phone and, contrary to popular belief, the percentage of households having videos is below the national average.

Austin Mitchell may well have a point when he says that 'air passengers landing at Newcastle are invited to put their watches back twenty years and the area has the feel of the 1960s without their prosperity' (Mitchell, 1986, p.68). It is not just a question of economics, though; it is also a matter of ideas and attitudes. These are hard to measure but part of the picture comes from statistics on voting behaviour, trade unionism and strikes (Table 7.2). The area undoubtedly remains loyal to the Labour Party as shown at the last General Election in 1987 and at local elections in 1988 which saw a significant swing to Labour in Tyneside. Allied to this, a high proportion of people are in trade unions and the area still has a relatively high incidence of strikes, though much lower than in the past.

TABLE 7.2. POLITICS, TRADE UNIONS AND STRIKES, NORTHERN REGION, UK AND SOUTH EAST

	NORTHERN REGION	UK	SOUTH EAST
POLITICS			
General Election, 1987:			
Proportion voting Labour	51.5%	30.8%	22.3%
Proportion voting Conservative	28.2% (Tyneside)	42.3%	52.2%
TRADE UNIONS			
Proportion of employees in a trade union, 1984.	72%	58%(GB)	45%
STRIKES			
Days lost per 1000 employees, 1986	215	89	41

Sources: Politics: Butler and Kavanagh, 1988 and *Dods Parliamentary Companion*, 1988.
Trade Unions: *Employment Gazette*, May 1988.
Strikes: *Regional Trends*, 23 (1988).

As elsewhere, Tyneside has the virtuous and the wicked. Around 7% to 9% attend church on Sunday in Tyne & Wear—a figure thought to be similar to the national average—though in the region as a whole 83% identify with the Christian faith by claiming a denominational affiliation. Churches have been closing in Tyneside but the number of church members has stabilised and there are signs of new growth (Longley and Spearing, 1986). By contrast, crime has been growing rapidly—a real boom industry in the area (Table 7.3), with a particularly high level of burglary, theft and criminal damage.

TABLE 7.3. CRIME IN THE NORTHERN REGION, ENGLAND AND SOUTH EAST

	NORTHERN REGION	ENGLAND	SOUTH EAST
Notifiable offences[1] per 100,000 popn.	9,648	7,764	7,706
Increase in notifiable offences, 1981–6	+41.6%	+28.1%	+24.3%

Source: Regional Trends, 23 (1988).
Note: 1. Notifiable offences recorded by the police. Around half these offences are theft and handling stolen goods.

Looking at averages and overall trends can be misleading, hiding from view the Andy Capps and also the yuppies. Tyneside has areas of considerable affluence and of severe poverty, great variations in unemployment rates (Chapter 3) and in premature mortality (Chapter 6). Indeed, divisions *within* Tyneside are as wide as any North-South divide. Henry Mess noted the contrasts between the 'pleasanter places' where the 'well-to-do' lived and the 'one-class towns' like Jarrow, Hebburn and Felling, and these contrasts remain sixty years later. Ponteland, for example, an affluent suburb just outside Newcastle's boundary is a sort of Henley-on-Tyne, a world away from the Geordie stereotype. But, even so, there are proportionately fewer affluent households in the North than in any other region and only Northern Ireland has a larger percentage of very poor households (Table 7.4). Tynesiders may feel a great loyalty to their area and feel satisfied with their quality of life but materially, at least, they are worse off than most of their counterparts in the rest of Britain.

TABLE 7.4. INCOME DISTRIBUTION, NORTH, UK AND SOUTH EAST, 1985–86

	NORTHERN REGION	UK	SOUTH EAST
Proportion of households with average weekly income:			
Below £80	26.9%	21.5%	16.9%
Above £375	8.5%	15.3%	23.5%

Source: Regional Trends, 23 (1988)

The Rich and the Poor

The old 'ruling class'

'. . . no longer do a few individual dynasties visibly control the factories, the banks, and the local council. But what clearly emerges from examining the 1930s and the post-war years of state intervention is not an erosion of dynastic influence but rather a subtle accommodation to change, which has enabled individual family members to move into commanding positions within the region and within the wider national economy' (Benwell CDP, 1978, p.7).

The epic report by the Benwell Community Development Project in 1978, *The Making Of A Ruling Class*, which traced the exodus of the old Newcastle and Tyneside industrial families from the city and conurbation, where they made their fortunes, to the estates of the Tyne Valley and beyond—where they effortlessly eased into the aristocracy—is an essential starting point for any study of the Tyneside establishment.

Most of the industries that made the original fortunes for the Joiceys, Dickinsons, Strakers, Ridleys, Armstrongs and the rest—coal, iron foundries, lead, engineering—may have declined or disappeared but, as the report showed, the business involvement of these families is still strong.

'The most notable change was the movement of later generations of the families into the finance capital sector, into banking, insurance, investment holding companies, property companies, building societies and into professions—stockbroking and the law—that were money-management oriented. It was a movement that distanced them from the point of production . . . and created a group within the capitalist class—'finance capital'—whose interests did not always coincide with industrial capital' (Benwell CDP, 1978, p.58).

Mess himself had noted that 'the feudal tradition is strong in Northumberland, and there is not the sharp divorce between it and the new industrialism which is found in most areas . . .' while Austin Mitchell has voiced a familiar criticism:

'the North East was betrayed, let down by the original leaders who made it, the captains of industry who never thought about the future, a usual local trait. They made money, built monoliths, sold out, leaving the land that made them; they to retire, it to rot' (Mitchell, 1986, p.74.).

Yet in the world of 'public service' this old ruling class still wields considerable influence as part of the Tyneside 'establishment'. While the

Benwell report noted that these families gradually lost control of local government, it emphasised that they came to have a dominating influence in the non-elected State machinery and other important regional institutions 'through which large amounts of state funds have been channelled'—such as the new town corporations, water and hospital authorities.

Sir Michael Straker, member of one of these elite Tyneside families, exemplifies the public service orientation of the old ruling class. A former chairman of Newcastle Area Health Authority, Peterlee and Aycliffe Development Corporation, and the Newcastle and Gateshead Water Company—a private utility/monopoly founded by the old dynasties—he now chairs the Northumbrian Water Authority, and the newly-privatised 'Go Ahead Northern' bus company. Sir Michael, who farms at High Warden, near Hexham, has been called 'the original quango man'. He is frank, welcoming, and says he has a high regard for the Labour politicians he regularly sits alongside at the development corporation and elsewhere.

The Straker family's original interests were in the Durham coalfield, and up to 1943 the Strakers ran the old Robert Stephenson and Hawthorn's locomotive works at Forth Banks in Newcastle. He is not entirely happy with some of the inferences in the Benwell study—still a talking point among the great and the good—but willingly discusses his family tree which is attached to the report . . . 'he went into banking, he stayed in the coal industry; that man (John Straker, 1815–1885) was a coal owner, and no doubt he made some money. He was successful and did things that present people would say were outrageous, but they were the standard practice at that time. He financed his children no doubt—one to stay in coal, one into engineering and one into banking—and I suppose they all helped each other. I always joke that we are no smart, well-bred family. We're just a bunch of pitmen but we managed to get our snouts above the ground'.

Sir Michael acknowledges the criticism levelled at the old families, but thinks much of it is misplaced and unfair. 'People have often . . . said that many of the people who made a lot of money out of the North hadn't been re-investing the money in this part of the world. That's a bit of an unfair criticism because since the last war the taxation has been fairly aggressive until the last five years or so and the opportunities for honourable people who were paying their dues to reinvest in any substantial form . . . were not very great'.

Sir Michael thinks that Britain is 'riddled with a social structure', but insists the edges are becoming generally more blurred. And yet . . . 'It's still very much part of life, and more so here than the South . . . I don't know whether the South is any better for it, but money governs things down there. I don't think that's quite as true up here. People tell me we've got a lot of entrepreneurs up here, a lot of wealthy people around prepared to have a go'. If that is the case, which establishment do *they* slip in to?

The new rich

Are the *new* rich on the periphery, snubbed by the old ruling class and sometimes (but not always) treated with suspicion by the ruling Labour class? Take John Hall, chairman of the small family company that developed the Gateshead MetroCentre and then bought Lord Londonderry's Wynyard estate, near Stockton—or Joe Robertson, a younger Tyneside millionaire who owns a fast expanding pubs-to-property empire.

Hall first. He clearly feels excluded, snubbed by the establishment. 'They must look at me as a usurper. I am not a member of clubs or establishments. I don't believe in them. I'm not a Mason. I'm not anything. They've never done anything for me. I've done it for myself. But you have to recognise there is a power group there. I have to deal with them as I move forward. But I'm not going to toe their party lines'.

But do they resent his success? 'Oh yes. My greatest critics were my professional people in the early days—the establishment— but I'm not going to mention any names. I didn't have one supporter from any of them because I'm John Hall from a pit village [Ashington] and what the hell does he know. I was not part of the scene. I didn't give them the business. I've had battles galore with them'.

John Hall has, however, been appointed as a member of the Tyne and Wear Urban Development Corporation and is on the CBI's national Inner City Task Force. Hall recognises there is a risk of being 'sucked into the establishment'. He adds: 'You think you're going onto these boards for what you've done but it may be there are ulterior motives to make sure, in a sense . . . that you don't become part of the competition. If this area is to survive it hasn't got to have cliques. It has got to be more open, like the American system where it's easier to move round'.

Joe Robertson, boss of the City Leisure group, insists he does not aspire to be a member of any establishment—'not in the slightest, but I like all these people. I don't think there's the great rift you imagine. I suppose there are the type that wear Barbour jackets and green wellies but they are a type of person as opposed to a monetary class. Maybe their offspring become estate agents—that's what they all seem to do if they cannot get a decent job'.

Robertson, former sales assistant, trainee cinema manager, ship's steward, rock group manager and mirror manufacturer, recently sold his seven 'high profile' city centre bars—Berlins, Maceys, Luckies, and so on—to a Leicester concern, although he reckons his group still has property worth over £6 million in the centre of Newcastle. He believes he is the man that has brought style to the once dingy bars of Newcastle—revolutionised a drinking culture, if you like—and says there are a lot of people in his mould making a lot of money in Tyneside. 'We just happen to be more visible'.

Unlike John Hall, Joe Robertson says he is not in the business of building up a family empire—a dynasty. (In an interview, Hall said he would prefer his grandson to go to Harvard Business School and to get 'experience of life . . . there is no way I want my son to just get the wealth and sit back and rest . . .'). Robertson says: 'The money I make, I'm not keeping it to pass onto my son and daughter. I'm not building up the family business, the dynasty. I'm just an entrepreneurial, fast-moving businessman and I need to do deals now. I just want to make money and have a good time'. He would like a private plane so he can commute to a house in the South of France, which he visits most weekends.

An unashamed right winger, who has all the trappings of wealth— Bentley, and white Mercedes, with personalised number plates, flat in London's Park Lane—Robertson, born in the West end of Newcastle, says he accepts Tyneside has its 'haves' and 'have-nots'. 'There are some very impoverished conditions I see in the West End and Byker; people who are really living on the breadline. I went into a couple of charity shops at Christmas and some people were shopping for second-hand kids' toys. I felt terrible. But I'm a great charity supporter. I give a lot of money away because you've got to remember where you came from. We give jobs to people who walk in the door. I think that's important. I've probably created 1500 jobs and invested £20 million over the last few years.'

The poor

The new MetroCentre shopping development lies barely half a mile from the offices of the Scotswood Credit Union in the west end of Newcastle. The families, and the unemployed, queuing for their Giro cheques at the nearby post office, can easily spot this retail wonderland over the Tyne; they can even take a special bus there. But few bother. 'It's like Disneyland', says Brian Tate, unemployed shipyard worker and chief cashier of the Credit Union, who is about to launch a similar enterprise in nearby Fenham. He is nearer the mark than he thinks. Disneyland? A few weeks after we spoke, 'Metroland', labelled 'Europe's first indoor theme park', opened at the MetroCentre.

The Credit Union, formed in 1983 as a co-operative venture to counter loan sharks, began as a savings club and subsequently offered low interest loans (at 1% a month). It has over 200 people on the books. In 1987 they took £15,000 and were able to lend a similar amount. The majority of members are unemployed on an estate where they count the number of people in work; Brian Tate reckons only about 20% of the men have regular jobs. He says employment has halved in the last 10 years. Economic recovery? Joe Caffrey, a community worker who helped form the Union, says there is little sign of that; just widespread disenchantment with 'the system'. 'About 80% don't vote in local elections', he says. 'It's not apathy. People just don't relate to the democratic process.'

The people in the Credit Union's offices (a converted house used as a council neighbourhood office) may speak the same dialect as John Hall or Joe Robertson; the Union officials may be as nimble at number crunching on a pocket calculator. They are certainly as articulate as any property developer/speculator. They are well-read. Many have (redundant) skills, too. But they represent the 'down side' of the Tyneside economy and of the retail/credit boom. Things may be getting better . . . for some. Brian Tate has strong views about the great divide in society:

> 'It's not just a North-South split. It's between the people in work and the unemployed. People in work are better off than they were five years ago but people without work are worse off, and are going to get poorer. Some of them, on the face of it, are concerned, but when it comes to wage bargaining . . . well . . . let's say they had an option . . . take no increase so that the firm could employ more workers. I've got a fair idea of the way people on the shop floor would vote. They tell the media they are concerned. But in the end they want the money. This is where the trade unions are falling down. They fail to represent people out of work and I feel the Labour Party is now turning its back on the unemployed and areas of high unemployment. Yes, there have been slumps before, but in the old days they were slumps in the market. Now the old skills have gone'.

The Credit Union represents a positive response to the tensions engendered by a split society, while the darker side to the retail boom is debt. At the last count, 17,611 court summonses were issued in Newcastle against people who could not repay loans, an increase of 10% over the previous 12 months. Over 10,000 warrants were issued by Courts allowing bailiffs to seize goods from householders. Tony Flynn, chairman of the city's social services committee commented: 'For those on low incomes, credit is much easier to obtain these days—just go into a store, without any surety, and they oblige'.

At the Citizens Advice Bureau in Newcastle's Cruddas Park, Brian Ritchie, the manager, points to a steady rise in people facing debt problems, from rent arrears to final demands from credit card companies. One unemployed woman, highlighted by *The Journal* at the end of 1987, had debts of more than £4,000 and no ready way of paying them off. She is not exceptional.

Newcastle City Council established in 1983 a 'Money Matters Project', a specialist debt counselling service, which advises people how to cope with mounting bills. Welfare rights officers help people reschedule their debts and write to creditors pleading for flexibility and understanding; it often works. The Social Services Department has produced several fairly typical case studies. Take Mr. and Mrs. L, a couple with two children aged four and seven. They were wholly dependent on supplementary benefit after Mr. L. lost his job almost a year ago. They had debts of £1,112, low by comparison with many on the 'Money Matters' register. Although the County Court ordered the couple to repay £43.33 monthly, they were unable to meet this legal requirement and faced electricity and gas disconnection until a debt counsellor stepped in.

Labour historian Ben Pimlott notes that 'the reality of modern unemployment is not manifested in dole queues or marching men'. He points out that the scene that greets any visitor who steps off a train at Newcastle is of a still flourishing commercial and cosmopolitan city with boutiques and wine bars and a new underground system. Where are the unemployed? They are out of view, scattered through a hundred council estates, sitting in clubs, or slumped in front of television sets. The unemployed and the poor are often not very visible nor are they organised or vociferous—and they are 'not so much powerless as politically non-existent' (Pimlott, 1985).

The poor become visible; hundreds of unemployed people and pensioners queued for free butter from the European Community's 'butter mountain' in 1987. This queue was at the Salvation Army, North Shields. (*Newcastle Chronicle & Journal*).

Politics

'See the people on the city streets
They're tired, angry and cold;
And you can only take so much;
Before something will explode'.

(Ian McCallum, 1988)

Ian McCallum, a young Tyneside singer/musician, from Sunniside, Gateshead, who leads a rock band called simply 'McCallum', feels angry. A place like Ponteland may ooze affluence, but the places he knows well are downtrodden and he wonders why his fellow Tynesiders accept their lot without a fight. So he writes, with more hope than confidence: 'We're hard people; we believe in what is right; we're hard people; we can learn to stand and fight'. Actually, he's not convinced 'we' can.

McCallum loves Tyneside, but hates the apathetic streak lodged deep in the subconscious of its natives. Why don't they stand and fight or, put another way, why did Tyneside escape the inner-city disturbances of 1981? Of course there are many reasons, not least that the summer riots of Toxteth, Brixton, Chapeltown (Leeds) and St. Pauls (Bristol) were more an outcry by an oppressed Afro-Caribbean community against authority generally and police in particular than a spontaneous reaction against unemployment. When McCallum sings . . . 'Will you turn your back on history . . . will you burn the bridges and factories that our lives were built upon . . .' he is certainly touching a raw nerve.

Perhaps, on reflection, we should not be surprised by what some perceive as the endemic apathy of Tyneside. The industries of the conurbation have been in decline for as long as most can remember—shipbuilding, for instance, has long been characterised by short time working and casualisation, while coal has been running down for much of the century—and unemployment was no new phenomenon to some when Mrs. Thatcher came to power.

Jeremy Beecham, moderate leader of Newcastle City Council for ten years, who identifies closely with the Hattersley wing of his party, has one answer. He believes Tyneside has a level of social stability which other conurbations do not enjoy. There is, he says, 'a greater sense of community and less alienation. In spite of all the difficulties, people have still a [council-provided] level of provision which, even now, makes life tolerable—and in the East and West End of Newcastle [the poorest areas on every social indicator] there is a wealth of voluntary activity.'

Ian McCallum, and his left-wing friends, would not necessarily share Mr. Beecham's sentiments. 'People see high unemployment as wrong but they're not prepared to do anything about it. There's a horrible pride thing up here; you know—we're the best, living in the best part of the country'. I don't understand why they can't see they can change things if they want to.'

Certainly Tynesiders generally accept their lot in an area dominated by a conservative political machine, which happens to be Labour and is funded largely by two powerful unions which tend to pull the strings. Tyneside—like the wider North East—is one of Labour's traditional bastions but has never been noted for its political radicalism. The party sits securely on generally large majorities. All four Tyneside Councils are Labour-controlled and all the parliamentary constituencies, with the exception of Tynemouth, are held by Labour MPs. This strength has bred complacency, over-dependence on a union machine—notably the General, Municipal and Boilermakers Union (GMB)—and weakness where the party should be strong: at the grass roots. In her recent critique of the party, Hilary Wainwright is commenting on Newcastle but it could apply to other parts of Tyneside: 'A powerful combination of inertia and union machine politics has kept the whole party . . . at a very low political temperature; sometimes so cold that it has been mistaken for dead' (Wainwright, 1987, p.138). With trade union delegations wielding disproportionate power on local party General Management Committees (GMCs), Joe Mills, Newcastle-based Northern Regional Secretary of the Transport and General Workers' Union, and chairman of the Northern Labour Party, recognises the challenge ahead. 'Some people in the South have said to me that the Labour Party lacks buzz . . . this is because people up here have been Labour supporters for so long. But I've got to say that with the development of new employment practices, and with more share and house ownership and other forms of social advancement, people are going to look to Labour to be changing its attitude'.

Mr. Mills, a centre-right winger of some influence nationally in his union, believes the party must change, and become more responsive to the ordinary membership, if it is to withstand the challenge from another political force. Significantly, he fears a revived Social and Liberal Democratic Party more than the Conservatives. But the Conservative party—which controlled Newcastle, at regular intervals, until 1973—has begun to take urban and inner city areas much more seriously and has appointed a specialist organiser-cum-publicist on Tyneside.

The Labour Party's organisation in the region has appeared moribund, and anxious lay officials recognise it needs bringing back to life. There have been several disagreements with senior party officials in London over the direction the party should take in the North East. Some activists complain they, and their supporters, are treated as little more than voting fodder. 'One of the problems we have is that not many union leaders want to give up the authority they have within the party', says Mills who, unlike other union leaders, favours a one-member-one-vote system for selecting parliamentary candidates. 'Tragically, we've got a lot of unions who believe that because they pay the piper they've got to call the tune and until we overcome that dilemma I think the party will continue to be weak.

Trade union leaders have got to encourage more participation by the lay people instead of wanting to dominate the party'.

This could be taken as a sideswipe at the GMB, the dominant union in the constituencies. For the Kinnock leadership, the union is often seen to be using its power constructively; increasing its delegates on GMCs to snuff out a far left or Militant challenge, for instance, and ensuring the selection of its sponsored candidates. The GMB usually gets its way.

Andrew (Andy) Cunningham, the old regional GMB boss, who was gaoled in the aftermath of the Poulson affair in the early 1970s, may have wielded considerable power but Tom Burlison, the union's current regional secretary, has built a more efficient machine. 'After the Cunningham affair, the union lost heart in many ways. Representation in the party dropped significantly. The Cunningham episode demoralised people. They felt inhibited . . . I'd say we now have more influence than Andy Cunningham and it's more sustained'.

But the Labour Party's power base in the local authorities has been steadily, and quite severely, eroded by the present government. By the second term of Conservative Government in 1983, Mrs. Thatcher returned to power determined to clip the wings of local government—particularly Labour-controlled councils—which she regarded as unacceptable outposts of dissent. Her main target was the Greater London Council, but six other English metropolitan county councils, including Tyne and Wear, were also regarded as superfluous. In March 1986, they were abolished; their powers were handed back to the district councils or to joint boards comprising councillors from each district. A few tears were shed but, by and large, the district council leaders were privately happy to assume full control of their domains again. But the attack on local government continues: Newcastle, traditionally a high-spending (and centre-right) authority was rate-capped for the third year running in 1988 and Gateshead suffered a similar fate. In addition, the establishment of a new quango, the Tyne and Wear Urban Development Corporation, has the effect of side-stepping local democracy and imposing Whitehall solutions to the area's problems.

Sixty years ago, when local democracy was stronger, it was apparent to Mess that Newcastle's dominance of the conurbation—'a natural hegemony of the Tyne as far back as history has anything to say'—had soured relations with its municipal neighbours. 'Newcastle was for centuries inclined to use its powers selfishly . . .' While neighbouring councils looked to Newcastle as the area's natural metropolis, he said, they were nevertheless jealous of it, resenting its claims and aspirations.

The creation of the Tyne and Wear County did at least bring some political cohesion to a conurbation which, more than 20 years ago, had been regarded as the ideal size for a single unitary authority. The County Council's structure plan, which set out strategic planning objectives for

Tyne and Wear County Council. In spite of protests, the County Council was abolished in 1986, and with it went strategic planning for the conurbation as a whole. The new Tyne and Wear Urban Development Corporation, a government-created quango, now takes the lead in large-scale economic regeneration projects. (*TUSIU*).

the medium term, could at least serve to override petty parochial rivalries. But in its dying days, the County Council could not halt a significant breach in that plan—the approval, by Gateshead Council, of the massive MetroCentre retail and leisure development at Dunston. And the MetroCentre could be seen not so much in the context of Labour-controlled Gateshead providing a much needed outlet for the conurbation's shoppers, but more as a thinly disguised onslaught on the dominance of Newcastle and its Eldon Square shopping centre.

Behind the scenes, the Labour politicians of Newcastle and Gateshead often seem to be in competition with one another. Newcastle's response to the MetroCentre was the 'Armstrong Centre' scheme, across the river at Elswick. This proposal, opposed by Newcastle's own planners and sections of the left on the Council, was to be a 'unique centre for commerce, light industry, leisure and retail'. But it never really came off and had to be bailed out by the new Development Corporation. 'It is difficult to comprehend the financial logic of this scheme—other than its overwhelming recommendation that it is not in Gateshead', complains Jon Davies, a Newcastle University lecturer and former city councillor. In a

Thatcherite climate, Davies sees what he regards as a new political development . . . 'left-wing/Labour authorities . . . slipping fairly easily into a much more explicit and deliberate partnership with capitalism and capitalists'. He thinks left-wing councils, 'under conditions not of their choosing', are making history through parochial rivalry, and distinctly uncomradely competition and conflict (Davies, 1988). We should perhaps remember, however, that, back in the 'sixties, and 'seventies, some of our 'municipal capitalists' were busy stitching up city and town centre redevelopment schemes, as well as housing contracts, with property companies, pension funds, building firms, and dubious consultant architects—remember John Poulson—bringing to Tyneside another reputation: municipal corruption.

With a steady erosion of local political power—County Council abolition, tight expenditure controls on councils and rate-capping—the government is now increasingly setting the political agenda and, perhaps, drawing Labour into a trap. Although the Party opposed the creation of an Urban Development Corporation for Tyne and Wear, it has accepted seats on the board: Regional Party Chairman Joe Mills has joined, along with the deputy leader of South Tyneside Council, Sep Robinson. The government will, no doubt, draw the maximum credit for any success the Corporation may have although, according to one senior councillor . . . 'all they've done is go around all the local authorities asking for any development schemes we've got on the shelf and can't afford to implement because the government has cut back our resources'.

Fortunately the Corporation's chief executive, Alistair Balls, former regional director of the Departments of the Environment and Transport, has made clear that he sees his task, first and foremost, as job creation—underpinning the fragile economy of the Tyne and Wear riverside areas—rather than a London Docklands-style property development-led exercise. Joe Mills comments: 'At the first board meeting I made absolutely clear I would be consulting with all councils in the area and taking soundings from them . . . fortunately the board [chaired by Paul Nicholson, chairman of the Vaux brewery and hotels group] is made up of what I call northern nationalists who realise the strength of local councils and realise they're in a Labour area'. Mills describes his involvement as a 'damage limitation exercise' to prevent a London Docklands-style redevelopment.

There is another fear. One leading councillor, who declined to be named, said he had no immediate objections to the Corporation's strategy. But he feared that it might later flex its muscles, take on local councils—for it is a planning authority in its own right, with powers of compulsory purchase—and force a further erosion of local democracy.

At the moment, though, the Labour Movement still has considerable power in Tyneside in spite of government attacks on local authorities and the trade unions. This moderate, right-wing Labour Movement, far from being a spent force, is an integral and effective part of the local establishment along with the remnants of Tyneside's old 'ruling class'. These twin establishment pillars sit together on the same committees or quangos and, by all accounts, get on famously. As we earlier described, a new phenomenon has developed on Tyneside—a 'let's-sink-our-political-differences-in-the-interests-of-promoting-the-region' philosophy—which has already produced some interesting side effects. When, for instance, government proposed the abolition of automatic Regional Development Grants in 1988, it was difficult to find an over-critical voice in the Labour establishment. It is as if the word has gone out: 'Don't be too critical chaps, or you may rock the boat and damage our promotional efforts'.

In the eyes of some left-wingers, this new consensus also means that Labour quango men are actively encouraging non-union firms to invest in the area—and Joe Mills, for one, has faced some criticism from left-wingers in his union. Is he, then, an establishment man? 'I regard myself as someone from the Labour movement trying to make the North work and one of the problems is that you've got to be part of the organised establishment being created to do that—such as the Urban Development Corporation and the new regional promotional agency, the Northern Development Company. It has become quite apparent that to make the North reasonably successful again we've got to sit beside people who in the past we probably wouldn't have been in the same room with . . . there's a new sort of establishment being created based on the needs of the area'.

Conclusion

In March 1988, the Minister of State for Employment, John Cope, came to Felling to inaugurate a £2 million job creation project in an old clothing factory-cum-warehouse which had been closed by the Burton Group a few years ago. The project was described as a pace-setting initiative between the public sector (which will be contributing £1.3 million) and industry (which has to raise £700,000). Gateshead Council, rate-capped and strapped for cash, has even chipped in with 15% of the cost. Seventy men, described as the 'long-term unemployed', and attached to the Manpower Services Commission's Community Programme, are now converting the building into 50 small workshops for an enterprise called 'Design Works'. The aim is to encourage young entrepreneurs to set up shop and turn the place into a 'centre for design excellence' in conjunction with a local enterprise agency, Project North East.

At the ceremony, attended by Burton's Chairman, Sir Ralph Halpern, other captains of industry, and a host of local guests, Mr Cope talked enthusiastically of an upturn in Tyneside's fortunes; William McAlpine, boss of the well-known construction company (which is managing the workforce) said that commendable things could be achieved when government, local councils, and business worked together. Inside the factory shell, the publicity was lavish. Sir Ralph was bullish: 'I have no doubt that the prosperity we see in the South East will spread to the North East and beyond'. Design Works, therefore, was symbolic of a 'thrusting, thriving enterprise society that would take Britain into the 21st century'.

This, then, is what we might call the official vision for Tyneside. To paraphrase the Prime Minister . . . 'the men who made the area great [the 19th century industrialists] can do so again, given the right incentives . . .' The answer, in short, lies in the creation of small businesses, with a little pump-priming by government agencies.

In many ways this Design Works project illustrates the gulf between officialdom and reality. Thus: we know Tyneside has its problems, but they won't be solved by continually highlighting the 'down side' of the economy. So—talk optimistically, create a new climate of confidence, and things will improve, as John Hall has shown at the MetroCentre.

And the reality? Surely the economy must be improving—why else would the official jobless statistics show that unemployment had dropped by 15% in Tyne and Wear in the past year?. An unemployed building worker, now on his second Community Programme project, strongly disagreed: 'Not likely,' he replied. 'Take away all these schemes and things would be just as bad. Where are the real jobs?' Undoubtedly, new jobs are being created even in Tyneside, but many are part-time, low-paid and in the retail, leisure and catering industries.

Ben Pimlott noted the outward prosperity of Tyneside, and the underclass tucked away in the council ghettoes; scratch below the surface of a bustling Newcastle, and it is not hard to find a level of poverty which would have doubtless appalled Mess and which should be an affront to any civilised society. But a cautionary note. This is not a specifically Tyneside phenomenon. Those of us who regularly visit other conurbations—Clydeside, Greater Manchester, the West Midlands for instance and, yes, London—know all too well the poverty that afflicts much of the nation. (Can anyone recall a more depressing entrance to our national capital, or a more telling indictment on our society, than the foyer and exterior of King's Cross—the squalor, litter, the beggars, amid the surrounding fast food outlets, less than two miles from the world's most prosperous financial centre?)

In outlining the divide in Tyneside society, while pointing out the conurbation's attractions, it is important to dispel the myth of an 'industrial wasteland or desert'—perhaps a reasonable assumption from afar, considering the rapid decline of our manufacturing industry. It is important, too, to attack the tiresome stereotype of a second-rate region well behind the prosperous South East. Tyneside has its strengths: a relatively clean river, once again; a cleaner and healthier environment, courtesy of the Clean Air Acts; and magnificent countryside on the doorstep. Newcastle may have been disfigured, to some extent, by the hideous concrete structures of the 'sixties, and torn apart by a horrendous motorway quite out of scale with the city centre, while parts of Gateshead would still fit Priestley's unflattering description of a 'town built by an enemy of the human race'. But go to Tynemouth, or North and South Shields, witness the great improvements to the fabric of these towns—the bustling fish quay, the attractive waterfront areas and, most important, the (still) working river. A shadow of its former self, perhaps, but an asset which the new Tyne and Wear Development Corporation has begun to exploit. It is just a pity that our democratic institutions, the local councils—so out of favour with an increasingly centralist government— could not have been given the resources to do the job.

What would Henry Mess have made of Tyneside in 1988? Certainly, he would have commended the great physical improvements to the conurbation—major improvements to housing, transport, and environment. But we believe he would have been concerned by the continual failure to tackle Tyneside's more deep-seated economic problems caused, in part, by the concentration of power and wealth at the centre—and only reinforced by tax cuts favouring the rich and the gradual dismantling of regional policy.

Tyneside, and the wider North East, is right to publicise its strengths and attractions. But that must never be at the expense of obscuring the many problems that remain. It is a question of balance.

REFERENCES

Benwell Community Development Project (CDP) (1978) *The Making of a Ruling Class.* Newcastle: Benwell CDP.
Butler, D. and Kavanagh, D. (1988) *The British General Election of 1987.* London: Macmillan.
Central Statistical Office (1988) *Regional Trends,* 23. London: HMSO.
Davies, J.G. (1988) From Municipal Socialism to . . . Municipal Capitalism? *Local Government Studies,* 14, 2, 19–22.
Longley, D. and Spearing, M. (1986) *Tyne and Wear Christian Directory.* Bromley, Kent: MARC Europe.
Millward, N. and Stevens, M. (1988) Union Density in the Regions. *Employment Gazette,* May 1988, 286–295.
Mitchell, A. (1986) 'The North East' in Critchley, J. (ed), *Britain: a View from Westminster.* Poole: Blandford Press.
Newcastle Chronicle and Journal (1987) *The North East Marketing Pocket Book.* Newcastle: Chronicle and Journal.
Pimlott, B. (1985) Unemployment and 'the Unemployed' in North East England. *Political Quarterly* 56 (4), 346–360.
Priestley, J.B. (1934) *English Journey.* London: Heinemann.
Tyne Tees Television (1987) *Marketing Yearbook 1987.* Newcastle: Tyne Tees TV.
Wainwright, H. (1987) *Labour: A Tale of Two Parties.* London: Hogarth Press.

8

CONCLUSIONS

Fred Robinson and John Goddard

Change: Past and Present

Enormous economic and social changes have taken place over the past sixty years. Tyneside in the 1920s still had the economic structure which had powered its growth in the nineteenth century—though a structure clearly shaken by the deepening economic depression. And Tyneside was still suffering the problems and deprivations brought about by rapid industrialisation, like squalid, overcrowded housing and serious outbreaks of disease. Subsequently, in the 'hungry thirties' conditions were to become generally worse, not better, until war, once again, revived Tyneside.

The post-war years saw the creation of the welfare state and a massive increase in public sector provision and intervention—on a scale which Mess would have found unimaginable in the 1920s. Then there was the 'long boom' of the 1950s and a period of prosperity—perhaps false prosperity—in Tyneside in the 1960s. In the 1970s things went badly wrong, as large sections of the economy began to fall apart. High unemployment, as severe as in the 1930s, was again seen in Tyneside. It was abundantly clear by the early 1980s that the economy was undergoing fundamental structural changes, shattering old certainties and generating new social pressures.

Today, Tyneside is still reeling from the economic upheaval of the last few years, trying to find ways of adjusting to change. Reading Mess's book, one is struck by the sense of stagnation, out of which the best hopes were for gradual, marginal improvements. Although there are certainly many signs of stagnation in Tyneside today, change is widely seen as necessary, inescapable, and is even actively sought. Tyneside, as a minor outpost in a global economy in the throes of change, is reflecting and responding to powerful external forces. The area's social fabric, too, is subject to major external forces; Tyneside's local culture is overwhelmed by national mass culture and the changes in lifestyles it promotes. Similarly, though Tyneside may, in its provincial way, lag behind 'The South' in experiencing new social stresses and strains it does, nevertheless, share in them: it has the problems of crime and drug addiction, for example, seen elsewhere. In addition, we are in a period when government is pushing very hard for change at every level, seeking radical revisions to the social security system, local taxation, the health service, education and housing and also promoting the 'enterprise culture' and private sector approaches to economic and social problems. Again, Tyneside is by no means insulated or isolated from these pressures for change.

To say that we live in a period of rapid (and accelerating) change may sound like cliché; in every age commentators have perhaps said much the same. Indeed, in this region, a major planning document published over twenty years ago laid great stress on this theme, underlined by its title 'Challenge of the Changing North'. But it can be argued that change now really is all-pervasive and fundamental. It emerges as a major element in all the chapters of this book. The old and familiar is being swept away. Tyneside's traditional industries are nearly gone; council housing is being marginalised and privatised. Education is undergoing major changes, as is the health service through privatisation. Change is equally prevalent in other aspects of life, such as the rise in violent crime; the decline of organised religion; the rising rate of divorce. Long-established landmarks such as the 1944 Education Act or the commitment to maintaining full employment are becoming obsolete. And all these changes affect people in their everyday lives. Economic change has forced people to revise their expectations, live with uncertainty, perhaps consider self-employment. Social change has made single-parent families commonplace and shifted social life from the pub or club to the home video.

Obviously, change is by no means always 'a good thing', nor is it always welcomed. Looking back to the 1920s does show us why we should count our blessings; most of us enjoy far greater material comforts, better housing, education and health—we live longer too. On the other hand, we harbour doubts about change and question whether the quality of life, in the broadest sense, is really so much better now than it was then. We hanker after the past, the supposed certainties of the old close-knit communities of working class life in Tyneside. The highly successful Beamish Museum in County Durham, includes amongst its exhibits a 'town' set in the 1920s, which sparks off this nostalgia—even though most visitors to Beamish are too young to have known the 1920s. Beamish may be a 'packaged' and unreal version of the 1920s and our conceptions of the period may be very partial and romanticised; but many people certainly do refer back to images of this past which, at the least, serve to tarnish their views of the present.

The 1980s have seen such profound and rapid change that even the 1970s have become 'history' and attitudes or expectations of a decade ago seem old-fashioned or irrelevant. Ten years ago some revival of Tyneside's manufacturing industries at least seemed possible, if difficult; today, we appear to have largely accepted that Tyneside's economic future must be based on the service sector, not manufacturing. Even ten years ago, most

The Jarrow March to London, 1936; a plea for help for the unemployed. It did not bring much help but it effectively served to highlight the issue – and has become one of the most potent images of the 1930s. (*Newcastle Chronicle & Journal*).

The Jarrow March, 1986. The same banner was used but this was not a nostalgic re-enactment or a part of the 'heritage industry'. Fifty years on, high unemployment is again a major problem and, again, the march publicised the issue but produced no action. (*Newcastle Chronicle & Journal*).

Tyneside school-leavers found jobs, while nowadays most go on to the Youth Training Scheme. Perhaps the greatest change in perception, built up slowly but surely since the late 1970s, concerns the role of the state. Then, the state was expected to solve problems and meet needs; now, we are encouraged to look more and more to the private sector for solutions and resources—be it in education, housing, health services, transport, the utilities, or even the prisons, art galleries and libraries. The list of candidates for some form of privatisation is continually expanding. Moreover, the accent now is on *individual* freedom and endeavour—consumer choice, 'self-reliance' and 'enterprise', rather than on *social* benefits and objectives—like equality of opportunity and the safety-net of the welfare state.

All the contributors to this book pass comment on the desirability or otherwise of those changes which have taken place and consider further changes now appearing on the horizon. Within a long-term perspective, there is certainly a shared recognition of undeniable material progress since the 1920s. But there is distinct uneasiness about recent and future change. In part, this may be an uneasiness which stems from the removal of the familiar—a fear of change itself. However, it does go much deeper than that: it is, perhaps above all, a concern that economic and social inequalities are becoming more marked and more deeply entrenched.

In the labour market, there are deep and widening divisions, most notably between those in work and the unemployed—but also between the skilled and unskilled, the well-paid and the low-paid, and between men and women. The resulting substantial and growing differences in household income are translated into significant differences in access to all kinds of goods and services. And, as efforts are made to reduce state provision in education, housing, health and perhaps many other services, access becomes increasingly a matter of economic power, with the more affluent being able (and encouraged) to pay for better services. All this goes against the grain of the post-war welfare consensus, especially in a Labour stronghold like Tyneside which has depended so strongly on the state to soften the blows of economic decline.

The great fear is that a large and powerless 'underclass' will become a permanent feature of the economic and social structure of Tyneside (and, indeed, of other cities as well). Such a fear can hardly be easily dismissed when it is apparent that this underclass already exists. There is poverty in Tyneside, there are many whose everyday experience is of basic survival on low social security benefits—here it is worth restating that nearly half the unemployed have been out of work for over a year. The people of this underclass, left stranded by economic change, are largely excluded from the wider society, an exclusion emphasised by their being concentrated in certain areas of the conurbation. They have not had the rising standards of living enjoyed by many white-collar workers or derived quick profits from buying shares in industries being privatised, nor can they pay to opt out of public sector education, health care or housing. Their position continues to weaken and it is difficult to imagine an economic revival which would be sufficient to reintegrate this underclass. Part-time low-paid jobs and 'workfare' schemes would serve neither to lift them out of poverty nor restore their status. The signs are that this underclass—marginalised, ignored, even maligned—will remain; the unanswerable question is whether they will remain quiescent or threaten the stability of the social structure.

A further underlying theme in the preceding chapters is the disadvantage and deprivation of Tyneside in comparison with other parts of the country. This is nothing new; its persistence over the past sixty years makes it all the more disturbing and dispiriting. People in Tyneside and the North East can, quite legitimately, point to the area's many virtues, such as a reasonably civilised pace of life, generally adequate and affordable housing, and easy access to fine coast and countryside. Nevertheless, the 'North-South divide' is a reality and Tyneside is cast in the uncomfortable role of 'poor relation'. On most economic and social indicators—and especially unemployment rates—Tyneside's position is poor relative to national averages and the area very disadvantaged in comparison with the South. The gap between a quite prosperous South and a declining North still suffering the effects of recession, appears to be widening—just as the division between the 'haves' and 'have nots' within Tyneside grows and deepens. Reducing inequality (or, alternatively, 'managing' inequality so that resultant tensions are defused) would thus seem to pose a major challenge for the future.

The Future

One of the most important aspects of the changes we have discussed is that nearly all of them are a consequence of *external* forces and decisions. Most of the economy is controlled from headquarters outside the area, primarily in London, and Tyneside's branch operations have little autonomy and all too often are seen as dispensable. In Mess's time there was a large measure of local control and locally-based capital and even some industrialists having at least a degree of loyalty and commitment to the area. Today, most of that has gone, as have the local financial and commercial institutions. This has been a long-term process, culminating now in the internationalisation of production. The parallel centralisation of government has been much more recent. The past sixty years saw the rise and massive expansion of local government while the last decade has witnessed the reversal of that process. Local government is now firmly constrained by central government and has little room for manoeuvre. This process of externalisation of control can be seen in many other spheres; for example, in relation to culture, ideas, lifestyles and the formation of opinion, television provides a London-based view with very little regional input.

In short, then, Tyneside is in a highly dependent position; it would not be an overstatement to say that, in many ways, it is a colony controlled by London. This in itself severely limits the options for locally influencing the pattern of change and *creating* the future rather than just reacting (often belatedly) to events. Moreover, local institutions have been too weak to challenge the power of the centre and promote locally-based alternatives. In the field of economic development policy, for instance, there is a plethora of relatively weak organisations with overlapping concerns, little co-ordination and no clear strategy. Local government, even though comprising moderate and 'realistic' Labour administrations, is diminished, belittled and ignored by the Conservative central government. The private sector also lacks power and local commitment. Back in the 1960s, T. Dan Smith, then leader of Newcastle City Council, gave Tyneside some prominence and 'clout' in national politics and offered some kind of vision (flawed, but ambitious) for the future. Since his departure (on account of involvement in corruption), no-one has taken his place. Today, there is a serious absence of leadership and vision in Tyneside, and there are no local leaders with access to national centres of power.

There are, however, opportunities. Large amounts of money from central government and also from the European Community continue to be spent on a wide variety of projects in Tyneside. The Manpower Services Commission spends £1 million a week and the new Urban Development Corporation may spend up to £160 million in Tyne and Wear over the next six years. Private sector investment can also be attracted to the area, as developer John Hall has clearly demonstrated with the MetroCentre scheme. Inner cities are high on the political agenda and there is a certain new enthusiasm for 'doing something'—even the private sector is, at last, beginning to respond.

But can these opportunities be grasped by the area so that the people of Tyneside benefit and their needs and aspirations are met? It *may* be possible to wrest some power back from the centre but this means building up local institutions powerful enough, and committed enough, to do so.

The absence of institutions or powerful coalitions of interests at the local level does actually pose problems for the centre, since it can mean that centrally-imposed policies—in economic development or education, for example—may prove ineffective, unsuccessful and inappropriate when implemented in the local situation. There is no doubt that a great deal of public money has been spent ineffectively in Tyneside, with little to show for it. One reason for this is the failure to tailor policy action to local needs, and part of this failure stems from the absence of vociferous

Tyneside institutions to establish and articulate what is needed. Thus local institutions can contribute to the achievement of cost effectiveness in government programmes and contribute to their successful implementation—these are aims which the centre certainly recognises as important. Local institutions, with sufficient insight and vision to identify needs and opportunities can thus promote the effective use of MSC funds or launch suitable initiatives in health, education and housing. It is worth bearing in mind, too, that the centre is dependent on local institutions to implement schemes and programmes, a position which does give some power to the local level.

All this is not to deny the constructive contribution of locally-based interests in Tyneside. There are many examples of the creative use of resources, many small-scale local initiatives growing out of local concerns. But, we would argue, there has not been enough creativity nor has there been much coherence—and the abolition of the County Council has not helped, by removing one mechanism for coherence and co-ordination at the 'strategic' level. Initiatives, and projects have emerged on an *ad hoc* basis, often by chance and without a great deal of forethought. This is perhaps most evident in relation to urban regeneration policies which Tyneside has tended to copy from others without much consideration of their relevance to the specific local circumstances.

A key condition for the resurgence of Tyneside must be the restoration and development of local sources of power able to articulate Tyneside's needs and challenge external institutions. A great provincial conurbation must not accept the role of quiet, compliant colony for it will be ignored and will miss opportunities. It is now essential to create dialogues between the many different interests in Tyneside and develop some coherent view of how Tyneside should respond to change. Fundamentally, a vision is needed of a desirable future for Tyneside, focusing attention on how that future is to be attained.

One of Mess's main recommendations was the creation of a Council of Social Service for Tyneside to be representative of the various agencies, foster co-operation, co-ordination and efficiency, and make united representations on behalf of social service agencies. It seems to us that a similar 'Council', though much more broadly-based, would now be helpful as a way of focusing on Tyneside's future. Such organisations have already been set up in some cities to take stock of the present and look to the future.

What we have in mind is *not* a 'talking shop' of elites. Elites tend to create bureaucracies, new agencies and grandiose projects (like unwanted marinas and science parks) while much-needed small scale community-based initiatives (like welfare rights projects) are left underfunded and accorded low priority. Rather, what is needed is community representation spanning many different interests and concerns, firmly

T. Dan Smith points to the future for Newcastle City Centre. Also in this
photograph, taken in the mid 1960s are Arne Jacobsen, the architect; the City
Council's Planner, Sir Wilf Burns; and City Architect George Kenyon. A variation
on this theme – but without the high-rise hotel – emerged as the Eldon Square
development. (*Amber Films*).

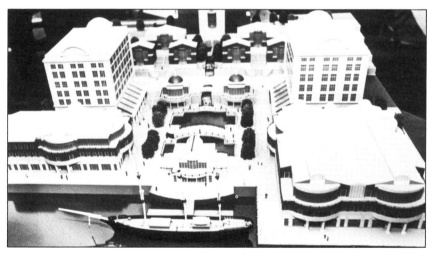

The future for Newcastle's Quayside – model of part of the £108 million
redevelopment of the East Quayside area, planned for completion in the
mid-1990s. This part of the development includes offices, a hotel, exhibition
centre, shopping and leisure facilities grouped around a central square. Tyne and
Wear Urban Development Corporation selected this private sector scheme in
1988, and is to contribute up to £20 million of public sector subsidy. (*Newcastle
Chronicle & Journal*).

rooted in the local community. It must not be just a 'talking shop'—though a proper dialogue between institutions, interests and individuals is vitally needed in Tyneside. It must be more than that, with a power to establish future directions for Tyneside based on a widely-acknowledged recognition that it can speak, with credibility, for Tyneside and its people.

Such an organisation—let us call it something like the 'Tyneside Council for the Future'—could perform many valuable functions. It could question and challenge the 'quangos' (such as the new Urban Development Corporation) and the bureaucracies (central and local government, the health authority) and companies. It could point to ways of making others more effective and more sensitive to local needs. It could be a sounding board for existing organisations trying to review their activities or develop in new directions. It could comment on how Tyneside should respond to new government initiatives (the City Technology Colleges, to take one example) and consider policy choices such as the priorities local authorities may have in economic development policy. Above all, a 'Council for the Future', could provide a forum for thinking about the future in a comprehensive way, embracing the whole of Tyneside and including a wide range of interests. Consensus is probably too much to hope for—indeed, conflicts of view are inevitable—but, at the least, a deeper understanding and fuller appreciation of the issues would be attained. Tyneside must regain some locally-based power, try to influence events and create a better future.

This modest proposal may easily be attacked. It might be argued that it would usurp the functions of local political institutions, particularly the local authorities. This is not so; the aim would be to have the local authorities playing a very active and important part in this broader and Tyneside-wide forum. In providing a broadly-based institution, this Council for the Future could provide a voice for Tyneside which might be listened to by central government at a time when the local authorities are being ignored. In addition, some might argue that such is the centralisation of economic and political power that any local institution seeking to threaten that power is bound to fail. This cannot be lightly dismissed; it may prove to be so, but it is worth making the attempt. And, as we have noted, central government does ultimately need local institutions and local knowledge to make policies relevant and effective and to implement them.

In a period of great change, presenting many threats and perhaps offering some opportunities, some vision of the way forward for Tyneside is absolutely vital. This must be founded on an appreciation of present problems—which we hope this book helps to provide. In our opinion, there is no point in trying to play down those problems on the grounds that they will serve to deter investors and sully Tyneside's 'image'. Tyneside must forcibly make the case that it has problems and needs help or it will not secure the resources it needs nor be given the priority it deserves. That said, the 'begging bowl' approach is very likely to be ineffective and even counterproductive. It is, therefore, necessary also to highlight Tyneside's many positive aspects and the opportunities available in the area.

The 'vision' for the future we hope for must be uniquely developed to address the particular problems and needs of Tyneside *and* meet local aspirations. A vision which aims to make Tyneside like South East England is not likely to be popular, nor is it feasible. Over-ambitious and over-blown grand conceptions, like T. Dan Smith's idea of Newcastle as the 'Brasilia of the North', are not wanted either; such 'visions' are basically shallow and ultimately unhelpful. What is needed, then, is a comprehensive and sensible view of what Tyneside should become, together with a realistic strategy (continually updated and revised) showing how to attain well-defined goals. Throughout, questions of inequality and social welfare must be at the top of the agenda.

In the concluding chapter of his book, Mess argued that Tyneside's problems would not solve themselves. Action was needed:

'The natural tendency is to say that nothing can be done just now, that the district must carry on as best it can till better times arrive. But there is no salvation in that direction. If Tyneside waits for the good old times to come back, it may wait for ever.'

Looking back over sixty years, it is heartening to see how much has been done and how much has been achieved. But new problems arise, new aspirations develop; Tyneside must now work towards a new and better future. Tyneside cannot wait for the good old times to come back, for it would surely wait for ever.

INDEX

Page numbers in italics refer to illustrations.